SHOP MANUAL

Auto Engine Performance

Job Sheets for Performance-Based Learning

Chris Johanson
Brandon Baldwin

Publisher
The Goodheart-Willcox Company, Inc.
Tinley Park, Illinois
www.g-w.com

Manufactured in the United States of America.

ISBN 979-8-89118-249-3

1 2 3 4 5 6 7 8 9 – 25 – 28 27 26 25 24 23

The Goodheart-Willcox Company, Inc. Brand Disclaimer: Brand names, company names, and illustrations for products and services included in this text are provided for educational purposes only and do not represent or imply endorsement or recommendation by the author or the publisher.

The Goodheart-Willcox Company, Inc. Safety Notice: The reader is expressly advised to carefully read, understand, and apply all safety precautions and warnings described in this book or that might also be indicated in undertaking the activities and exercises described herein to minimize risk of personal injury or injury to others. Common sense and good judgment should also be exercised and applied to help avoid all potential hazards. The reader should always refer to the appropriate manufacturer's technical information, directions, and recommendations; then proceed with care to follow specific equipment operating instructions. The reader should understand these notices and cautions are not exhaustive.

The publisher makes no warranty or representation whatsoever, either expressed or implied, including but not limited to equipment, procedures, and applications described or referred to herein, their quality, performance, merchantability, or fitness for a particular purpose. The publisher assumes no responsibility for any changes, errors, or omissions in this book. The publisher specifically disclaims any liability whatsoever, including any direct, indirect, incidental, consequential, special, or exemplary damages resulting, in whole or in part, from the reader's use or reliance upon the information, instructions, procedures, warnings, cautions, applications, or other matter contained in this book. The publisher assumes no responsibility for the activities of the reader.

The Goodheart-Willcox Company, Inc. Internet Disclaimer: The Internet resources and listings in this Goodheart-Willcox Publisher product are provided solely as a convenience to you. These resources and listings were reviewed at the time of publication to provide you with accurate, safe, and appropriate information. Goodheart-Willcox Publisher has no control over the referenced websites and, due to the dynamic nature of the Internet, is not responsible or liable for the content, products, or performance of links to other websites or resources. Goodheart-Willcox Publisher makes no representation, either expressed or implied, regarding the content of these websites, and such references do not constitute an endorsement or recommendation of the information or content presented. It is your responsibility to take all protective measures to guard against inappropriate content, viruses, or other destructive elements.

Image Credits. Front cover: BACHTUB DMITRII/Shutterstock.com, Happycreator/Shutterstock.com, Goodheart-Willcox Publisher

Introduction

The Shop Manual for *Auto Engine Performance* provides step-by-step instruction of all the tasks listed in the A8—Engine Performance area of the ASE Education Foundation Task List. Each job in this manual is a hands-on activity, and most jobs correspond to one or more of the ASE Education Foundation tasks. The jobs have been carefully organized and developed to increase your chances of passing the related ASE tests by helping you apply the information you have learned from the *Auto Engine Performance* textbook and in the classroom.

Using this Shop Manual

This shop manual guides you through all the ASE Education Foundation tasks in the A8—Engine Performance area, which include inspecting, testing, and diagnosing starting, charging, lighting, and accessory systems; removing and replacing self-contained components; and removing, overhauling, and reinstalling major components. The jobs are not correlated to specific textbook chapters but will be assigned when your instructor determines that you have sufficient knowledge to complete them.

When performing the jobs, follow these guidelines:

- Read the instructions carefully and proceed through the steps in the order they are presented.
- Refer to the proper service information to find specific procedures and specifications for the vehicle being serviced.
- Carefully read all notes, cautions, and warnings before proceeding.
- Record specifications and the results of diagnostic procedures in the spaces provided.
- Consult your instructor when directed to do so by this shop manual and when unsure of how to proceed.
- Never attempt a step if you are unsure how to perform it correctly.

Features of the Manual

The projects in this manual include a brief introduction about the type of service being performed, a list of the jobs included in the project, and a tools and materials list for the jobs.

The jobs in this manual are designed to be accomplished in one or two lab sessions. Checkboxes are provided in the left-hand column of the job so you can mark off tasks as they are performed. Blank spaces are provided for recording service-related information.

In addition, three types of special notices appear throughout the jobs in this manual. These notices point out special information or safety considerations for the task being performed. They are color coded according to the type of information being provided:

Tech Tip

Note features provide additional information, special considerations, or professional advice about the task being performed. Note features are blue.

Caution

Caution features appear near critical steps in a service procedure. These features warn the reader that failure to perform the task properly can lead to equipment or vehicle damage. Caution features are yellow.

Warning

Warning features also appear near certain critical steps in the service procedure. These features warn the reader that failure to perform the task properly could result in personal injury. Warning features are red.

If properly implemented, this manual will help you do well in your course, pass the related ASE certification tests, and find a job in the automotive industry.

Chris Johanson

Brandon Baldwin

Table of Contents

Project 1—Preparing to Service a Vehicle 9

Job 1—Perform Safety and Environmental Inspections 11

Personal Protective Equipment 11
Safety Data Sheets 12
Fire and Shop Safety 13
Electrical Safety 14
Vehicle System-Related Safety Considerations 16
Compressed Air Safety 16
Shop Cleanliness 17
Clothing Safety 17
Carbon Monoxide 17
Grinder and Drill Press Safety 18
Floor Jack and Jack Stand Safety 18
Hydraulic Lift Safety 19
Environmental Protection 20

Job 2—Identify and Interpret Vehicle Numbers 23

Locate the Vehicle Identification Number (VIN), Emissions Certification Label, and Refrigerant Identification Label 23
Locate Major Component Identification Numbers 26

Job 3—Find and Use Service Information 27

Use the Internet to Obtain Service Information 27
Use an SDS to Determine the Safety and Environmental Hazards of a Substance 28
Derive Information from Vehicle Service History—Optional Task 29
Complete a Work Order 29

Job 4—Use a Scan Tool to Retrieve Diagnostic Trouble Codes 31

Obtain Freeze Frame Data 34
Clear Trouble Codes 34
Run Monitors 35

Job 5—Identify Hybrid Vehicle High-Voltage Components and Disable High-Voltage Systems 37

Locate High-Voltage System Components 37
Locate High-Voltage System Disconnects 38
Disable Hybrid Vehicle High-Voltage Systems 38

Project 2—Diagnosing General Engine Concerns 41

Job 6—Check for Engine Oil, Coolant, Fuel, and Vacuum Leaks 45

Visual Inspection 45
Powder Method 46
Black Light Method 46
Pressure Test a Cooling System 47
Check for Vacuum Leaks 48

Job 7—Diagnose Engine and Vehicle Performance, Noise, and Vibration Problems 55

Diagnose an Engine Performance and/or Drivability Problem 55

Job 8—Use a Scan Tool to Access and Reprogram a Vehicle Computer 63

Access the Vehicle Computer 63
Reprogram the Computer 65

Job 9—Use a Multimeter to Perform Pinpoint Sensor Tests 69

Test Sensor Resistance 69
Test Sensor Voltage 72
Test Sensor or Actuator Circuit Voltage Drop 73

Job 10—Use a Scope to Perform Pinpoint Sensor and Actuator Tests 75

Test a Sensor for Proper Waveform 76
Using a Low-Amp Clamp to View Actuator Waveforms 77

Job 11—Diagnose a Control Module and Module Communication Errors 81

Job 12—Perform a Vacuum Test, Power Balance Test, Compression Test, and Cylinder Leakage Test 87

Engine Vacuum Test 87
Power Balance Test 89
Static Compression Test 90
Running (Dynamic) Compression Test 91
Relative Compression Test 92
Cylinder Leakage Test 93

Job 13—Inspect and Test a Cooling System 97

Inspect Belts and Hoses 97
Inspect Other Cooling System Components 98
Pressure Test the Cooling System 100
Make Visual Tests for Leaks 101
Check the Coolant Pump 101
Check Coolant Temperature and the Operation of a Cooling Fan 102
Check Fan Shroud and Air Dams 103
Check for Combustion Leaks 103
Inspect the Engine Oil Cooler 104

Job 14—Use a Four- or Five-Gas Analyzer to Check Emission System Operation 107

Project 3—Diagnosing and Repairing an Ignition System 111

Job 15—Inspect and Test an Ignition System's Secondary Circuit Components and Wiring 113

Test for a Spark from the Secondary System 114
Read and Interpret Ignition System Waveforms 114
Check the Spark Plugs 115
Check the Spark Plug Wires 116
Check Distributor Components 116

Job 16—Inspect and Test an Ignition System's Primary Circuit Components and Wiring 121
Visually Inspect Primary Circuit Wiring 121
Make Resistance Checks of Wires and/or Connectors 122
Inspect Solid-State Components 122
Test the Ignition Module and/or ECM 123
Test Ignition Coil(s) 125
Check and Set the Initial Timing—Optional Task 125
Check the Timing Advance 126
Check Knock Sensor Operation 127

Project 4—Diagnosing and Servicing Fuel and Air Induction Systems 129
Job 17—Verify Fuel Quality 131
Inspect a Gasoline Sample for Contamination 131
Check for Excessive Alcohol in Gasoline 132
Inspect a Diesel Fuel Sample for Contamination 132
Measure the Diesel Fuel Cetane Rating 133
Check for Diesel Fuel Waxing 133
Job 18—Test and Replace Fuel Supply System Components 135
Remove, Check, and Replace Fuel Filters 135
Test Fuel Pressure (Electric Pump) 136
Test Electric Fuel Pump Relays 137
Test the Electric Fuel Pump's Amperage Draw 137
Test Electric Fuel Pump Waveforms 138
Replace an Inline Electric Fuel Pump 139
Replace an In-Tank Electric Fuel Pump 141
Test Mechanical Fuel Pump Pressure 142
Replace a Mechanical Fuel Pump 143
Job 19—Inspect and Service a Throttle Body 145
Check for Loose or Damaged Air Intake System Ducts or Hoses 145
Check the Spray Patterns in a Throttle Body Injection (TBI) System 146
Inspect and Service a Throttle Body 146
Job 20—Check Idle Speed Motor or Idle Air Control 149
Check Idle Speed Motor or Idle Air Control 149
Remove and Replace an Idle Speed Motor 150
Job 21—Check Fuel Injector Waveforms 153
Job 22—Perform a Fuel Injector Balance Test 157
Job 23—Remove and Replace a Fuel Injector 159
Job 24—Check Supercharger and Turbocharger Operation 163
Check a Supercharger 164
Check a Turbocharger 165
Check an Intercooler 166

Project 5—Diagnosing and Servicing an Exhaust System. 169
Job 25—Inspect and Test an Exhaust System 171
Check and Refill Diesel Exhaust Fluid (Diesel Vehicles Only) 171
Visually Inspect the Exhaust System and Check for Exhaust Leaks 171
Perform a Backpressure Test to Check for Exhaust Restriction 172
Job 26—Replace Exhaust System Components 177
Remove and Replace Exhaust Components 177
Use an Oxyacetylene Cutting Torch 180

Project 6—Diagnosing and Servicing Emission Control Systems 185

Job 27—Test and Service an EGR Valve 187

Remove and Replace an EGR Valve 188

Clean an EGR Valve and Passages 189

Job 28—Test and Service an Air Pump and Air Injection System 191

Test Air Pump and Air Injection System Valve Operation 191

Replace an Air Injection Pump 193

Replace a Vacuum Switching or Diverter Valve 193

Replace an Electrical Switching or Diverter Valve 193

Replace a Check Valve 194

Replace an Injector Tube Assembly 195

Job 29—Test and Service a Catalytic Converter 197

Test Catalytic Converter Operation 198

Replace a Catalytic Converter 200

Job 30—Test and Service Positive Crankcase Ventilation (PCV) Systems 203

Test and Service a PCV System 203

Job 31—Test and Service Evaporative Emissions Systems. 207

Using the Scan Tool to Give Direction to the Diagnosis on Vacuum-Based Systems 208

Using the Scan Tool to Give Direction to the Diagnosis on Pressure-Based Systems 210

Locate Evaporative Emissions System Leaks with a Smoke-Generating Machine 211

Project 7—Performing Engine-Related Service. 215

Job 32—Change Oil and Filter 217

Job 33—Repair Damaged Threads 221

Repair External Threads 221

Repair Internal Threads 223

Job 34—Test and Service Variable Valve Timing or Lift Components 225

Job 35—Service Valve Timing Components 229

Check Operation of a Variable Valve Timing Mechanism 229

Check Camshaft Drive Parts 230

Install Valve Timing Components 231

Job 36—Adjust Valves 235

Adjust Valves—Mechanical Valve Lifters 235

Adjust Valves—Hydraulic Valve Lifters 236

Job 37—Remove and Replace a Thermostat 239

Project 8—Diagnosing and Servicing Stop-Start Systems and Hybrid Vehicles 243

Job 38—Testing the Starting Battery on a Stop-Start System 245

Job 39—Testing a Stop-Start System 247

Job 40—Testing the Auxiliary Battery in a Hybrid 251

Job 41—Diagnosing the Cooling Motors of a Hybrid Vehicle 253

Testing the Inverter/Converter Coolant Pump 253

Testing a Battery Cooling Fan Motor 255

Job 42—Hybrid Vehicle Maintenance 257

PROJECT 1

Preparing to Service a Vehicle

Introduction

In this project, you will be introduced to some of the tasks that must be completed before a vehicle can be properly serviced. These tasks include evaluating safety considerations, properly identifying the vehicle being serviced, and locating and using appropriate service information.

Thousands of technicians are injured every year while on the job, and some are even killed. Most of these technicians were breaking basic safety rules before their accidents. The technicians that survived learned to respect safety precautions the hard way by experiencing a painful, but instructive, injury. Know how to avoid accidents—by studying and following shop safety rules.

The service technician is responsible for maintaining a safe workspace and performing service safely, but is also responsible for protecting the environment. You must follow all applicable environmental laws or risk heavy fines. In addition to the legal obligations, proper waste disposal and recycling will save money. In Job 1, you will locate and identify safety equipment and hazards in the shop. You will also identify the types of wastes generated by the shop and describe the proper procedures for waste disposal.

It is no longer sufficient to open the hood and visually identify an engine. You must use identifying numbers to determine the type of engine and drive train, specifications, part numbers, and which service operations can be performed. Some vehicle systems cannot be successfully serviced without finding and interpreting vehicle numbers. In Job 2, you will locate and interpret vital vehicle numbers.

Once the vehicle and its systems have been properly identified, you must locate the appropriate service information. In Job 3, you will locate and interpret service information.

With the prevalence of computer-controlled systems, the scan tool is essential for diagnosis. The information retrieved through stored diagnostic trouble codes helps the technician pinpoint problems in computer-controlled systems. In Job 4, you will connect and use a scan tool to retrieve stored trouble codes.

In Job 5, you will locate high-voltage system components and disconnects on a hybrid vehicle. You will also disable hybrid vehicle high-voltage systems.

Project 1 Jobs

- Job 1—Perform Safety and Environmental Inspections
- Job 2—Identify and Interpret Vehicle Numbers
- Job 3—Find and Use Service Information
- Job 4—Use a Scan Tool to Retrieve Diagnostic Trouble Codes
- Job 5—Identify Hybrid Vehicle High-Voltage Components and Disable High-Voltage Systems

Tools and Materials

The following list contains the tools and materials that may be needed to complete the jobs in this project. The items used will depend on the make and model of vehicle being serviced.

- One or more vehicles.
- A computer and the appropriate service-related software.
- Internet access.
- Technical service bulletin(s).
- Vehicle service history when available.
- One or more safety data sheets (SDS).
- Other service information.
- Safety glasses and other protective equipment.

Safety Notice

Before performing these jobs, review all pertinent safety information in the text and review safety information with your instructor.

Name ______________________________

Date ______________ Class ______________

Project 1: Job 1—Perform Safety and Environmental Inspections

After completing this job, you will be able to locate the shop's fire extinguishers, fire exit, and eye wash stations. You will be able to locate and properly use safety glasses and other shop safety equipment. You will also learn the general safety rules of an auto shop. You will learn the methods of preventing environmental damage through environmentally friendly work procedures.

Instructions

As you read the job instructions, answer the questions and perform the tasks. Record your answers using complete sentences. Ask your instructor for help as needed. A careful study of Chapter 3, *Safety and Environmental Protection*, will prepare you for some the procedures in this job.

Warning

Before performing this job, review all pertinent safety information in the text and discuss safety procedures with your instructor.

Procedures

Personal Protective Equipment

☐ 1. Eye protection (safety glasses or goggles) should be worn during any operation that could injure your eyes. See **Figure 1-1**. This includes, for example, hammering, drilling, grinding, and blasting, using compressed air, carrying a battery, or working around a spinning engine fan.

List five common tasks that require the use of safety goggles: ______________________________

____

____

Where are the safety glasses and goggles kept in your shop? ______________________________

____

____

Figure 1-1. Eye protection should be worn while working in the shop. A—Safety glasses. B—Safety goggles. C—Face shield.

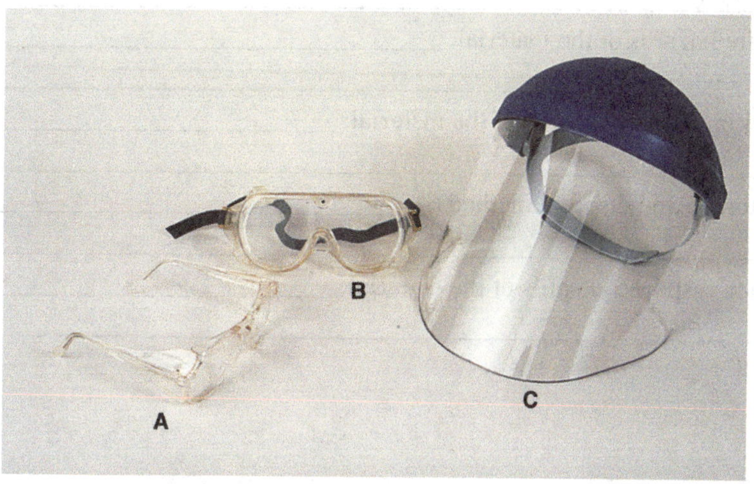

☐ 2. Hearing protection (earplugs or protective earmuffs) should be worn during any loud activities. These include tasks like hammering, operating pneumatic tools, and grinding.

List five common tasks that require the use of hearing protection: ____________________

____

____

Where are the earplugs and protective earmuffs kept in the shop? ____________________

____

____

☐ 3. Dust masks and respirators may be required performing certain tasks or working with certain chemicals.

Where are respirators and dust masks kept in the shop? ____________________

____

Safety Data Sheets

☐ 1. Walk through the shop and familiarize yourself with the chemicals stored there.

2. Find the safety data sheets for the chemicals in the shop. Look up information about the chemicals stored in the shop.

Were any chemicals improperly stored according to the safety data sheets?
Yes ___ No ___

If Yes, describe the chemicals and inform your instructor: ____________________

____

Were safety data sheets missing for any of the chemicals in the shop?
Yes ___ No ___

If Yes, describe the chemicals and inform your instructor: ____________________

____

☐ 3. Obtain an SDS from your instructor.

☐ 4. List the following information from the SDS.

General class of material covered by the SDS (if applicable): ____________________

Trade (manufacturer's) name for the material: ____________________

Chemical or generic name of the material: ____________________

Known breathing hazards of the material: ____________________

____

Known fire hazards of the material: ____________________

____

Known skin damage hazards of the material: ____________________

____

Proper storage and disposal methods: ____________________

____

Emergency response to spills of the material: ____________________

____

Name ______________________________

Fire and Shop Safety

☐ 1. Walk around the shop and locate all of the fire extinguishers, the fire exit, and fire alarms. Such information is crucial in the event of an emergency.

How many fire extinguishers and alarms are there in your shop? ______________________________

Where are the fire extinguishers located? ______________________________

What types of fire extinguishers are available in the shop? ______________________________

Where are the fire alarms? ______________________________

How do you leave the shop in case of a fire? ______________________________

☐ 2. To help prevent an emergency, memorize these important fire prevention tips:

- Always take actions to prevent a fire.
- Store gasoline-soaked and oily rags in safety cans, **Figure 1-2**.
- Wipe up spilled gasoline and oil immediately.
- Hold a rag around the fitting when removing a car's fuel line, **Figure 1-3**.

Figure 1-2. Special safety cans should be used to store oily rags.

Figure 1-3. This technician is using a shop rag to prevent fuel from leaking as he disconnects a fuel line.

☐ 3. Identify the location of safety equipment and special hazard areas within the shop.

Where are the eye wash stations located? ____________________

____

____

Where are first aid stations located? ____________________

____

____

What other special hazard areas exist within the shop? ____________________

____

____

How are the special hazard areas identified? ____________________

____

____

Electrical Safety

☐ 1. Check the shop for unsafe electrical conditions, such as damaged electrical cords and overloaded outlets.

Were any unsafe electrical conditions found? Yes ___ No ___

If Yes, describe them in as much detail as possible: ____________________

____

____

☐ 2. Make sure that all electrically operated tools and equipment with three-prong electrical plugs have their grounding prongs intact, **Figure 1-4**.

Do any tools or equipment have the grounding prong removed? Yes ___ No ___

If Yes, list the items: ____________________

____

Warning

Do not use tools or equipment on which the grounding prong has been removed.

Name ____

Project 1: Job 1 *(continued)*

Figure 1-4. The grounding prong has been broken off the electrical plug on the right. Do *not* use a piece of equipment if the grounding prong has been removed.

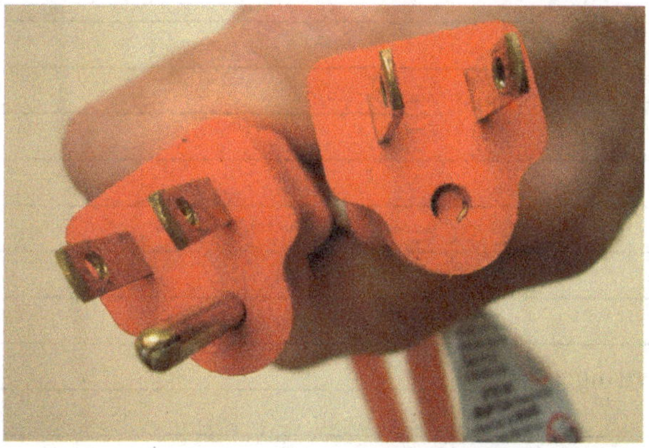

☐ 3. Obtain the use of a vehicle.

☐ 4. Check the following:

- Battery and battery terminal condition.
- Battery bracket and tray corrosion.
- Ignition secondary wiring condition.
- Condition of all visible wiring.
- Condition of hybrid vehicle high-voltage system wiring.

Warning

Hybrid high-voltage wires are orange, **Figure 1-5**. Follow all safety precautions when inspecting the insulation and connectors. Remember that these wires carry several hundred volts, and can deliver a lethal shock!

Were any defects found? Yes ___ No ___

If Yes, describe: ____

____

Figure 1-5. Be extremely careful when working around the orange high-voltage wires found on hybrid vehicles.

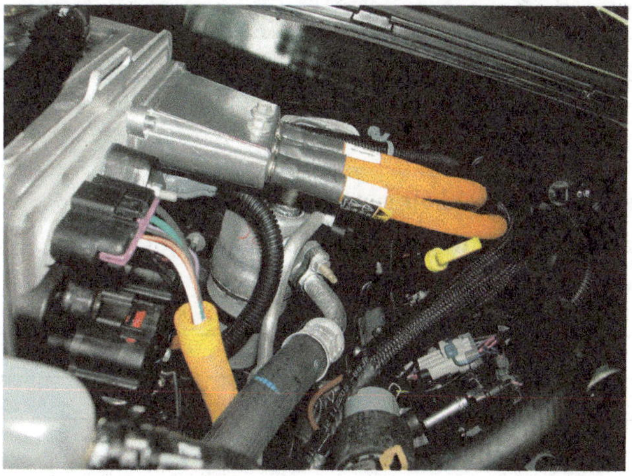

☐ 5. Describe the dangers posed by the following:

Damaged high-voltage wiring insulation: ____________________

____

____

Loose or corroded connections: ____________________

____

____

Battery gases: ____________________

____

____

Short-circuited wiring: ____________________

____

____

Careless handing of hybrid high-voltage system wiring: ____________________

____

____

Warning

Other potential sources of high voltage include ignition system secondary wiring, fuel injection system wiring, and high-intensity discharge (HID) lighting systems.

Vehicle System-Related Safety Considerations

☐ 1. Identify the special safety considerations associated with each of the following common vehicle systems:

Supplemental restraint systems (SRS): ____________________

____

____

Electronically controlled braking systems (ABS, TCS): ____________________

____

____

High-intensity discharge (HID) lighting systems: ____________________

____

____

Compressed Air Safety

☐ 1. Locate the shop's compressed air supply.

What is the air pressure setting on the shop compressor? ____________

Describe the dangers posed by compressed air: ____________________

____

____

____

Name ____________________

Project 1: Job 1 *(continued)*

Shop Cleanliness

☐ 1. Check the shop floor for unsafe conditions, including spills and trip hazards.
List any unsafe conditions: ____________________

☐ 2. Check the shop tools for cleanliness and organization.
List any ways that tool storage can be improved: ____________________

Clothing Safety

☐ 1. Different types of gloves are required for different service procedures.
List tasks that require leather gloves: ____________________

List tasks that require nitrile gloves: ____________________

List tasks that require electrically insulated rubber (electric lineman's) gloves: ____________________

List tasks for which mechanic's gloves would be appropriate: ____________________

☐ 2. Examine your clothing from a safety standpoint.
List and explain any changes that would make your clothing safer or better-suited in the shop:

☐ 3. Any technicians working in the shop should wear steel-toe safety boots, remove their jewelry, and, if they have long hair, tie it back, out of the way.
In your own words, explain the reasons for these safety precautions: ____________________

Carbon Monoxide

☐ 1. Locate the exhaust hoses in the shop.
Where are they located? ____________________

☐ 2. Locate the controls to operate the shop's exhaust fans.

Where are they located? ____

____

____

Grinder and Drill Press Safety

☐ 1. Go to the electric grinder and inspect it closely. Locate the power switch. Observe the position of the tool rest and face shield. Also, check the condition of the grinding wheel.

Is the electric grinder in the shop safe? Yes ___ No ___

If No, explain: ____

____

____

☐ 2. Locate and inspect the operation of the shop's drill press. Find the on/off button, feed lever, chuck, and other components.

List the safety precautions associated with operating a drill press: ____________________

____

____

Floor Jack and Jack Stand Safety

☐ 1. Check out a floor jack and a set of jack stands.

☐ 2. Without lifting a vehicle, practice operating a floor jack. Close the valve on the jack handle. Pump the handle up and down to raise the jack. Then, lower the jack slowly. It is important that you know how to control the lowering action of the jack.

In what direction must you turn the jack handle valve to raise the jack? ____________

To lower the jack? ____________

Warning

Ask your instructor for permission before beginning the next step. Your instructor may need to demonstrate the procedures to the class.

☐ 3. After getting your instructor's approval, place the jack under a proper lift point on the vehicle (frame, rear axle housing, suspension arm, or reinforced section of the unibody), **Figure 1-6**. If in doubt about where to position the jack, refer to the service information for the particular vehicle. Instructions will usually be given in one of the front sections of the service information.

Where did you position the floor jack? ____

____

☐ 4. To raise the vehicle, place the transmission in Neutral and release the emergency brake. This will allow the vehicle to roll as the jack goes up. If the vehicle cannot roll and the small wheels on the jack catch in the shop floor, the vehicle could slide off the jack.

☐ 5. As soon as the vehicle is high enough, place jack stands under the suggested lift points. Lower the vehicle onto the stands slowly. Check that they are safe. Then, remove the floor jack and block the wheels. It should now be safe to work under the car.

Where did you position the jack stands? ____

Name ____

Project 1: Job 1 *(continued)*

☐ 6. Raise the vehicle. Remove the jack stands. Lower the vehicle and return the equipment to the proper storage area.

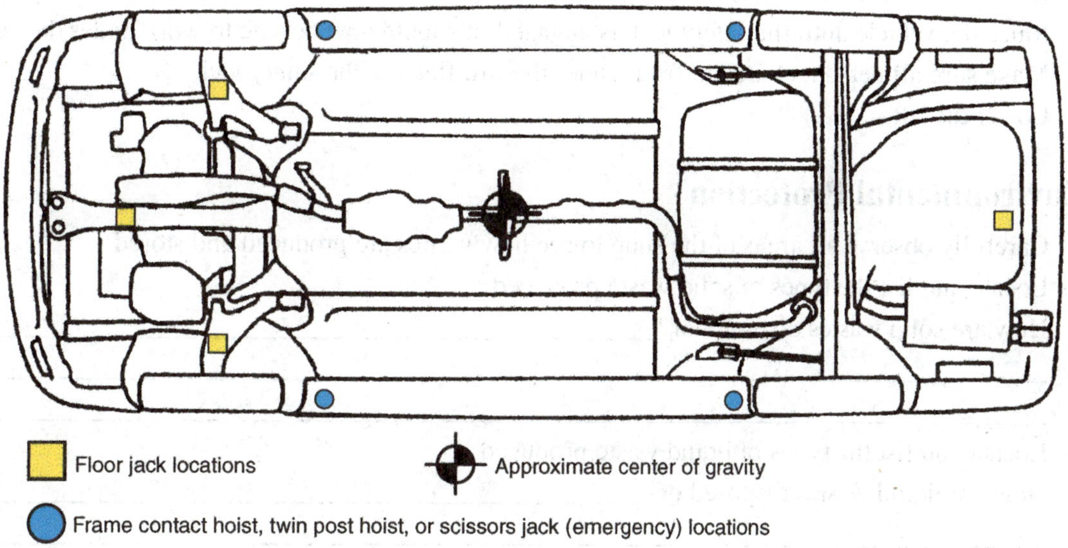

Figure 1-6. One manufacturer's recommended lift points are shown here. Consult the proper service information to determine the lift points for the specific vehicle you are working on.

Hydraulic Lift Safety

☐ 1. Obtain the use of one of the shop's hydraulic lifts.

☐ 2. Without lifting a vehicle, practice operating the lift controls.

☐ 3. Raise the lift and ensure that the lift's safety lock operates properly.

Does the lock operate properly? Yes ___ No ___

If Yes, go to step 4.

If No, consult your instructor before proceeding.

> **Tech Tip**
>
> The lift may be equipped with more than one safety lock.

☐ 4. After getting your instructor's approval, drive a vehicle onto the lift.

> **Tech Tip**
>
> If the rack is a drive-on type, skip steps 5 through 9.

☐ 5. Consult service information to determine the proper lift points for the vehicle.

☐ 6. Position the pads under the vehicle's lift points.

☐ 7. Raise the vehicle so that the pads lightly contact the vehicle's lift points.

☐ 8. Recheck the lift points to ensure that the pads are contacting them properly.
Are the pads contacting the frame at the proper points? Yes ___ No ___
If Yes, go to step 9.
If No, lower the rack and repeat steps 6 and 7.

☐ 9. Raise the vehicle until the safety lock is engaged. It should now be safe to work under the vehicle.

☐ 10. Make sure all personnel are out from under the lift. Release the safety lock.

☐ 11. Lower the lift.

Environmental Protection

☐ 1. Carefully observe all areas of the shop to see how wastes are produced and stored.

☐ 2. Locate and list the types of solid waste produced.
How are solid wastes disposed of? ____________________

____

____

☐ 3. Locate and list the types of liquid waste produced.
How are liquid wastes disposed of? ____________________

____

____

☐ 4. Locate and list types of gases or airborne particles produced.
How are these contaminates prevented from entering the atmosphere? ____________________

____

____

☐ 5. From the lists above, identify the types of solid and liquid waste that could be recycled:

____

____

Identify the materials that could be returned for a core deposit: ____________________

____

____

Do any Environmental Protection Agency (EPA) regulations apply to the wastes generated in the shop? Yes ___ No ___
If Yes, briefly summarize them: ____________________

____

Do any local and state regulations apply to the wastes generated by the shop? Yes ___ No ___
If Yes, briefly summarize them: ____________________

____

List any of the shop's waste disposal practices that require improvement:

____

Name ____________________

Project 1: Job 1 *(continued)*

Explain what improvements could be made: ____________________

____

____

Job Wrap-Up

- ☐ 1. Clean the work area and return any equipment to storage.
- ☐ 2. Did you encounter any problems during this procedure? Yes ___ No ___

  If Yes, describe the problems: ____________________

  ____

  What did you do to correct the problems? ____________________

  ____
- ☐ 3. Have your instructor check your work and sign this job sheet.

Performance Evaluation—Instructor Use Only

How would you rate this student's overall performance on this task/job?

4 Competent/Proficient. Able to perform all elements of the task/job successfully and independently.

3 Satisfactory performance of the task/job. Able to perform elements of the task/job with minimal instructor assistance.

2 Completed the task/job with significant instructor assistance.

1 Unsuccessfully attempted the task/job.

0 No exposure. Note reason below (absence, skill not covered, etc.).

Comments:

____

____

____

____

Instructor's Signature: ____________________

Notes

Name ____________________

Date ____________________ Class ____________________

Project 1: Job 2—Identify and Interpret Vehicle Numbers

After completing this job, you will be able to locate and interpret vehicle and vehicle subassembly numbers.

Instructions

As you read the job instructions, answer the questions and perform the tasks. Record your answers using complete sentences. Consult the proper service information and ask your instructor for help as needed.

Warning

Before performing this job, review all pertinent safety information in the text and discuss safety procedures with your instructor.

Procedures

☐ 1. Obtain a vehicle to be used in this job. Your instructor may specify one or more vehicles to be used.

Locate the Vehicle Identification Number (VIN), Emissions Certification Label, and Refrigerant Identification Label

☐ 1. Locate the vehicle identification number (VIN). On all vehicles built after 1968, the VIN will be visible in the lower driver's side corner of the windshield, **Figure 2-1**. On most vehicles built before 1968, the VIN will be located in the driver's side front door jamb, **Figure 2-2**.

Write the VIN here: ____________________

Figure 2-1. On all vehicles made after 1968, the VIN is located on the driver's side of the dashboard, where it can be clearly seen through the windshield.

Figure 2-2. The VIN on this older vehicle is installed inside the driver's side door jamb.

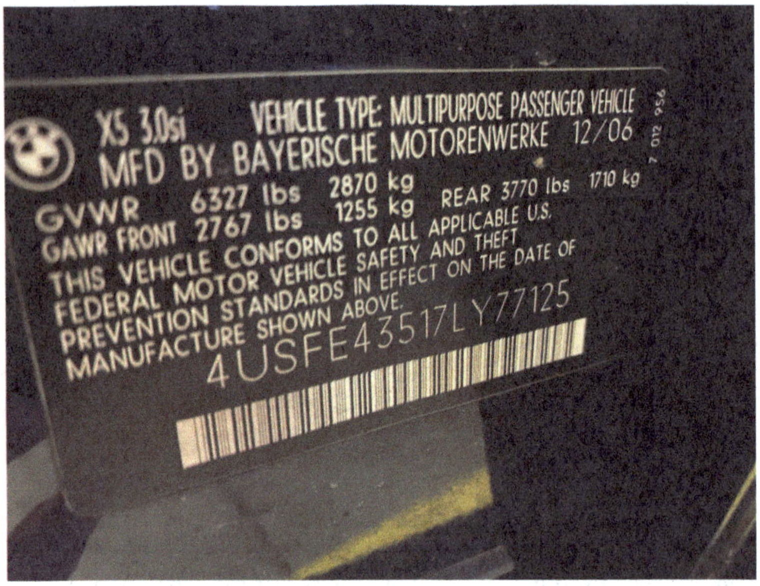

☐ 2. Open the vehicle hood or engine compartment cover and locate the vehicle's emissions certification label, **Figure 2-3**.

☐ 3. Answer the following questions:

What is the model year of the vehicle? ______________________________

What size engine does the vehicle have? ______________________________

What type of fuel does this engine require? ______________________________

Can the ignition timing be adjusted? Yes ___ No ___

Is this vehicle California emissions compliant? ______________________________

Tech Tip

If the vehicle is not equipped with air conditioning, skip the following step. Also, some older air-conditioned vehicles may not have a refrigerant identification label.

☐ 4. Return to the engine compartment and locate the refrigerant identification label, **Figure 2-4**. The refrigerant identification label may be on an air conditioner component or on the inner fender or strut housing.

What type of refrigerant is used in this vehicle? ______________________________

Name ______________________________

Project 1: Job 2 *(continued)*

Figure 2-3. The emission certification label.

Figure 2-4. The refrigerant label will be installed under the hood, but not necessarily near any air conditioner components.

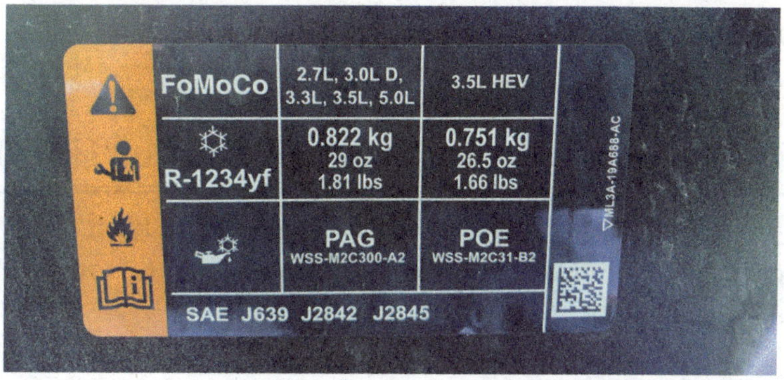

Tech Tip

Identification labels vary by manufacturer. Not all vehicles will have the same labels. Typical labels may be called *calibration labels*, *safety certification labels*, or *vehicle service parts labels*. Needed information may be included in the certification label rather than on separate labels.

☐ 5. Locate all of the vehicle identification labels on the vehicle. Labels may be found on the passenger side door or door pillar, under the vehicle hood, on the underside of the vehicle trunk lid, on the tailgate of a minivan or hatchback, and on the spare tire cover. In your own words, describe the types of labels and the information that they contain:

____

____

____

Locate Major Component Identification Numbers

☐ 1. Ask your instructor for information concerning which vehicle component to use for locating a component number.

☐ 2. Locate the component and record the component identification number(s):

____

☐ 3. In your own words, describe the purpose of these numbers: ______________________

____

____

____

☐ 4. Close the vehicle hood, trunk, and door and park the vehicle as directed by your instructor.

Job Wrap-Up

☐ 1. Clean the work area and return any equipment to storage.

☐ 2. Did you encounter any problems during this procedure? Yes ___ No ___

If Yes, describe the problems: ______________________________

____

What did you do to correct the problems? ______________________________

____

☐ 3. Have your instructor check your work and sign this job sheet.

Performance Evaluation—Instructor Use Only

How would you rate this student's overall performance on this task/job?

4 Competent/Proficient. Able to perform all elements of the task/job successfully and independently.

3 Satisfactory performance of the task/job. Able to perform elements of the task/job with minimal instructor assistance.

2 Completed the task/job with significant instructor assistance.

1 Unsuccessfully attempted the task/job.

0 No exposure. Note reason below (absence, skill not covered, etc.).

Comments:

____

____

____

____

Instructor's Signature: ______________________________

Name ______________________________

Date ____________________ Class ____________________

Project 1: Job 3—Find and Use Service Information

After completing this job, you will be able to locate, identify, and use diagnosis and repair information for a specific vehicle from a variety of sources. You will be able to complete a work order to include customer information, vehicle identifying information, customer concern, related service history, cause, and correction.

Instructions

As you read the job instructions, answer the questions and perform the tasks. Record your answers using complete sentences. Consult the proper service information and ask your instructor for help as needed.

Warning

Before performing this job, review all pertinent safety information in the text and discuss safety procedures with your instructor.

Procedures

☐ 1. Ask your instructor to assign a vehicle problem to diagnose or a service procedure to perform.

Describe the problem or procedure assigned: ______________________________

____

Use the Internet to Obtain Service Information

☐ 1. Ask your instructor to assign a vehicle problem.

Describe the type of problem assigned: ______________________________

____

☐ 2. Make arrangements to use the shop/school computer, or plan to use your personal computer or mobile device. Answer the following questions.

What type of computer or device are you using?

____

Is your connection to the Internet a wired connection, through Wi-Fi, or cellular data?

____

Which input/output capabilities does your device have? Check all that apply.

USB drive ___

SD card ___

Camera ___

Bluetooth ___

CD/DVD drive ___

Other ___

☐ 3. What Internet browser are you using?

____

☐ 4. Is any particular software or app required to access the service information? If so, make note of it.

____

Figure 3-1. This online service information provider allows you easily locate problem-specific service and repair information.

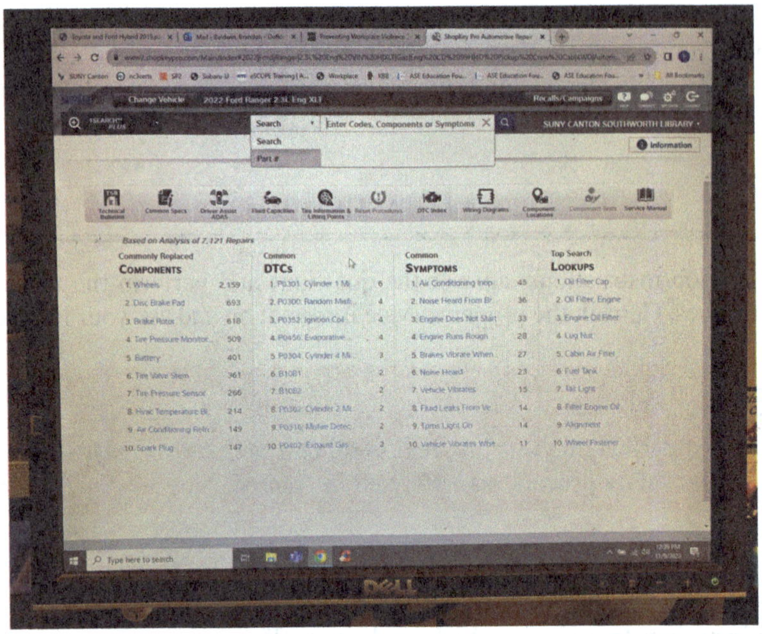

☐ 5. Obtain the needed website address from your instructor and make note of it.

____

☐ 6. Open the website to access the service information provider.

☐ 7. Locate service information related to the assigned task, **Figure 3-1**.

If asked to do so by your instructor, print out the selected information. Otherwise, summarize the service information.

____

____

____

____

____

Use an SDS to Determine the Safety and Environmental Hazards of a Substance

☐ 1. Locate an SDS or obtain an SDS from your instructor.

☐ 2. List the following information from the SDS:

General class of material covered by the SDS (if applicable): ____________________

Trade (manufacturer's) name for the material: ____________________

Chemical or generic name of the material: ____________________

Known breathing hazards of the material: ____________________

____

Known fire hazards of the material: ____________________

____

Known skin damage hazards of the material: ____________________

____

Name ____

Project 1: Job 3 *(continued)*

Proper storage and disposal methods: ______________________________

____

Emergency response to spills of the material: ______________________

____

Derive Information from Vehicle Service History—Optional Task

☐ 1. Obtain a vehicle service history from your instructor. This may consist of receipts for previous service, a journal of maintenance and repairs performed, or another type of service record.

☐ 2. Read the vehicle service history and answer the following questions.

Has the vehicle been properly maintained? Yes ___ No ___

How can you tell? ____

____

____

Does anything in the vehicle service history indicate a developing problem? Yes ___ No ___

If Yes, what is the problem? ______________________________________

____

☐ 3. Return any printed literature and safety data sheets to storage.

Complete a Work Order

Tech Tip

Your instructor may ask you to fill out additional work orders for other jobs in this manual.

☐ 1. Obtain a shop work order from your instructor.

☐ 2. Enter today's date in the proper space on the work order.

☐ 3. Enter the customer's name and address in the proper work order spaces. If the vehicle is a shop unit, enter the name and address of your school.

☐ 4. Record phone number(s) where the customer may be reached. If the vehicle is a shop unit, use the school phone number or create a number.

☐ 5. In the proper spaces on the work order, enter information about the vehicle, including the following:

- Make.
- Model.
- Year.
- Mileage.

☐ 6. Enter the vehicle's VIN in the proper space on the work order.

☐ 7. In the proper work order spaces, record the customer complaint(s) or other relevant customer remarks. Be brief but record all necessary information.

☐ 8. Record any vehicle service history that may help with diagnosis.

☐ 9. When repairs are complete, list the following in the appropriate work order spaces:

- Cause of the vehicle problem.
- Corrections made (repairs or adjustments performed).
- Parts installed and their price.

☐ 10. Add the parts prices and write the total in the parts total space on the work order.

☐ 11. Determine the total labor time of the above operations and write it in the appropriate space on the work order.

☐ 12. Multiply the total labor time by the labor rate for your area and write the total in the labor price space on the work order. Your instructor may furnish a labor rate to use.

☐ 13. If necessary, add the cost of shop supplies, such as lubricants and shop towels, in the appropriate space on the work order.

☐ 14. Add the parts, labor, and shop supply totals and write this amount in the proper space.

☐ 15. Calculate the sales tax:
- Determine the sales tax rate for your area.
- Multiply the parts, labor, and shop supply total by the tax rate to obtain the tax.

☐ 16. Add the tax to the parts and labor total and enter this total in the proper space on the work order.

☐ 17. Make other remarks on the work order as necessary. Examples of other remarks are the need for additional work or fasteners that must be retorqued after several use cycles.

☐ 18. Recheck your work and submit the completed work order to your instructor.

Job Wrap-Up

☐ 1. Did you encounter any problems during this procedure? Yes ___ No ___

If Yes, describe the problems: ______________________________

____

What did you do to correct the problems? ______________________________

____

☐ 2. Have your instructor check your work and sign this job sheet.

Performance Evaluation—Instructor Use Only

How would you rate this student's overall performance on this task/job?

4 Competent/Proficient. Able to perform all elements of the task/job successfully and independently.

3 Satisfactory performance of the task/job. Able to perform elements of the task/job with minimal instructor assistance.

2 Completed the task/job with significant instructor assistance.

1 Unsuccessfully attempted the task/job.

0 No exposure. Note reason below (absence, skill not covered, etc.).

Comments:

____

____

____

____

Instructor's Signature: ______________________________

Name ____________________

Date ____________________ Class ____________________

Project 1: Job 4—Use a Scan Tool to Retrieve Diagnostic Trouble Codes

After completing this job, you will be able to use a scan tool to retrieve diagnostic trouble codes.

Instructions

As you read the job instructions, answer the questions and perform the tasks. Record your answers using complete sentences. Consult the proper service information and ask your instructor for help as needed.

Warning

Before performing this job, review all pertinent safety information in the text and discuss safety procedures with your instructor.

Procedures

☐ 1. Obtain a vehicle to be used in this job. Your instructor may direct you to perform this job on a shop vehicle.

☐ 2. Obtain a scan tool and related service information for the vehicle selected in step 1.

Type of scan tool: ____________________

Tech Tip

The following procedure is a general guide to scan tool use. Scan tool manufacturers have varying ways of configuring their tools. Always obtain the service instructions for the scan tool that you are using. If the scan tool literature calls for a different procedure or series of steps from those in this job, always perform procedures according to the scan tool manufacturer's instructions.

☐ 3. If necessary, attach the proper test connector cable to the scan tool.

☐ 4. Ensure that the ignition switch is in the *Off* position.

☐ 5. Locate the diagnostic link connector (DLC). Most DLCs are accessible from the driver's seat. See **Figure 4-1**. If you cannot locate the DLC, refer to the vehicle's service information.

Location of the DLC: ____________________

____

Figure 4-1. A typical OBD II data link connector is shown here.

☐ 6. Attach the scan tool cable to the DLC. OBD II scan tools are powered from terminal 16 of the DLC; no other power connections are needed.

Caution

Make sure that the scan tool and cable do not interfere with any of the vehicle controls, such as the steering or brake pedal.

☐ 7. Observe the scan tool's screen to ensure that the scan tool is working properly. **Figure 4-2** shows a typical screen on an OBD II scan tool. Most scan tools will complete an internal self-check and notify the technician if there is a software or communication problem. Some scan tools will perform a self-test to verify that they are operating properly.

Tech Tip

If the scan tool indicates a software or communication problem, first make sure that the vehicle battery is not discharged. Low voltage can cause scan tool malfunctions.

☐ 8. Factory scan tools usually default to manufacturer data. Generic scan tools will provide the option of vehicle-specific information, which requires the VIN, or OBD II information. When using the generic scan tool, pick OBD II first. OBD II information is for the engine only and is accurate, meaning there is no fabricated or calculated data. Retrieve trouble codes from OBD II using Mode $03. If there are no trouble codes, see your instructor to create trouble codes by disconnecting a sensor or actuator.

Trouble Code	**Meaning**
____________________	____________________
____________________	____________________
____________________	____________________
____________________	____________________
____________________	____________________
____________________	____________________

Do not clear the trouble codes.

☐ 9. Back out of the trouble codes menu. Look at freeze frame data in Mode $02. Freeze frame data is a list of the data that existed when a code is set.

List the following common freeze frame data points:

RPM: _______

Engine temperature (ECT): _______

Airflow: _______

List other freeze frame data below that may be important to diagnosing the trouble codes found in step 8.

____

____

____

____

Name ____

Figure 4-2. A typical screen on an OBD II scan tool.

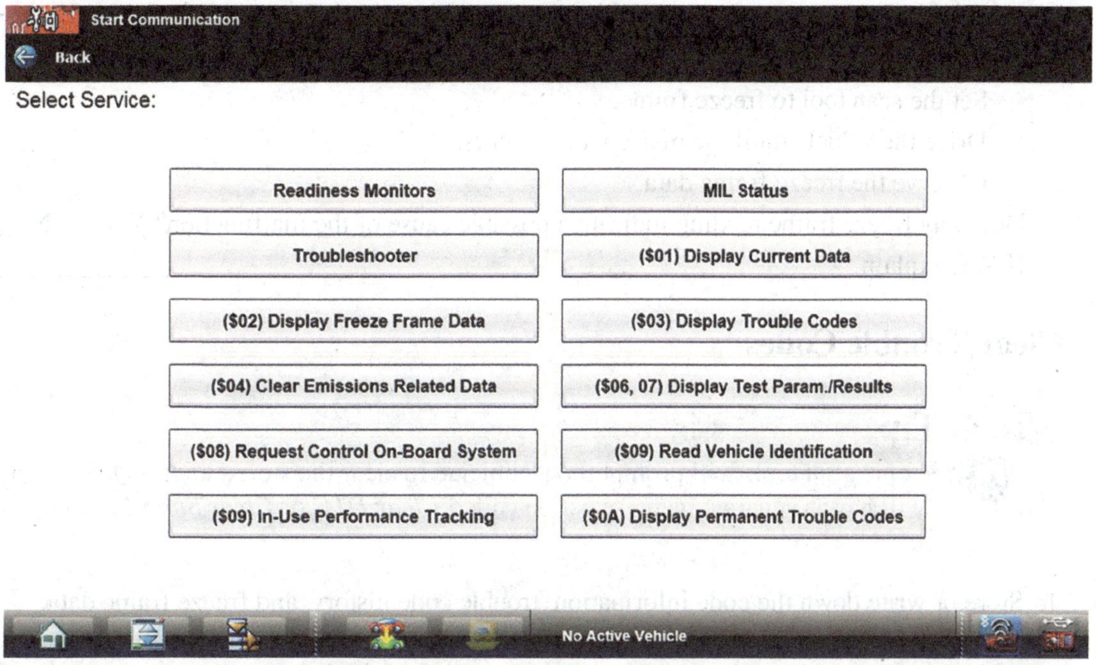

☐ 10. Back out of OBD II and enter scanner mode to access vehicle-specific codes. The scan tool will connect automatically if the vehicle is model year 2007 or newer; otherwise, vehicle information must be entered. List the codes found in scanner mode:

Trouble Code	**Meaning**
____________________	____________________
____________________	____________________
____________________	____________________
____________________	____________________
____________________	____________________
____________________	____________________

☐ 11. Look at freeze frame data in scanner mode. Again, only emissions-related codes will show. List the following common freeze frame data points:

RPM: _______

Engine temperature (ECT): _______

Airflow: _______

List other freeze frame data below that may be important to diagnosing the trouble codes found in step 10.

____

____

____

____

☐ 12. Compare the codes and freeze frame data in scanner mode to those in OBD II. Many will be the same, but list any that are different.

____

____

Obtain Freeze Frame Data

☐ 1. If a drivability problem is encountered based on the above steps, use the scan tool freeze frame feature to capture readings that occur at the time the malfunction occurs.
- Set the scan tool to freeze frame.
- Drive the vehicle until the malfunction occurs.
- Observe the freeze frame data.

Does any freeze frame reading indicate a possible cause of the malfunction? Yes ___ No ___

If Yes, explain. ____

Clear Trouble Codes

Tech Tip

Some scan tools will prompt the technician to clear the stored codes. Other scan tools will have a separate menu selection called *Clear DTC* or *Clear Stored Codes*.

☐ 1. Store or write down the code information, trouble code history, and freeze frame data.

Caution

On many OBD II systems, clearing the stored trouble codes also clears the record of all monitors (emission control system self-checks) performed. Do *not* clear the codes in states or counties that require periodic emissions inspections, as this will also clear the monitors. The monitors must reset before the vehicle will pass the emissions inspection.

☐ 2. Select the proper menu to clear codes. The menu should prompt you to clear codes.

☐ 3. Select *Yes* or *Enter* when prompted to clear codes. After a brief interval, the scan tool will tell you if the codes have been cleared.

Tech Tip

In some cases, the MIL light may flash while the scan tool is clearing the computer's memory.

☐ 4. After the scan tool indicates the codes have been cleared, recheck the computer's memory to ensure that the codes have been cleared.

☐ 5. If necessary, drive the vehicle or activate the system that caused the original code(s). Recheck the computer for codes after a few minutes of driving or system operation. Any code that resets is a hard code.

☐ 6. If your instructor directs you to do so, perform the following actions:
- Make further checks to isolate the problem(s) revealed by the trouble codes.
- Correct the problem(s) as necessary. Refer to other jobs as directed.
- Use the scan tool to confirm that the codes do not reset.

☐ 7. When the test is completed, turn the ignition switch to the *Off* position.

☐ 8. Remove the scan tool test connector cable from the diagnostic connector.

☐ 9. Detach the scan tool power lead from the accessory power outlet or battery terminals, if applicable.

Name____

Project 1: Job 4 *(continued)*

Run Monitors

Tech Tip

If the vehicle has an OBD II system, do *not* erase codes after repairs are completed. Erasing codes will also remove any monitors that have been run, which may cause the vehicle to fail its next emissions test.

☐ 1. After all repairs are complete, operate the vehicle to rerun the monitors. Running the monitors ensures that repairs have been successfully completed and no further service is needed. If any monitors fail, a trouble code will set, indicating the need for further service. When attempting to set the monitors, keep several points in mind:

- Some monitors are designed to run under certain ambient temperature conditions. In some parts of the United States, these temperatures may not be reached for many months, or ever.
- Monitors may not reset a trouble code until they have run several times. Therefore, it is not possible to determine the status of repairs without keeping the vehicle for an excessive amount of time.
- The vehicle may have to be returned to the owner before all monitors have reset.
- Most state emission inspections require a certain percentage, usually about 80%, of the monitors to have been run to pass inspection.

Job Wrap-Up

☐ 1. Clean the work area and return any equipment to storage.

☐ 2. Did you encounter any problems during this procedure? Yes ___ No ___

If Yes, describe the problems: ____

____

What did you do to correct the problems? ____

____

☐ 3. Have your instructor check your work and sign this job sheet.

Performance Evaluation—Instructor Use Only

How would you rate this student's overall performance on this task/job?

4 Competent/Proficient. Able to perform all elements of the task/job successfully and independently.

3 Satisfactory performance of the task/job. Able to perform elements of the task/job with minimal instructor assistance.

2 Completed the task/job with significant instructor assistance.

1 Unsuccessfully attempted the task/job.

0 No exposure. Note reason below (absence, skill not covered, etc.).

Comments:

____

____

____

____

Instructor's Signature: ___________________________

Name ______________________________

Date ______________________ Class ______________________

Project 1: Job 5—Identify Hybrid Vehicle High-Voltage Components and Disable High-Voltage Systems

After completing this job, you will be able to locate high-voltage system components and disconnects on a hybrid vehicle. You will also be able to disable hybrid vehicle high-voltage systems.

Instructions

As you read the job instructions, answer the questions and perform the tasks. Record your answers using complete sentences. Consult the proper service information and ask your instructor for help as needed.

Warning

Before performing this job, review all pertinent safety information in the text and discuss safety procedures with your instructor.

Procedures

☐ 1. Obtain a vehicle to be used in this job. Your instructor may direct you to perform this job on a shop vehicle.

☐ 2. Gather the tools needed to perform this job. Refer to the tools and materials list at the beginning of the project.

Locate High-Voltage System Components

Warning

Hybrid vehicles produce extremely high voltages! To avoid potentially fatal shocks, perform steps 1 and 2 on every hybrid vehicle before beginning any service operations. Check the manufacturer's service information for exact procedures.

☐ 1. Using the manufacturer's service information, identify the vehicle low- and high-voltage circuits.

☐ 2. Locate the high-voltage components and cables on the vehicle.

Tech Tip

The high-voltage cables on many hybrid vehicles are covered with orange insulation for easy identification, **Figure 5-1**.

Figure 5-1. Orange covers are used to identify hybrid high-voltage cables.

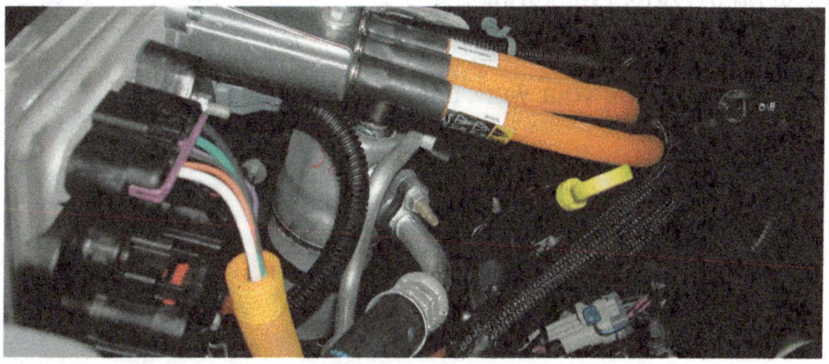

Locate High-Voltage System Disconnects

☐ 1. Check the vehicle service information for exact location of the disconnect device as applicable:
   - Auxiliary battery negative terminal.
   - Service disconnect plug.
   - Specific high-voltage circuit control fuse or control relay.

> **Warning**
> Wear insulated rubber gloves when working near any of the above electrical components.

☐ 2. Note the type of disconnect device and its location.
   Device: ______________________________
   Location: ______________________________

Disable Hybrid Vehicle High-Voltage Systems

☐ 1. Identify the vehicle low- and high-voltage circuits as explained earlier in this job.

☐ 2. Disable the high-voltage circuit by one of the following methods:
   - Disconnect the auxiliary battery negative terminal clamp.
   - Remove the service disconnect plug.
   - Remove the high-voltage circuit control fuse or control relay specifically designed to disable the high-voltage system.

> **Warning**
> Wear insulated rubber gloves when removing any of the above electrical components.

☐ 3. Wait at least five minutes to allow the full discharge of the high-voltage condensers.

☐ 4. Use a voltmeter or multimeter to test the high-voltage cables for low or zero voltage. Less than 12 volts is considered safe.

Job Wrap-Up

☐ 1. Clean the work area and dispose of old parts.

☐ 2. Did you encounter any problems during this procedure? Yes ___ No ___
   If Yes, describe the problems: ______________________________
   ____
   What did you do to correct the problems? ______________________________
   ____

☐ 3. Have your instructor check your work and sign this job sheet.

Name ____

Project 1: Job 5 *(continued)*

Performance Evaluation—Instructor Use Only

How would you rate this student's overall performance on this task/job?

4 Competent/Proficient. Able to perform all elements of the task/job successfully and independently.

3 Satisfactory performance of the task/job. Able to perform elements of the task/job with minimal instructor assistance.

2 Completed the task/job with significant instructor assistance.

1 Unsuccessfully attempted the task/job.

0 No exposure. Note reason below (absence, skill not covered, etc.).

Comments:

____

____

____

____

Instructor's Signature: ____

Notes

PROJECT 2

Diagnosing General Engine Concerns

Introduction

The most important part of engine performance service is determining what is wrong. It is almost impossible to service modern vehicles without knowing how to diagnose them. As you work through the jobs in this project, you will diagnose a variety of common engine concerns.

Usually, oil and coolant leaks will not affect engine performance until the fluid level is low enough to cause overheating or mechanical damage. On the other hand, fuel leaks are dangerous, may cause loss of fuel pressure, and may result in performance problems. Vacuum leaks have the most effect on engine operation. These leaks create a lean air-fuel mixture and cause loss of performance, rough idling, and overcompensation by the electronic control system. In Job 6, you will check for engine oil, coolant, fuel, and vacuum leaks.

Noise, vibration, and harshness (commonly called NVH) problems are frequent sources of complaints. Modern vehicles use more lightweight materials than older vehicles, which allows more NVH to reach the passenger compartment. Also, all of the drive train components of front-wheel drive vehicles are located at the front of the vehicle near the passenger compartment. Vans, pickup trucks, and SUVs have large sheet metal stampings that amplify any NVH developed by the moving parts. In Job 7, you will locate and correct NVH complaints and diagnose engine performance problems.

Scan tools are an important diagnostic instrument. Every vehicle system is controlled by, or sends input to, the on-board computer. This information can only be accessed with a scan tool. The on-board diagnostic systems on modern vehicles make it relatively easy to identify vehicle components that are causing driveability problems. If a scan tool returns a trouble code that indicates a sensor error, pinpoint tests of the sensor can be used to determine whether the sensor error is a result of a faulty sensor or is a symptom of another problem. You will access a vehicle computer, download diagnostic codes, and reprogram the computer in Job 8. In Job 9, you will follow up on diagnostic trouble codes by performing pinpoint sensor tests with a multimeter. You will perform additional pinpoint sensor tests with a scope in Job 10.

Newer vehicles with OBD II systems may contain several on-board modules (computers) to control the engine, transmission/transaxle, anti-lock brakes, and various body systems, such as keyless entry and theft protection. A computer that controls a vehicle system or systems is called a control module. The OBD II system controls communication between these modules. Problems occurring in the modules or the associated wiring can be difficult to track down. A scan tool must be used to begin diagnosing these problems. In Job 11, you will diagnose control module problems and communication errors between various vehicle modules.

Underneath all of the electronic devices on a modern engine are mechanical parts that would be recognized by a technician from 100 years ago. Before assuming that a problem is in one of the high-tech areas of the vehicle, it is often necessary to use a variety of diagnostic tests to eliminate the engine's internal parts as the source of problems. You will perform a vacuum test, power balance test, engine compression test, and cylinder leakage test in Job 12.

The cooling system removes about one-third of the heat produced by the engine. If the cooling system is neglected, the engine can overheat and be damaged in a short time. Lack of cooling system maintenance can affect vehicle driveability and heater operation. In Job 13, you will inspect and perform diagnostic tests on a cooling system.

Exhaust gas analyzers are used to measure the gases exiting the engine and, therefore, the air-fuel ratio and engine condition. Exhaust gas analyzers are invaluable for diagnosing performance, driveability, and emissions problems. In many states and cities, the technician must be able to use an exhaust gas analyzer to perform required emissions-compliance inspections. In Job 14, you will use an exhaust gas analyzer to check exhaust gases and interpret the results.

Project 2 Jobs

- Job 6—Check for Engine Oil, Coolant, Fuel, and Vacuum Leaks
- Job 7—Diagnose Engine and Vehicle Performance, Noise, and Vibration Problems
- Job 8—Use a Scan Tool to Access and Reprogram a Vehicle Computer
- Job 9—Use a Multimeter to Perform Pinpoint Sensor Tests
- Job 10—Use a Scope to Perform Pinpoint Sensor and Actuator Tests
- Job 11—Diagnose a Control Module and Module Communication Errors
- Job 12—Perform a Vacuum Test, Power Balance Test, Compression Test, and Cylinder Leakage Test
- Job 13—Inspect and Test a Cooling System
- Job 14—Use a Four- or Five-Gas Analyzer to Check Emission System Operation

Tools and Materials

The following list contains the tools and materials that may be needed to complete the jobs in this project. The items used will depend on the make and model of vehicle being serviced.

- Vehicle in need of performance diagnosis.
- Vehicle in need of emission testing.
- Vehicle with an NVH problem.
- Applicable service information.
- Four- or five-gas analyzer.
- Dye and black light.
- Talcum powder.
- Cooling system pressure tester.
- Carburetor cleaner.
- Propane enrichment device.
- Electronic leak detector.
- Smoke-generating machine.
- Scan tool and adapters.
- Scan tool operating instructions.
- Multimeter.
- Hand tools.
- Air-powered tools.
- Safety glasses and other protective equipment.

Safety Notice

Before performing these jobs, review all pertinent safety information in the text and review safety information with your instructor.

Notes

Name ____

Date ______________________________ Class ______________________

Project 2: Job 6—Check for Engine Oil, Coolant, Fuel, and Vacuum Leaks

After completing this job, you will be able to check an engine for fluid and vacuum leaks.

Instructions

As you read the job instructions, answer the questions and perform the tasks. Record your answers using complete sentences. Consult the proper service information and ask your instructor for help as needed.

Warning

Before performing this job, review all pertinent safety information in the text and discuss safety procedures with your instructor.

Procedures

☐ 1. Obtain a vehicle to be used in this job. Your instructor may direct you to perform this job on a shop vehicle or engine.

☐ 2. Gather the tools needed to perform the following job. Refer to the tools and materials list at the beginning of the project.

Visual Inspection

Caution

Before performing any work under the hood of a vehicle, always place covers over the fenders to prevent scratches and dings.

☐ 1. Inspect the top of the engine for leaks. Such leaks will usually be visible at the point of leakage.

- Common upper-engine oil leak points are valve covers, timing covers, and the oil filler cap.

Are any oil leaks found? Yes ___ No ___

If Yes, list the locations of the oil leaks: ____

____

- Common upper-engine fuel leak points are fuel fittings, hose clamps, and pressure regulators.

Are any fuel leaks found? Yes ___ No ___

If Yes, list the locations of the fuel leaks: ____

____

- Common upper-engine coolant leak points are hoses, hose fittings, radiator seams, and the radiator cap.

Are any coolant leaks found? Yes ___ No ___

If Yes, list the locations of the coolant leaks: ____

☐ 2. Obtain a drop light or other source of illumination.

☐ 3. Examine the underside of the vehicle for evidence of oil or grease. Slight seepage is normal.

Is excessive oil or grease observed? Yes ___ No ___

If Yes, where does the oil/grease appear to be coming from? ____

____

Tech Tip

Airflow under the vehicle will blow leaking oil backward. The leak may be some distance forward from where the oil appears.

Powder Method

- [ ] 1. Thoroughly clean the area around the suspected leak.
- [ ] 2. Apply talcum powder to the clean area.
- [ ] 3. Lower the vehicle from the lift and drive it several miles or carefully run it on the lift for 10–15 minutes.
- [ ] 4. Raise the vehicle (if necessary) and check the area around the suspected leak.

Warning

The vehicle must be raised and supported in a safe manner. Always use approved lifts or jacks and jack stands.

Does the powder show streaks of oil, fuel, or coolant? Yes ___ No ___

If Yes, which type of fluid is leaking and where does it appear to be coming from? ____________

____

Black Light Method

- [ ] 1. Ensure that the engine has enough oil and coolant. Add oil or coolant as needed.
- [ ] 2. Add fluorescent dye to the unit through the filler plug, being careful not to spill dye on the outside of the engine.
- [ ] 3. Lower the vehicle from the lift and drive it several miles, or carefully run it on the lift for 10–15 minutes.
- [ ] 4. Raise the vehicle, if necessary.

Warning

The vehicle must be raised and supported in a safe manner. Always use approved lifts or jacks and jack stands.

- [ ] 5. Turn on the black light and direct it toward the area around the suspected leak. See **Figure 6-1**.

Figure 6-1. When necessary, a black light can be used to locate leaks. (Tracer Products Division of Spectronics Corporation)

Name ____

Project 2: Job 6 *(continued)*

Does the black light show the presence of dye? Yes ___ No ___

If Yes, where does the dye appear to be coming from? ___________________________

____

☐ 6. Consult your instructor about the steps to take to correct the leak. Steps may include:
- Tightening fasteners.
- Replacing gaskets or seals.
- Replacing a cracked, broken, or punctured part.

Steps to be taken: ____

____

____

☐ 7. Make the necessary repairs.

Pressure Test a Cooling System

☐ 1. Obtain a cooling system pressure tester.

☐ 2. Check the condition of the radiator cap. Install the cap on the tester, **Figure 6-2**. Adapters may be needed to properly test the cap. Pump up pressure until the pressure levels off. A pressure specification should be printed somewhere on the cap. The radiator cap should hold this pressure without allowing it to drop.

Does the radiator cap pass the pressure test? Yes ___ No ___

If No, replace the radiator cap.

☐ 3. Remove the radiator cap from the pressure tester and install the pressure tester on the radiator filler neck, **Figure 6-3**. If the system is very low on coolant, first add coolant to make the job of pressurizing easier.

Figure 6-2. Install the pressure cap on the pressure tester. Adapters may be needed, as shown here. (Jack Klasey)

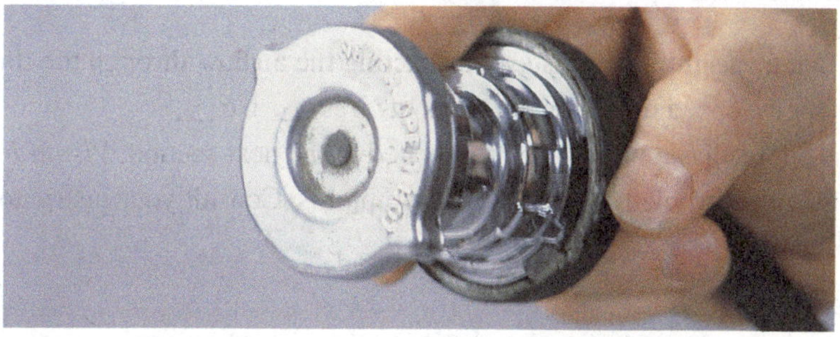

Figure 6-3. Install the pressure tester on the radiator filler neck. (Jack Klasey)

☐ 4. Pump up the pressure tester until the cooling system has been pressurized to the rating on the radiator cap. Carefully observe the cooling system for leaks. If no leaks are visible and the pressure holds for two minutes, the system is not leaking.

Does the cooling system pass the test? Yes ___ No ___

If No, consult your instructor for the steps to take to correct the leak. Steps may include any of the following:

- Tightening fasteners.
- Replacing gasket or seal.
- Replacing a cracked, broken, or punctured part.

Steps to be taken: ____

____

____

☐ 5. Make repairs as needed.

☐ 6. Recheck to ensure that the leak has been corrected.

Caution

If you add water to the cooling system for diagnostic testing, make sure you drain the system and refill it with the proper antifreeze-water mixture before releasing the vehicle to its owner.

Check for Vacuum Leaks

Tech Tip

Depending on equipment and vehicle availability, your instructor may assign some of the subtasks below instead of the entire series.

☐ 1. Confirm that a vacuum leak exists by restricting the airflow through the throttle valve.

Does the engine speed up and/or smooth out? Yes ___ No ___

If Yes, the engine has a vacuum leak. Proceed to the next section, *Visual Inspection*.

If No, some other problem is causing the symptoms. Consult your instructor as to what steps to take next.

Visual Inspection

☐ 1. Visually inspect vacuum hoses and connections. Look for disconnected, loose, or cracked hoses; broken fittings; damaged gaskets; loose fasteners; worn throttle shaft; and loose injector O-rings.

☐ 2. If the leak is severe with no obvious cause, check for an EGR valve that is stuck open.

Tech Tip

If necessary, check suspect vacuum-operated components by using a vacuum pump. Apply vacuum to various vacuum hoses and diaphragms to determine whether they hold vacuum.

Sound Method

☐ 1. Obtain an automotive stethoscope or length of vacuum hose.

☐ 2. Position the stethoscope or hose so that you can hear clearly, then search for the leak while the engine is running.

Name ____

Project 2: Job 6 *(continued)*

Tech Tip

This method usually works only on large or unusually noisy leaks.

Ultrasound Method

☐ 1. Obtain an ultrasound leak detector and calibrate it.

☐ 2. Start the engine and allow it to idle.

☐ 3. Pass the probe of the leak detector along the suspected leak area as the engine operates.

Does the detector find any leaks? Yes ___ No ___

If Yes, describe the location: ____

____

Hydrocarbon Richening Method

Warning

All of the substances used in this step are highly flammable. Use extreme caution and do *not* allow any flames, sparks, or other source of possible ignition in the immediate vicinity.

☐ 1. If the engine has an idle speed control governed by the ECM, disconnect the idle speed control solenoid or motor.

☐ 2. Start the engine and allow it to idle.

☐ 3. Apply a petroleum-based substance to the suspected leak area as the engine operates. Any one of the following methods is acceptable:

- Use a squirt can to apply automatic transmission fluid or light motor oil.
- Spray aerosol carburetor cleaner (most common method), **Figure 6-4**.
- Use a propane bottle attached to a length of rubber hose to direct a flow of propane.

Caution

Richening the mixture for long periods can damage the catalytic converter. Perform this step as quickly as possible.

Figure 6-4. Spray carburetor cleaner around the suspected leak while monitoring engine operation.

If a leak is present, engine speed should increase slightly and engine operation will become smoother when any of the hydrocarbons enter the leak. If transmission fluid or motor oil is used, white smoke will exit from the tailpipe(s).

Does the engine speed up and smooth out when one of the hydrocarbons is introduced to a certain location? Yes ___ No ___

If Yes, describe the location: ______________________________

____

Scan Tool Method

☐ 1. If a vacuum leak is slight, it may be difficult to detect a corresponding change in engine speed. When you suspect such a leak, connect a scan tool and use Mode $01 in OBD II to look at data. If the vehicle has a MAP sensor, look at the MAP sensor data. If there is no vacuum leak, vacuum on the MAP sensor will read approximately 35 kPa or approximately 10" Hg. When there is a vacuum leak, the numbers will be higher than 35 kPa or lower than 10" Hg.

☐ 2. Depress the throttle 50% and once again look at the MAP sensor data.

What is the MAP sensor vacuum with the throttle depressed 50%?

There will be less vacuum as the throttle is opened. Did the engine run better as you opened the throttle? Yes ___ No ___

If not, there is not a vacuum leak. *As the throttle is opened, a vacuum leak has less of an impact because the intake vacuum is decreasing as intake air volume is increasing.*

☐ 3. Turn the engine off. Move the ignition key back into the RUN position so data can be read again.

What is the MAP sensor vacuum with the engine off?

Since there is no vacuum when the engine is off, there is full atmospheric pressure in the intake manifold. This is equivalent to full throttle. When the throttle is wide open, full atmospheric pressure can enter the manifold.

Based on MAP sensor vacuum readings, does this vehicle exhibit signs of a vacuum leak?

Yes ___ No ___

If Yes, explain why? ______________________________

____

____

____

☐ 4. Still using the scan tool, look at the downstream oxygen sensor. This can be either bank 1, sensor 2 or bank 2, sensor 2 on engines with more than one cylinder head. When the vehicle is fully warmed up, the downstream oxygen sensor(s) will hover around 500 mV. If there is a vacuum leak and not a misfire, the downstream oxygen sensors will read lean, meaning under 400 mV but proportional to the severity of the leak. The worse the leak, the lower the oxygen sensor voltage.

What is the voltage of the downstream oxygen sensor(s)?

Bank 1, sensor 2 voltage: ______________________________

Bank 2, sensor 2 voltage: ______________________________

Explain what happens to the voltage of the downstream oxygen sensors as the throttle is opened?

____

____

____

Does this engine have a vacuum leak? Yes ___ No ___

Name ____________________

Project 2: Job 6 *(continued)*

☐ 5. To find the location of the vacuum leak, introduce the throttle body cleaner as previously discussed to areas around the intake plenum, injectors, vacuum tubing, and anything connected to intake manifold vacuum. Wait approximately 2 seconds for the downstream oxygen sensors to react, as the cleaner will need to make its way through the intake, through the combustion chamber, and then down the exhaust. Of course, if you hear the engine rpm change, you have found the leak and can use the downstream oxygen sensors to verify when they go rich, meaning above 600 mV.

Where is the vacuum leak on this engine? ____________________

____

____

What is needed to fix the vacuum leak on this engine? ____________________

____

____

Exhaust Analyzer Method

☐ 1. Locate the proper specifications for CO, HC, and O_2 at idle for this engine.

CO: ____________________

HC: ____________________

O_2: ____________________

☐ 2. Install the exhaust gas analyzer into the vehicle tailpipe.

☐ 3. Start and calibrate the exhaust gas analyzer.

☐ 4. Start the engine and allow readings to stabilize.

☐ 5. Note the readings to determine whether they indicate a vacuum leak.

- Large leaks affecting most cylinders will cause a very low CO reading and slightly higher, fluctuating HC and O_2 readings.
- A leak that affects only a few cylinders will cause high, fluctuating HC and O_2 readings. CO reading will be normal or slightly low.

Record the readings in the following spaces:

CO: ____________________

HC: ____________________

O_2: ____________________

☐ 6. Compare the CO, HC, and O_2 readings with the specifications obtained in step 1.

Do the readings indicate a vacuum leak? Yes ___ No ___

☐ 7. Use a propane bottle attached to a length of rubber hose to direct a flow of propane at suspected leak points. When propane is introduced into the leak, the following will happen:

- Idle will smooth out and possibly increase.
- HC and O_2 will drop.
- CO will rise.

Is there an improvement in idle speed and smoothness and/or a change in the HC/CO/O_2 readings? Yes ___ No ___

Smoke Machine Method

☐ 1. Obtain a smoke machine and set it to test for vacuum leaks.

☐ 2. If necessary, connect the shop air or nitrogen source to the smoke machine.

☐ 3. Set the flow and pressure on the smoke machine as necessary.

☐ 4. Install the smoke machine output hose on a fitting on the intake manifold or plenum. Use adapters as needed to ensure a leak-proof seal.

☐ 5. Start the flow of smoke into the intake system.

☐ 6. Carefully observe the entire engine air intake system for signs of smoke. Locations to concentrate on include the areas around the throttle body and manifold/plenum to engine gaskets, injector seals, vacuum fittings, EGR valve hoses and fittings, and vacuum hoses.

Caution

Fuel vapors will be present. Use a caged drop light or other safe light source to illuminate suspected areas, if necessary.

Is smoke observed at a potential leak point? Yes ___ No ___

If Yes, list the location(s): ______________________________

____

☐ 7. Consult your instructor about what steps to take and repair leaks as necessary, **Figure 6-5**.

Needed repairs: ______________________________

____

☐ 8. If approved by your instructor, correct the leak.

Briefly explain what you did to make repairs: ______________________________

____

____

☐ 9. Recheck to ensure that leaks have been corrected.

Are all vacuum leaks eliminated? Yes ___ No ___

If Yes, go to step 10.

If No, recheck for additional vacuum leaks.

☐ 10. Clear any trouble codes that were set during the testing and repair procedures.

Figure 6-5. Sometimes a vacuum leak can be easily corrected by reattaching a vacuum hose or retorquing the intake manifold fasteners, as shown here.

Name ____

Tech Tip

Before returning a vehicle to a customer, always inspect the work area and passenger compartment to ensure that all tools, parts, and debris related to the service have been picked up. Some companies may want the disposable floor mats and protective covers left in place until the customer takes possession of the vehicle. Always prepare the vehicle in accordance with your company or school's policy.

Job Wrap-Up

☐ 1. Clean the work area and return any equipment to storage.

☐ 2. Did you encounter any problems during this procedure? Yes ___ No ___

If Yes, describe the problems: ____

____

What did you do to correct the problems? ____

____

☐ 3. Have your instructor check your work and sign this job sheet.

Performance Evaluation—Instructor Use Only

How would you rate this student's overall performance on this task/job?

4 Competent/Proficient. Able to perform all elements of the task/job successfully and independently.

3 Satisfactory performance of the task/job. Able to perform elements of the task/job with minimal instructor assistance.

2 Completed the task/job with significant instructor assistance.

1 Unsuccessfully attempted the task/job.

0 No exposure. Note reason below (absence, skill not covered, etc.).

Comments:

____

____

____

____

Instructor's Signature: ____

Notes

Name ____

Date ______________________ Class ______________________

Project 2: Job 7—Diagnose Engine and Vehicle Performance, Noise, and Vibration Problems

After completing this job, you will be able to diagnose an engine or vehicle performance, noise, or vibration problem.

Instructions

As you read the job instructions, answer the questions and perform the tasks. Record your answers using complete sentences. Consult the proper service information and ask your instructor for help as needed.

Warning

Before performing this job, review all pertinent safety information in the text and discuss safety procedures with your instructor.

Procedures

☐ 1. Obtain a vehicle to be used in this job. Your instructor may direct you to perform this job on a shop vehicle.

☐ 2. Gather the tools needed to perform this job. Refer to the tools and materials list at the beginning of the project.

☐ 3. Gather the necessary service information to perform these procedures. Service information may include:

- Service information, in either printed or electronic format.
- Diagnosis manuals, in either printed or electronic format.
- Troubleshooting charts.
- Factory hotlines.
- Internet resources.

Diagnose an Engine Performance and/or Drivability Problem

Tech Tip

Some performance and driveability problems are not caused by an engine defect and may be out of the scope of this job. The procedures below will isolate driveability problems to the engine or determine that the problem is not engine related. If the testing below indicates that the defect is not connected to the engine, consult your instructor before proceeding.

☐ 1. Question the vehicle driver and note the driver's description of the problem.

____

____

____

Project 2: Job 7—Diagnose Engine and Vehicle Performance, Noise, and Vibration Problems *(continued)*

Symptoms

Into which of the following categories does the problem fall?

- Driveability and performance, for instance rough idle or poor acceleration. ___
- Sounds, for instance detonation or squealing. ___
- Odors, for instance a gasoline or exhaust smell in the passenger compartment. ___
- Poor fuel economy. ___
- Failed emissions test. ___

Are any of the following exhaust colors or odors associated with the problem?

- Black color. ___
- White color. ___
- Blue color. ___
- Raw gas odor. ___
- Burned odor. ___
- Oil or antifreeze odor. ___
- Other (describe): ____

____

Acceleration

Under which engine conditions does the problem occur?

- When accelerating. ___
- When decelerating. ___
- At a fixed speed (explain): ____

____

Road Conditions

Does the problem vary with the type of road surface? Yes ___ No ___.

If Yes, the problem is most likely not in the engine.

Temperature Conditions

Does the problem vary with engine temperature, such as a problem during warm-up that disappears when the engine reaches operating temperature? Yes ___ No ___.

Does the problem vary with outside air temperature, such as detonation that occurs only on very warm days? Yes ___ No ___.

Steering

Does the problem occur when driving straight ahead or during turns?

- Driving straight ahead. ___
- During turns. ___
- Makes no difference. ___

What types of noises or vibrations are experienced?

- Knocking noises. ___
- Whining noises. ___
- Steering wheel pulsation or binding. ___
- Other (describe):

____

Name ____

Project 2 Job 7 *(continued)*

Brakes

Does the problem occur or increase in severity when the brakes are applied? Yes ___ No ___

If Yes, what type of symptoms are reported?

- Noises. ___
- Pulsation of the brake pedal. ___
- Other (describe): ____

____

Drive Train

Does the problem occur only in a certain transmission gear or transfer case position? Yes ___ No ___

If Yes, which of the following apply?

- Slippage when changing gears. ___
- Gear hunting. ___
- Problem in one gear only. ___
- Other (describe): ____

____

Does the problem occur only when the manual clutch is being engaged or disengaged? Yes ___ No ___

If Yes, what symptoms are reported?

- Shudder. ___
- Grabbing. ___
- Slipping. ___
- Other (describe): ____

____

Does the problem occur only when the torque converter lockup clutch is engaged? Yes ___ No ___

If Yes, what symptoms are reported?

- Shudder. ___
- Failure to engage. ___
- Constant engagement/stalling when the vehicle is brought to a stop. ___
- Other (describe): ____

____

Accessories

Which vehicle accessories are operating or turned on when the problem occurs?

- Cruise control. ___
- Steering/suspension controls. ___
- ABS/traction controls. ___
- Air conditioner, heater, or ventilation system. ___
- Security system. ___
- Aftermarket accessories. ___
- Other (describe): ____

____

☐ 2. Road test the vehicle and try to match the conditions under which the problem is reported to occur.

Can the problem be duplicated? Yes ___ No ___

If Yes, describe the problem in your own words. Be as specific as possible: ____________________

____

____

____

Tech Tip

Use precise terms such as: hesitation when starting, surging during cruise, detonation, slow cranking when hot, and so on. Do *not* use vague terms such as "shot," "busted," or "had it."

Does your description of the problem agree with the driver's description of the problem?
Yes ___ No ___

If No, explain why: ____

____

☐ 3. Review the appropriate service information and any available service records for the vehicle.

Does the service information address the specific problem? Yes ___ No ___

If Yes, explain: ____

____

____

____

Does the repair history provide a clue to the cause of the problem? Yes ___ No ___

If Yes, explain: ____

____

____

____

Does the service information provide clues to the cause of the problem? Yes ___ No ___

If Yes, explain: ____

____

____

____

☐ 4. Check for obvious problems by performing the following checks:

- Make a visual inspection of the engine compartment. Check for obvious problems, such as disconnected wires or vacuum lines, broken connectors or parts, sticking throttle linkages, clogged air filters, and modifications to the engine mechanical, fuel, or ignition systems.

List any problems found: ____

____

____

- Check the electrical system for problems. Typical checks are for battery physical and electrical condition, starter amperage draw, and charging system voltage and amperage output.

List the electrical checks made and any problems found: ____________________

____

____

Name ____

Project 2: Job 7 *(continued)*

- Make visual inspections at other applicable points on the vehicle. For example, check for exhaust system components that are loose or vibrating against other components.

List the other areas checked and any problems found: ______________________

____

- Retrieve any trouble codes that may have been set. Refer to Job 4 as needed.

List the codes: ____

____

Can any defects found in this step be the cause of the problem determined in step 2?
Yes ___ No ___

Explain your answer: ____

____

____

____

☐ 5. Determine which component or system is causing the problem by performing the following tasks:

Tech Tip

In cases where an obvious problem is located before all steps are completed, your instructor can approve the elimination of some steps.

- Obtain the proper service information and other service information. ___
- Use the service information to compare the problem with trouble codes retrieved. ___
- Obtain needed test equipment. ___
- Familiarize yourself with the common sources of NVH complaints. **Figure 7-1** shows some typical causes of NVH complaints on a modern vehicle.
- Check engine systems. ___
- Check exhaust system. ___
- Check steering and suspension systems. ___
- Check drive train systems. ___
- Check motor and transmission/transaxle mounts. ___
- Check heater/air conditioner. ___
- Check other accessories as applicable. ___

List any abnormal conditions or readings that are not within specifications: ______________

____

____

____

____

Do you think this could be the cause of the problem? Yes ___ No ___

Explain your answer: ____

____

____

____

____

☐ 6. Eliminate any duplicate causes of problem by checking components that could cause the findings found in step 5.

- Make physical checks.

Describe the checks made and list any defective components or systems detected: ______________

____

____

- Make electrical checks.

Describe the checks made and list any defective components or systems detected: ______________

____

____

Do you think these defects could be the cause of the original problem? Yes ___ No ___

Explain your answer: ____

____

____

☐ 7. Isolate and recheck causes of the problem by performing the following:

- Recheck damaged components.
- Repeat electrical checks.

Did the rechecking procedure reveal any new problems or establish that the suspected components were in fact good? Yes ___ No ___

If Yes, explain: ____

____

Figure 7-1. Common areas of NVH complaints in vehicles with different powertrain arrangements. A—Rear-wheel drive. B—Front-wheel drive. C—Four-wheel drive.

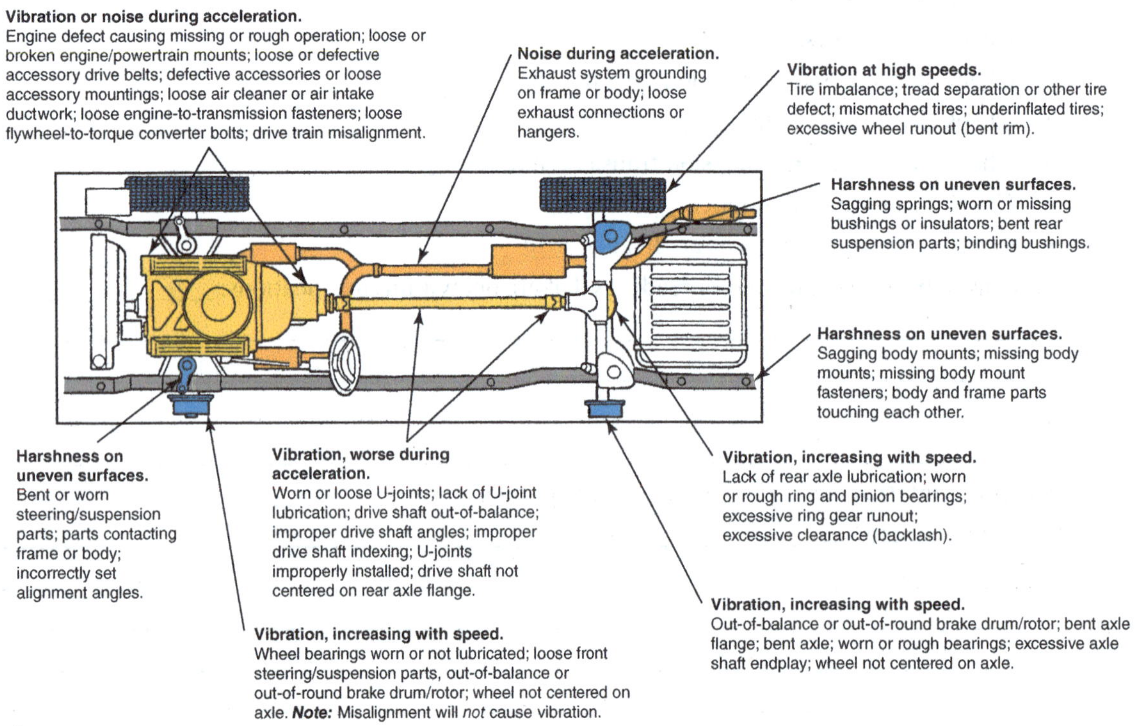

A

(continued)

Name ____________________

Project 2: Job 7 *(continued)*

If there are any differences with the conclusions in step 5, what is the reason? ____________________

____

Figure 7-1. (continued) Common areas of NVH complaints in vehicles with different powertrain arrangements. A—Rear-wheel drive. B—Front-wheel drive. C—Four-wheel drive.

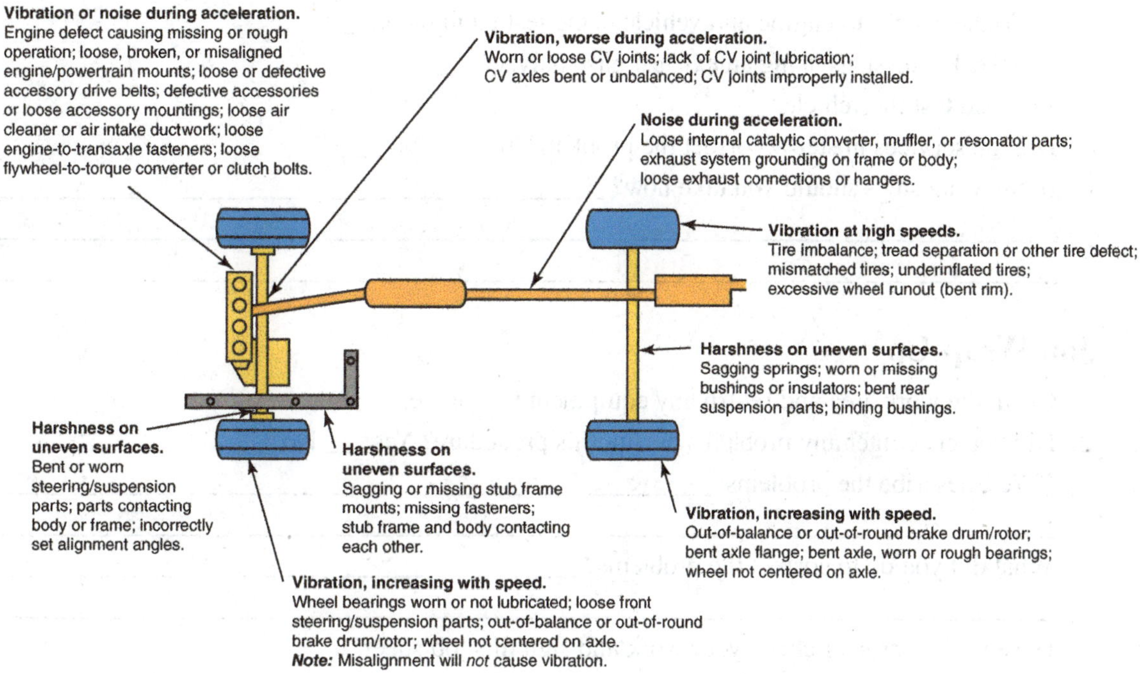

B

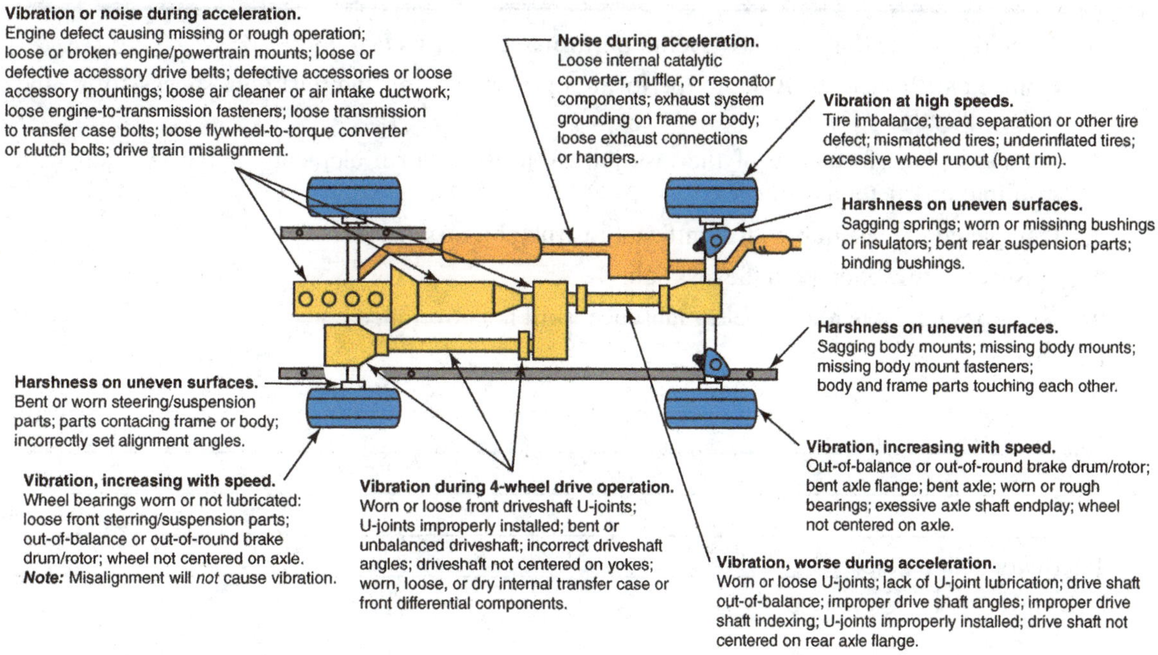

C

☐ 8. Correct the defect by making necessary repairs or adjustments.

Describe the services performed: ____________________

____

____

____

☐ 9. Recheck system operation by performing one or more of the following:

- Make checks to engine and vehicle using test equipment. ___
- Check emissions using an exhaust gas analyzer. ___
- Road test the vehicle. ___

Did the services in step 9 correct the problem? Yes ___ No ___

If No, what steps should you take now? ____________________

____

____

Job Wrap-Up

☐ 1. Clean the work area and return any equipment to storage.

☐ 2. Did you encounter any problems during this procedure? Yes ___ No ___

If Yes, describe the problems: ____________________

____

What did you do to correct the problems? ____________________

____

☐ 3. Have your instructor check your work and sign this job sheet.

Performance Evaluation—Instructor Use Only

How would you rate this student's overall performance on this task/job?

4 Competent/Proficient. Able to perform all elements of the task/job successfully and independently.

3 Satisfactory performance of the task/job. Able to perform elements of the task/job with minimal instructor assistance.

2 Completed the task/job with significant instructor assistance.

1 Unsuccessfully attempted the task/job.

0 No exposure. Note reason below (absence, skill not covered, etc.).

Comments:

____

____

____

____

Instructor's Signature: ____________________

Name ______________________________________

Date ____________________ Class ____________________

Project 2: Job 8—Use a Scan Tool to Access and Reprogram a Vehicle Computer

After completing this job, you will be able to use a scan tool to access a vehicle engine or powertrain computer for diagnosis purposes.

Instructions

As you read the job instructions, answer the questions and perform the tasks. Record your answers using complete sentences. Consult the proper service information and ask your instructor for help as needed.

Warning

Before performing this job, review all pertinent safety information in the text and discuss safety procedures with your instructor.

Procedures

- ☐ 1. Obtain a vehicle to be used in this job. Your instructor may direct you to perform this job on a shop vehicle.
- ☐ 2. Gather the tools needed to perform this job. Refer to the tools and materials list at the beginning of the project.
- ☐ 3. Obtain a scan tool and related service information for the vehicle selected in step 1.

  Type of scan tool: ______________________________

Tech Tip

There are many kinds of scan tools. The following procedure is a general guide to scan tool use. Always obtain the service instructions for the scan tool that you are using. If the scan tool literature calls for a different procedure or series of steps from those in this procedure, always perform procedures according to the scan tool literature.

Access the Vehicle Computer

- ☐ 1. Attach the proper test connector cable and power lead to the scan tool.
- ☐ 2. Ensure that the ignition switch is in the *Off* position.
- ☐ 3. Locate the correct diagnostic connector.

  Diagnostic connector location: ______________________________
- ☐ 4. Attach the scan tool test connector cable to the diagnostic connector, using the proper adapter if necessary.
- ☐ 5. Attach the scan tool power lead to the accessory power outlet or battery terminals, if necessary.

Tech Tip

OBD II scan tools are powered from terminal 16 of the diagnostic connector.

- ☐ 6. Observe the scan tool screen to ensure it is working properly.
- ☐ 7. Enter vehicle information as needed to program the scan tool. Many scan tools can be programmed with the proper vehicle information by entering the vehicle identification number (VIN).

Project 2: Job 8—Use a Scan Tool to Access and Reprogram a Vehicle Computer *(continued)*

☐ 8. Turn the ignition key to the *On* position.

☐ 9. Retrieve trouble codes and list them below.

Trouble codes: ____

____

Tech Tip

Vehicle computer systems in good condition will produce a single code to indicate that the engine is not running. If more than one code is produced, check with your instructor before continuing. The computer system and vehicle may have defects that are beyond the scope of this job.

☐ 10. Use the scan tool or factory service information to determine the meaning of the codes.

Code	Defect
__________	______________________________
__________	______________________________
__________	______________________________
__________	______________________________
__________	______________________________

☐ 11. Start the engine.

☐ 12. Have another student drive the vehicle while you record the following information. If a particular reading is not available, write "NA" in the space.

- Idle rpm: __________
  Is the idle speed within specifications? Yes ___ No ___
- Intake air temperature: __________
  Is the air intake temperature within specifications? Yes ___ No ___
- MAF sensor reading: __________
  Is the MAF sensor reading within specifications? Yes ___ No ___
- MAP sensor reading: __________
  Is the MAP sensor reading within specifications? Yes ___ No ___
- Fuel trim counts at idle: __________ At cruising speed: __________
  Are the fuel trim counts within specifications? Yes ___ No ___
- Does the torque converter lockup clutch apply at cruising speed? Yes ___ No ___
  Speeds at which the shift solenoids are energized:
  First: ______________________________
  Second: ______________________________
  Third: ______________________________
  Fourth: ______________________________
- Coolant temperature at the end of the test: __________°F or °C (circle one)
- Other readings as required by your instructor.

Type of Reading	Value (Include Units of Measure)	Within Specifications?
______________	______________	Yes ___ No ___
______________	______________	Yes ___ No ___
______________	______________	Yes ___ No ___
______________	______________	Yes ___ No ___

Name ____

Project 2: Job 8 *(continued)*

☐ 13. When the testing is complete, turn the ignition switch to the *Off* position.

☐ 14. If your instructor directs, make further checks to isolate the problem(s) revealed by the trouble codes or other readings. Refer to Job 9 and Job 10 as needed.

☐ 15. If your instructor directs, repair the problem(s) as necessary. Refer to other jobs as directed.

Reprogram the Computer

☐ 1. Determine the method to be used to reprogram the vehicle computer.

Which reprogramming method will be used? Upload-download ___ Pass through ___

☐ 2. The methods for reprogramming the computer are covered in the following two sections of the job. Follow the procedure in the appropriate section and disregard the other procedure.

Upload-Download Method

> **Tech Tip**
>
> This method is sometimes referred to as indirect programming.

☐ 1. If not done previously, ensure that the ignition switch is in the *Off* position and connect the scan tool to the vehicle diagnostic connector.

☐ 2. Observe the scan tool screen and ensure that the tool is operating properly.

☐ 3. If necessary, use the scan tool keypad to enter vehicle information.

☐ 4. Turn the ignition switch to the *On* position if necessary.

☐ 5. Download the existing ECM programming into the scan tool.

Briefly describe the steps taken to download the programming. Be sure to include menus selected and scan tool keys operated. ____

____

____

____

☐ 6. When downloading is complete, turn the ignition switch to the *Off* position and disconnect the scan tool from the vehicle diagnostic connector. **Figure 8-1** shows a scan tool with downloaded ECM programming.

☐ 7. Take the scan tool to the Internet connection, modem, or programming computer.

☐ 8. Access the programming database.

Database name: ____

☐ 9. Download the updated programming into the scan tool.

Briefly describe the steps taken to begin the downloading process: ______________________

____

____

____

> **Tech Tip**
>
> Several minutes may be needed to overwrite the existing programming. The computer and/or scan tool will indicate the finish of the downloading process.

Figure 8-1. This scan tool is performing an over-the-air (OTA) update. This is a scripted operation that provides instructions as it progresses.

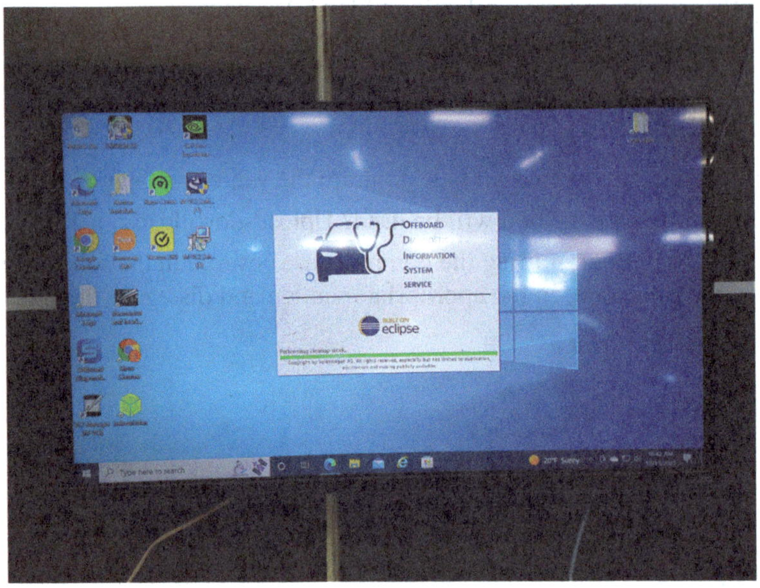

☐ 10. When the new programming has been installed in the scan tool, unplug the tool and take it to the vehicle.

☐ 11. Plug the scan tool into the diagnostic connector and, if necessary, turn the ignition switch to the *On* position.

☐ 12. Operate the scan tool as necessary to install the new programming into the vehicle ECM.

Briefly describe the steps taken to install the new programming, including scan tool menus selected:

____

____

____

☐ 13. After reprogramming is complete, start the engine and test drive the vehicle to ensure that the new programming has been properly entered.

Does operation of the ECM and vehicle indicate that the new programming has been properly installed? Yes ___ No ___

If No, describe the problem(s): ____

____

What could be the reason for the problem(s)? ______________________________________

____

____

Tech Tip

After reprogramming, many ECMs must go through a relearn procedure to properly control idle speed and other vehicle functions. This may take several minutes of driving. Some manufacturers require the technician to perform a specific series of relearning steps. Consult the manufacturer's service information for these procedures.

☐ 14. Park the vehicle and turn the ignition switch to the *Off* position.

☐ 15. Unplug the scan tool from the diagnostic connector.

Name ____

Project 2: Job 8 *(continued)*

Pass-Through Method

Tech Tip

This method is sometimes referred to as direct programming, flash reprogramming, or J2534 programming.

☐ 1. Park the vehicle at a place in the shop where it can be attached to the Internet connection using the available connecting cables.

☐ 2. If not done previously, ensure that the ignition switch is in the *Off* position.

☐ 3. Connect the scan tool or reprogramming tool to the vehicle diagnostic connector.

☐ 4. Attach the scan tool or reprogramming tool to the Internet connection using correct cables. This connection is usually made through an Internet-ready computer, **Figure 8-2**.

☐ 5. Turn the ignition switch to the *On* position if necessary.

☐ 6. Use the computer (and scan tool if required) to access the remote reprogramming website.
Name of website: ____

☐ 7. Follow website instructions to reprogram the vehicle ECM.
Briefly describe the steps taken to reprogram the ECM: ______________________
____
____

Tech Tip

Several minutes may be needed to overwrite the existing programming. The website will indicate when the program has finished downloading.

☐ 8. After reprogramming is complete, exit the website and turn the ignition switch to the *Off* position.

☐ 9. Unplug the scan tool or reprogramming tool from the vehicle diagnostic connector and remove it from the vehicle.

Figure 8-2. The reprogramming tool shown here is usually called a J2534 tool. Connection methods vary but usually consist of attaching one cable from the diagnostic connector to the tool, and another from the tool to the computer.

☐ 10. Start the engine and test drive the vehicle to ensure that the new programming has been properly entered.

Does operation of the ECM and vehicle indicate that the new programming has been properly installed? Yes ___ No ___

If No, describe the problem(s): ____

____

____

What could be the reason for the problem(s)? ______________________________________

____

____

Tech Tip

After reprogramming, many ECMs must go through a relearn procedure to properly control idle speed and other vehicle functions. This may take several minutes of driving. Some manufacturers require the technician to perform a specific series of relearning steps. Consult the manufacturer's service information for these procedures.

☐ 11. If necessary, disconnect the scan tool or reprogramming tool from the computer.

☐ 12. Turn off the computer and return any cables to storage.

Job Wrap-Up

☐ 1. Return the scan tool to storage.

☐ 2. Clean the work area and return any equipment to storage.

☐ 3. Did you encounter any problems during this procedure? Yes ___ No ___

If Yes, describe the problems: ____

____

What did you do to correct the problems? ______________________________________

☐ 4. Have your instructor check your work and sign this job sheet.

Performance Evaluation—Instructor Use Only

How would you rate this student's overall performance on this task/job?

4 Competent/Proficient. Able to perform all elements of the task/job successfully and independently.

3 Satisfactory performance of the task/job. Able to perform elements of the task/job with minimal instructor assistance.

2 Completed the task/job with significant instructor assistance.

1 Unsuccessfully attempted the task/job.

0 No exposure. Note reason below (absence, skill not covered, etc.).

Comments:

____

____

____

____

Instructor's Signature: ____

Name ____________________

Date ____________________ Class ____________________

Project 2: Job 9—Use a Multimeter to Perform Pinpoint Sensor Tests

After completing this job, you will be able to use a multimeter to test sensors.

Instructions

As you read the job instructions, answer the questions and perform the tasks. Record your answers using complete sentences. Consult the proper service information and ask your instructor for help as needed.

Warning

Before performing this job, review all pertinent safety information in the text and discuss safety procedures with your instructor.

Procedures

- [ ] 1. Obtain a vehicle to be used in this job. Your instructor may direct you to perform this job on a shop vehicle.
- [ ] 2. Gather the tools needed to perform this job. Refer to the tools and materials list at the beginning of the project.
- [ ] 3. Obtain a multimeter and related service information for the vehicle selected in step 1.

Type of multimeter: ____________________

Tech Tip

There are many kinds of multimeters. The following procedure is a general guide to multimeter use. Always obtain the service instructions for the multimeter that you are using. If the multimeter literature calls for a different procedure or series of steps from those in this procedure, always perform procedures according to the multimeter literature.

Caution

Be sure that the multimeter that you are using is a high-impedance type. An older, low-impedance multimeter can allow too much current to flow through the sensor being tested, possibly causing damage.

Test Sensor Resistance

Tech Tip

The following general rules apply to sensor resistance specifications:

- Many sensors will have a resistance specification given as a range, such as 600–900 ohms. Any reading within this range is considered correct.
- The resistance of many sensors varies with engine variables such as temperature, throttle position, manifold vacuum, airflow, and engine speed.
- Sensors that do not have a published resistance specification should not be tested.

☐ 1. Attach the test leads to the proper multimeter outlets.

☐ 2. Turn the multimeter on and set it to read resistance.

☐ 3. If the sensor will be tested on the vehicle, ensure that the ignition switch is in the *Off* position.

☐ 4. Locate the sensor to be tested.

Sensor being tested: ______________________________

Sensor location: ______________________________

☐ 5. Obtain the sensor resistance specification and write it in the space below.

Sensor resistance specification ____________ at ____________

Tech Tip

Use the second space to record a value that will affect resistance. Examples are percent of throttle opening for a throttle position sensor, or actual temperature of a temperature sensor. These values can be varied to check how the sensor reacts to changes in the value that it is measuring.

☐ 6. Place the leads of the multimeter on the appropriate terminal(s) of the sensor to be tested. This can be done with the sensor in the vehicle, as in **Figure 9-1**, or removed from the vehicle, as in **Figure 9-2**. Make sure that you place the leads on the proper terminals. For a single terminal sensor, place one lead on the terminal and the other on the body of the sensor. On units with more than one terminal, such as the one in **Figure 9-3**, check the service information and place the leads on the appropriate terminals.

☐ 7. Observe and record the resistance reading on the multimeter.

Resistance: ________ ohms at ____________

Tech Tip

Use the following spaces to show whether resistance changes in reaction to changes in the value that is being measured. For instance, MAP sensor values should change smoothly as vacuum is applied to the sensor. Consult your instructor about performing operations to change the values being measured.

Figure 9-1. This sensor is being checked while it is still installed on the vehicle. Be sure that you are checking the right sensor. For instance, this engine has two coolant temperature sensors, one connected to the ECM and another connected to the temperature gauge.

Name ____

Project 2: Job 9 *(continued)*

Resistance: _________ ohms at ____________________
Resistance: _________ ohms at ____________________
Resistance: _________ ohms at ____________________
Resistance: _________ ohms at ____________________

Figure 9-2. This sensor has been removed from the vehicle for testing.

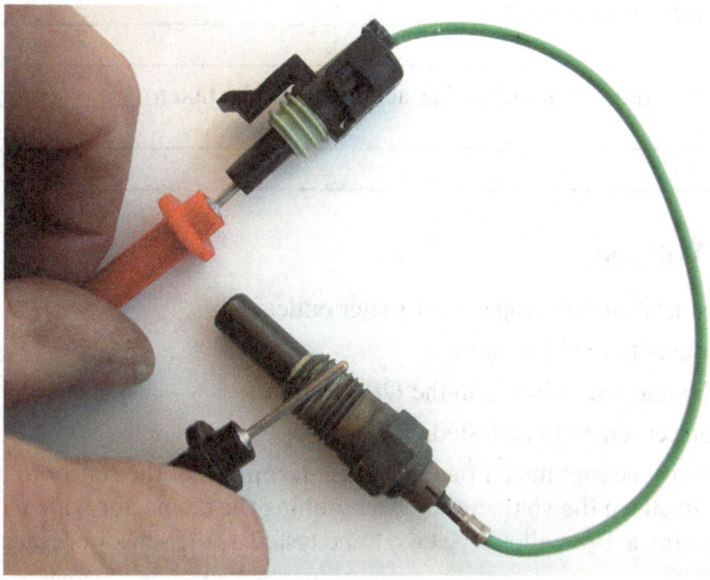

Figure 9-3. Before testing a sensor with several terminals, be sure that you are checking the proper terminals.

☐ 8. Compare the resistance to specifications.

Is the resistance correct? Yes ___ No ___

If Yes, consult your instructor.

Is the reading too high or infinity? Yes ___ No ___

If Yes, what does this indicate? ____

____

Is the reading too low or zero? Yes ___ No ___

If Yes, what does this indicate? ____

____

Based on the resistance readings, what action should be taken? ____________________

____

____

Test Sensor Voltage

☐ 1. Attach the test leads to the proper multimeter outlets.

☐ 2. Set the multimeter to read voltage.

☐ 3. Ensure that the ignition switch is in the *Off* position.

☐ 4. Locate the correct sensor to be tested.

☐ 5. Place the leads of the multimeter on the correct terminals of the sensor to be tested. It may be necessary to attach the voltmeter by backprobing the connector with a T-pin as shown in **Figure 9-4**. Using a T-pin allows voltage to be tested as the sensor operates.

Caution

Most manufacturers caution against piercing wire insulation. Damage to the insulation allows moisture to enter the wire, causing corrosion and high resistance.

Figure 9-4. To make voltage tests of some sensors, it may be necessary to back probe the connector using a T-pin so the sensor to be tested as it operates.

Name ____

Project 2: Job 9 *(continued)*

☐ 6. Turn the ignition switch to the *On* position.

☐ 7. Observe and record the multimeter voltage reading.

Voltage: _____ volts

Is the voltage within specifications? Yes ___ No ___

If Yes, proceed to step 8.

If No, determine whether the loss in voltage is caused by the sensor itself or a problem with the reference voltage supplied to the sensor. This can usually be determined by unplugging the sensor and noting the reference voltage.

Is the reference voltage normal? Yes ___ No ___

If Yes, the problem is in the sensor. Consult your instructor, and replace the sensor as directed.

If No, there is a battery, ECM, or wiring problem. Consult your instructor and correct the problem as directed before continuing.

☐ 8. Start the engine.

☐ 9. Observe and record the multimeter voltage reading.

Voltage: _____ volts

☐ 10. Compare the voltage readings to specifications.

Is the voltage within specifications? Yes ___ No ___

☐ 11. Vary the test conditions or take other readings as necessary to determine whether sensor voltages are correct. The following are examples of how test conditions might be varied or additional readings might be required, depending on the sensor being tested:

- Increasing engine speed to check throttle position, air flow, and engine speed sensors.
- Placing a load on the engine to check MAP sensors.
- Driving the vehicle to check vehicle speed sensors.

☐ 12. Describe the actions performed in step 11 and record the voltage reading.

Action performed	**Voltage reading**	**Voltage specification**
______________	__________	__________
______________	__________	__________
______________	__________	__________
______________	__________	__________

Are the voltage readings within specification? Yes ___ No ___

If No, what action should be taken? ____

____

☐ 13. When the testing is complete, turn the ignition switch to the *Off* position.

☐ 14. If your instructor directs, make further checks to isolate the problem(s) revealed by the other readings.

☐ 15. If your instructor directs, repair the problem(s) as necessary. Refer to other jobs as directed.

Test Sensor or Actuator Circuit Voltage Drop

☐ 1. Attach the test leads to the meter outlets for reading voltage.

☐ 2. Set the multimeter to read DC voltage.

☐ 3. Ensure that the ignition switch is in the *On* position.

☐ 4. Locate the sensor or actuator to be tested.

☐ 5. Locate the correct wiring diagram associated with this circuit so that the beginning and end of the circuit are found in the cavities of the connectors of the ECU and the component.

☐ 6. Back probe the connector cavities of the wires in question. Polarity of the meter may not matter to you if you are only looking for voltage drop in the wire.

☐ 7. With the circuit operating, the goal is to be as close to 0 mV as possible, as voltage loss, signal voltage loss, or ground loss makes the sensor signal accuracy lower or the actuator output lower.

Reference or power wire voltage drop: _____

Signal wire voltage drop: _____

Ground wire voltage drop: _____

☐ 8. Acceptable voltage drop loss is under 200 mV on a non-computer circuit and under 100 mV for a computerized circuit.

Did any of the wires have an unacceptable voltage drop? Yes ___ No ___

☐ 9. If any of the wires had an unacceptable voltage drop, what was the reason for the excessive voltage drop?

____

____

____

____

Job Wrap-Up

☐ 1. Return the multimeter to storage.

☐ 2. Clean the work area and return any equipment to storage.

☐ 3. Did you encounter any problems during this procedure? Yes ___ No ___

If Yes, describe the problems: ____

____

What did you do to correct the problems? ____

☐ 4. Have your instructor check your work and sign this job sheet.

Performance Evaluation—Instructor Use Only

How would you rate this student's overall performance on this task/job?

4 Competent/Proficient. Able to perform all elements of the task/job successfully and independently.

3 Satisfactory performance of the task/job. Able to perform elements of the task/job with minimal instructor assistance.

2 Completed the task/job with significant instructor assistance.

1 Unsuccessfully attempted the task/job.

0 No exposure. Note reason below (absence, skill not covered, etc.).

Comments:

____

____

____

____

Instructor's Signature: ____

Name ______________________________

Date ____________________ Class ____________________

Project 2: Job 10—Use a Scope to Perform Pinpoint Sensor and Actuator Tests

After completing this job, you will be able to use a scope to test sensors.

Instructions

As you read the job instructions, answer the questions and perform the tasks. Record your answers using complete sentences. Consult the proper service information and ask your instructor for help as needed.

Warning

Before performing this job, review all pertinent safety information in the text and discuss safety procedures with your instructor.

Procedures

☐ 1. Obtain a vehicle to be used in this job. Your instructor may direct you to perform this job on a shop vehicle.

☐ 2. Gather the tools needed to perform this job. Refer to the tools and materials list at the beginning of the project.

☐ 3. Obtain a scope and related service information for the vehicle selected in step 1. **Figure 10-1** shows a typical modern 4-channel scope.

Type of scope used: ______________________________

Tech Tip

There are many kinds of automotive scopes. A scope may be called a waveform meter, DSO, or pulse meter. The following procedure is a general guide to scope use. Always obtain the service instructions for the scope that you are using. If the scope literature calls for a different procedure or series of steps from those in this procedure, always perform procedures according to the scope literature.

Figure 10-1. This is a modern 4-channel scope. This scope allows up to four different waveforms to be tested at one time.

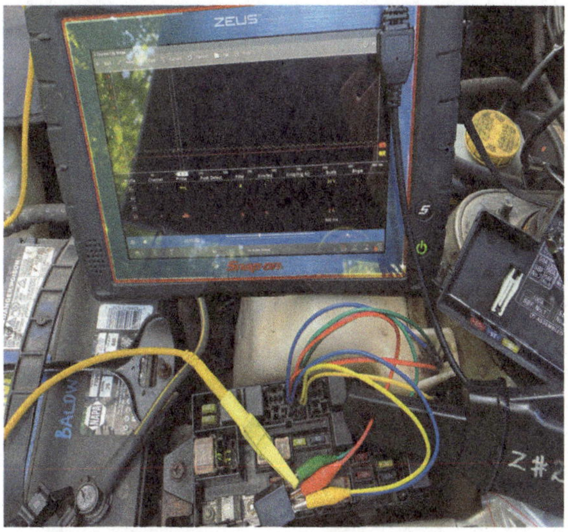

Test a Sensor for Proper Waveform

☐ 1. Attach the proper test connector cable and power lead to the scope.

☐ 2. Ensure that the ignition switch is in the *Off* position.

☐ 3. Locate the correct sensor to be tested.

Sensor being tested: ______________________________

Sensor location: ______________________________

☐ 4. Attach the scope leads to the sensor and other engine components as necessary.

Typical connections include sensor leads, positive and negative battery leads, engine rpm pickup, and inductive current pickup. Many scopes have provisions for attaching probes to individual spark plug wires and fuel injector harnesses.

Tech Tip

It may be necessary to attach the scope through jumper wires as shown in **Figure 10-1**. Using this type of testing arrangement allows the pattern to be observed as the sensor operates.

☐ 5. Turn the scope on and observe the screen or control lights to ensure that the scope is working properly.

☐ 6. Adjust the scope settings as needed.

☐ 7. Turn the ignition key to the *On* position or start the vehicle as needed.

☐ 8. Read the sensor scope pattern, varying test conditions as needed. The following are examples of how test conditions might be varied depending on the sensor being tested:

- Increasing engine speed to check throttle position, air flow, and engine speed sensors.
- Placing a load on the engine to check MAP sensors.
- Driving the vehicle to check vehicle speed sensors.

Describe any changes made to the testing conditions: ______________________________

____

____

☐ 9. Draw the pattern as it appears on the scope.

Name ____

Project 2: Job 10 *(continued)*

☐ 10. Draw the pattern of a properly functioning sensor.

☐ 11. Compare the patterns.

Does the observed pattern match the pattern of a properly functioning sensor? Yes ___ No ___

If No, what action should be taken? ____

____

____

☐ 12. When the testing is complete, turn the ignition switch to the *Off* position.

☐ 13. Remove the scope test leads from the vehicle.

☐ 14. If your instructor directs, make further checks to isolate the problem(s) revealed by the trouble codes or other readings.

☐ 15. If other sensors are being tested, draw and compare the observed and specified patterns on a separate sheet of paper.

☐ 16. If your instructor directs, repair the problem(s) as necessary. Refer to other jobs as directed.

Using a Low-Amp Clamp to View Actuator Waveforms

☐ 1. Obtain a vehicle with a working engine for this job. Your instructor may direct you to perform this job on a shop vehicle.

☐ 2. Attach a low-amp clamp to the scope.

☐ 3. Locate the actuator to be tested.

Actuator being tested: ____

Actuator location: ____

☐ 4. To get the low-amp clamp around the wire of the single actuator, such as an injector, an ignition coil, or a relay, a portion of the electrical tape or harness may need to be cut back. Another option is to use a wiring diagram to locate a fuse that feeds multiple injectors, coils, or relays. A fused jumper wire can be installed in place of the fuse and the low-amp clamp can be connected around the jumper wire. See **Figure 10-2**.

Which method did you use? ____

Figure 10-2. Although this low-amp clamp is being used to check the fuel pump, the method can be used when checking injectors or ignition coils at the fuse box.

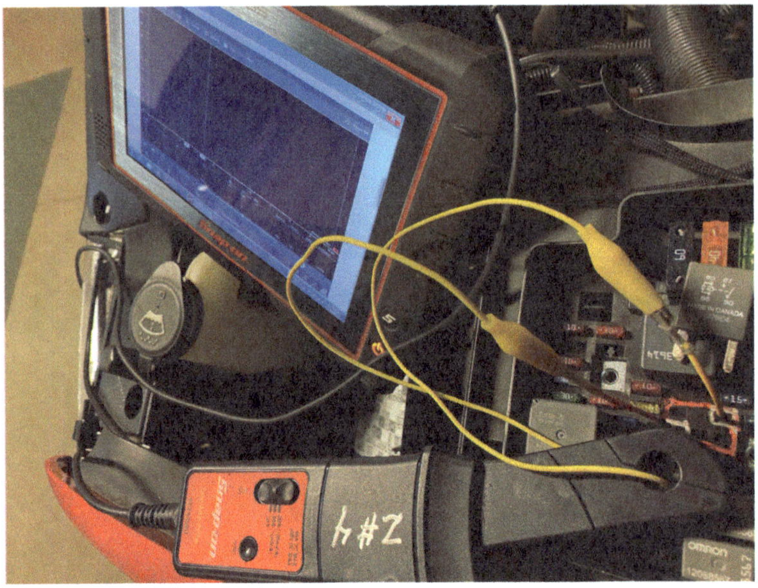

☐ 5. Set the scope up to read the low-amp clamp.

Tech Tip

The low-amp clamp reads the magnetic field around a wire and amplifies it. The signal the amp clamp produces is proportional to the current in the wire. Therefore, the clamp sends a voltage to the scope. If your scope does not have an amp-clamp function, then select DC millivolts to read the amp clamp.

☐ 6. Start the engine and allow it to run. Some scopes have an auto-find feature that can be used, such as guided component tests. This feature walks the user through the setup step-by-step, showing which scope leads to use and where to place these leads. If your scope does not have these features, then a safe place to start to find your waveform is 50 volts by 50 milliseconds. Change the voltage (called scale) and the time (called sweep) to obtain one waveform on the screen. The waveform should fill most of the screen.

For an injector, a coil, and a relay, the waveform should have a ramp, a plateau, and a falling edge. See the red waveform of **Figure 10-3**.

Note that there is a slight indentation approximately 2/3 of the way up the ramp of the red waveform in **Figure 10-3**. This is the indication that the pintle of the injector moved to allow fuel to pass. A relay would have the same indentation to show the connection moved. If there is no indentation, the injector, relay, or even a solenoid did not operate. If you are testing an ignition coil, there would be little to no indentation.

The ramp is evidence that the magnetic field is building. The plateau shows that the magnetic field is being maintained. The falling edge is the field collapsing at the end of the operation. If the ramp is anything but a slope, the coil of wires in the component are shorted or open: replace the part.

☐ 7. Test an ignition coil using a low-amp clamp and draw the ramp on a separate sheet of paper.

☐ 8. Test a fuel injector using a low-amp clamp and draw the ramp on a separate sheet of paper.

☐ 9. Test a relay or solenoid using a low-amp clamp and draw the ramp on a separate sheet of paper.

Name ____

Project 2: Job 10 *(continued)*

Figure 10-3. This scope screenshot shows waveforms produced by a fuel injector. The red waveform represents current, while the yellow waveform represents voltage.

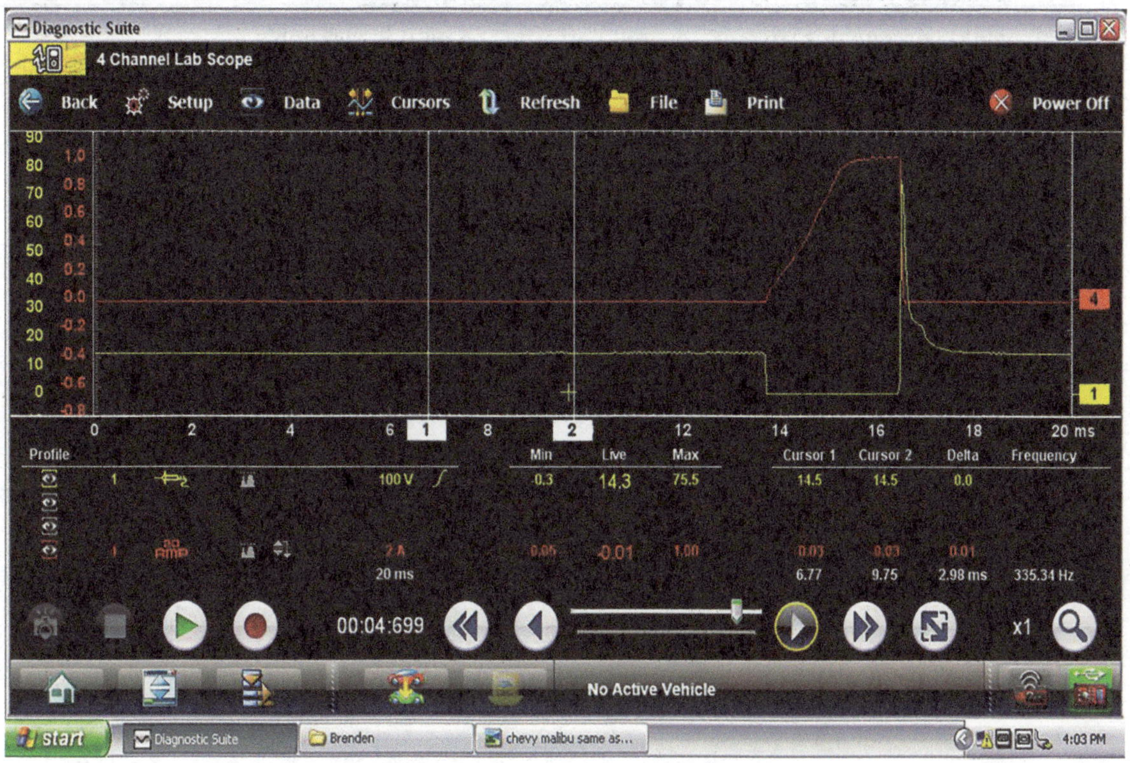

☐ 10. Were any of your components open or shorted? Yes ___ No ___

☐ 11. If Yes, list the components and explain how you determined they were open or shorted.

____

____

☐ 12. Once the testing is complete, turn the ignition switch to the *Off* position.

☐ 13. Remove any jumper wires and the amp clamp from the vehicle.

☐ 14. Remember to turn off the amp clamp to save the battery.

☐ 15. Turn off the scope.

Job Wrap-Up

☐ 1. Return the scope to storage.

☐ 2. Clean the work area and return any equipment to storage.

☐ 3. Did you encounter any problems during this procedure? Yes ___ No ___

If Yes, describe the problems: ____

____

What did you do to correct the problems? ____

____

____

☐ 4. Have your instructor check your work and sign this job sheet.

Performance Evaluation—Instructor Use Only

How would you rate this student's overall performance on this task/job?

4 Competent/Proficient. Able to perform all elements of the task/job successfully and independently.

3 Satisfactory performance of the task/job. Able to perform elements of the task/job with minimal instructor assistance.

2 Completed the task/job with significant instructor assistance.

1 Unsuccessfully attempted the task/job.

0 No exposure. Note reason below (absence, skill not covered, etc.).

Comments:

____

____

____

____

Instructor's Signature: ____

Name ______________________________

Date ____________________ Class ____________________

Project 2: Job 11—Diagnose a Control Module and Module Communication Errors

After completing this job, you will be able to diagnose control module problems and inter-module communication errors.

Instructions

As you read the job instructions, answer the questions and perform the tasks. Record your answers using complete sentences. Consult the proper service information and ask your instructor for help as needed.

Warning

Before performing this job, review all pertinent safety information in the text and discuss safety procedures with your instructor.

Procedures

Tech Tip

There are many kinds of scan tools. The following procedure is a general guide to scan tool use. Always obtain the service instructions for the scan tool that you are using. If the scan tool literature calls for a different procedure or series of steps from what is in this procedure, always perform procedures according to the scan tool literature.

☐ 1. Obtain a vehicle to be used in this job. Your instructor may direct you to perform this job on a shop vehicle.

☐ 2. Gather the tools needed to perform this job. Refer to the tools and materials list at the beginning of the project.

☐ 3. Obtain a scan tool and related service information for the vehicle selected in step 1.

Type of scan tool: ______________________________

☐ 4. Attach the proper test connector cable and power lead to the scan tool.

☐ 5. Ensure that the vehicle's ignition switch is in the *Off* position.

☐ 6. Locate the correct diagnostic connector.

Describe the diagnostic connector location: ______________________________

____

☐ 7. Attach the scan tool test connector cable to the diagnostic connector. If necessary, install the proper adapter.

☐ 8. Attach the scan tool power lead to the accessory power outlet or battery terminals as needed.

Tech Tip

OBD II scan tools are powered from terminal 16 of the diagnostic connector.

☐ 9. Observe the scan tool screen to ensure the scan tool is working properly.

☐ 10. Enter vehicle information as needed to program the scan tool. Many scan tools can be programmed with the proper vehicle information by entering the vehicle identification number (VIN). If the scan tool can read the VIN from the vehicle computer, skip this step.

☐ 11. Turn the vehicle's ignition switch to the *On* position.

☐ 12. Determine whether the scan tool communicates with the computer module. If the scan tool pulls up a screen similar to the one shown in **Figure 11-1**, the scan tool and module are communicating.

Do the module and scan tool communicate? Yes ___ No ___

If Yes, go to step 13.

If No, go to step 17.

☐ 13. Retrieve trouble codes and list them in the space provided.

Trouble codes: ____

Tech Tip

If more than one code is produced, check with your instructor before continuing. The module and vehicle may have defects that are beyond the scope of this job.

☐ 14. Turn the ignition switch to the *Off* position.

☐ 15. Determine the meaning of the codes by referring to one of the following sources:

- **Generic OBD II codes:** Refer to a listing of generic OBD II trouble codes. These codes always have a zero following the U, such as U0XXX.
- **Manufacturer-specific codes:** Refer to the manufacturer's service information. These codes always have a number other than zero following the U, such as U1XXX, U2XXX, etc.

Do any of the codes indicate a loss of communication between modules? Yes ___ No ___

If Yes, list them in the space provided, and then go to step 16: ______________________________

____

If No, go to step 17.

If the trouble code cannot be found in a list of generic trouble codes or in the manufacturer's service information, there are two possible reasons:

- The trouble code has been added since the list was compiled.
- An internal vehicle computer problem is causing a nonexistent code.

Figure 11-1. This scan tool is performing an OTA (over-the-air) update. This is a scripted operation that provides instructions as it progresses.

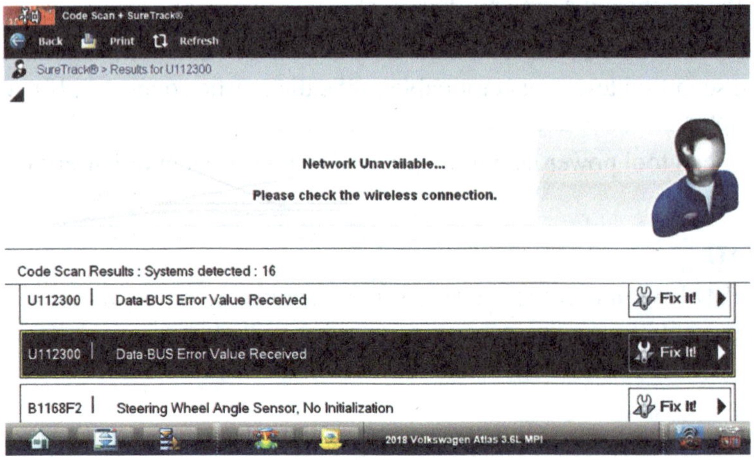

Name ____

Tech Tip

Class 2 serial data codes always begin with the letter U.

Code **Defect**

U ____________ ______________________________

U ____________ ______________________________

U ____________ ______________________________

U ____________ ______________________________

U ____________ ______________________________

☐ 16. Use the appropriate service information to determine which steps to take to deal with a particular class 2 serial data trouble code. These steps may include:

- Removing the battery negative terminal and checking various wire and module resistance readings with a multimeter.
- Inspecting fuses.
- Checking for battery voltage on input wires.
- Checking module grounds.
- Checking for module wiring that is disconnected or has high resistance.

What problems are found? ______________________________

____

____

What should you do to correct them? ______________________________

____

____

☐ 17. Use the scan tool to attempt to communicate with other vehicle modules.

Do the various modules communicate? Yes ___ No ___

If Yes, go to step 23.

If No, go to step 18.

☐ 18. Turn the vehicle's ignition switch to the *On* position.

☐ 19. Using a DVOM, ensure that power is available to both sides of all module fuses. Place a check mark next to the results of your tests.

- Test light illuminates on both sides of all fuses. ___ Go to step 20.
- Test light illuminates on one side of a fuse. ___ Go to step 21.
- Test light does not illuminate on either side of a fuse. ___ Go to step 22.

☐ 20. Using a test light, check for power at the module input wire.

Is power available at the module? Yes ___ No ___

If Yes, go to step 23.

If No, repair the wire between the fuse and the module and recheck module operation. Go to the *Job Wrap-Up* section of this job after verifying the problem has been resolved.

☐ 21. Replace the fuse and recheck module operation. Go to the *Job Wrap-Up* section of this job after verifying the problem has been resolved.

Caution

If the fuse is blown, you must determine what caused the electrical overload. Do *not* simply replace the fuse and let the vehicle go.

☐ 22. Back probe the system wiring until the reason for the lack of power is determined. Repair the wire or connector between the battery and fuse and recheck operation. Go to the *Job Wrap-Up* section of this job after verifying the problem has been resolved.

☐ 23. Use a DVOM to check the ground at the module.

Is the module properly grounded? Yes ___ No ___

If Yes, go to step 24.

If No, repair the ground wire(s) as needed and recheck module operation. Go to the *Job Wrap-Up* section of this job after verifying the problem has been resolved.

☐ 24. Replace the module and recheck its operation.

Caution

Ensure that the ignition switch is in the *Off* position and the battery negative cable is removed before replacing the module. Follow all static electricity precautions outlined by the vehicle manufacturer.

Job Wrap-Up

☐ 1. Clean the work area and return any equipment to storage.

☐ 2. Did you encounter any problems during this procedure? Yes ___ No ___

If Yes, describe the problems: ______________________________

____

What did you do to correct the problems? ______________________________

____

☐ 3. Have your instructor check your work and sign this job sheet.

Name ____

Project 2: Job 11 *(continued)*

Performance Evaluation—Instructor Use Only

How would you rate this student's overall performance on this task/job?

4 Competent/Proficient. Able to perform all elements of the task/job successfully and independently.

3 Satisfactory performance of the task/job. Able to perform elements of the task/job with minimal instructor assistance.

2 Completed the task/job with significant instructor assistance.

1 Unsuccessfully attempted the task/job.

0 No exposure. Note reason below (absence, skill not covered, etc.).

Comments:

____

____

____

____

Instructor's Signature: ____

Notes

Name ____

Date ____________________ Class ____________________

Project 2: Job 12—Perform a Vacuum Test, Power Balance Test, Compression Test, and Cylinder Leakage Test

After completing this job, you will be able to perform a vacuum test, power balance/running compression test, static compression test, and cylinder leakage test as part of the diagnostic process.

Instructions

As you read the job instructions, answer the questions and perform the tasks. Record your answers using complete sentences. Consult the proper service information and ask your instructor for help as needed.

Warning

Before performing this job, review all pertinent safety information in the text and discuss safety procedures with your instructor.

Procedures

- [ ] 1. Obtain a vehicle to be used in this job. Your instructor may direct you to perform this job on a shop vehicle or engine.
- [ ] 2. Gather the tools needed to perform the following job. Refer to the tools and materials list at the beginning of the project.

Engine Vacuum Test

- [ ] 1. Attach a vacuum gauge to the engine. The easiest way to do this is to remove an engine vacuum line and attach the vacuum gauge hose. If a vacuum line cannot be removed or if removing any hose would affect engine operation, the gauge should be connected to the vacuum circuit without interrupting it. This can be accomplished by removing one of the engine's vacuum lines, inserting a length of vacuum hose with a T fitting, and then attaching the vacuum gauge hose to the open nipple on the fitting. It can also be accomplished by removing a fitting from the intake manifold and temporarily installing a hose fitting that allows the gauge to be connected between the vacuum line and the manifold.
- [ ] 2. Start the engine and allow it to idle.
- [ ] 3. Refer to the chart in **Figure 12-1** to diagnose engine problems. If necessary, increase engine speed to make further checks.

  What conclusions can you make from reading the vacuum gauge? ____________________

  ____

  ____

  ____

  ____

  ____

- [ ] 4. Turn off the engine.
- [ ] 5. Remove the vacuum gauge and reattach vacuum hoses or fittings as necessary. If you used a T fitting to attach the vacuum gauge hose, remove the T fitting and reconnect the vacuum line.

Figure 12-1. Compare the vacuum gauge readings for the engine you are testing with the readings shown here.

Vacuum Gauge Readings

Note: White needle indicates steady vacuum. Red needle indicates fluctuating vacuum.

Needle steady and within specifications.

Cause: Normal vacuum at idle.

Needle very low and steady.

Cause: Vacuum or intake manifold leak.

Needle normal at idle, but fluctuates as engine speed is increased.

Cause: Weak valve spring.

Needle jumps to almost zero when throttle is opened and comes back to just over normal vacuum when closed.

Cause: Normal acceleration and deceleration reading.

Needle slowly drops from normal as engine speed is increased.

Cause: Restricted exhaust (compare at idle and 2500 rpm).

Needle steady, but low at idle.

Cause: Improper valve or ignition timing.

Needle has small pulsation at idle.

Cause: Insufficient spark plug gap.

Needle occasionally makes a sharp fast drop.

Cause: Sticking valve.

Needle regularly drops 4 to 8 inches.

Cause: Blown head gasket or excessive block-to-head clearance.

Needle slowly drifts back and forth.

Cause: Improper air-fuel mixture.

Needle drops regularly; may become steady as engine speed is increased.

Cause: Burned valve, worn valve guide, insufficient tappet clearance.

Needle drops to zero when engine is accelerated and snaps back to higher than normal on deceleration.

Cause: Worn piston rings or diluted oil.

Name____

Project 2: Job 12 *(continued)*

Power Balance Test

Tech Tip

Some testers can measure the amount of power being produced by each engine cylinder without shorting the cylinders. Most of these testers will display cylinder power balance by a bar graph, as shown in **Figure 12-2**. If this type of tester is available, it should be used as it is less likely to damage the catalytic converter.

☐ 1. Attach a power balance testing or running compression test device. This can be a scan tool or engine analyzer with the capability of disabling the fuel injector on individual cylinders.

☐ 2. Start the engine and set the engine speed to fast idle before beginning the test.

☐ 3. Kill (disable) each cylinder in turn and record the engine speed as each cylinder is disabled.

Cylinder # 1: ______ rpm.	Cylinder # 2: ______ rpm.
Cylinder # 3: ______ rpm.	Cylinder # 4: ______ rpm.
Cylinder # 5: ______ rpm.	Cylinder # 6: ______ rpm.
Cylinder # 7: ______ rpm.	Cylinder # 8: ______ rpm.
Cylinder # 9: ______ rpm.	Cylinder #10: ______ rpm.
Cylinder #11: ______ rpm.	Cylinder #12: ______ rpm.

Figure 12-2. These power balance bar graphs show how power balance tests can help diagnose common engine problems. A—Power output varies between cylinders. This may indicate fuel mixture problems, a vacuum leak, or engine wear. This may be a normal reading on some engines. B—When two adjacent cylinders are low, the head gasket may be damaged or the distributor cap (if used) may be carbon tracked.

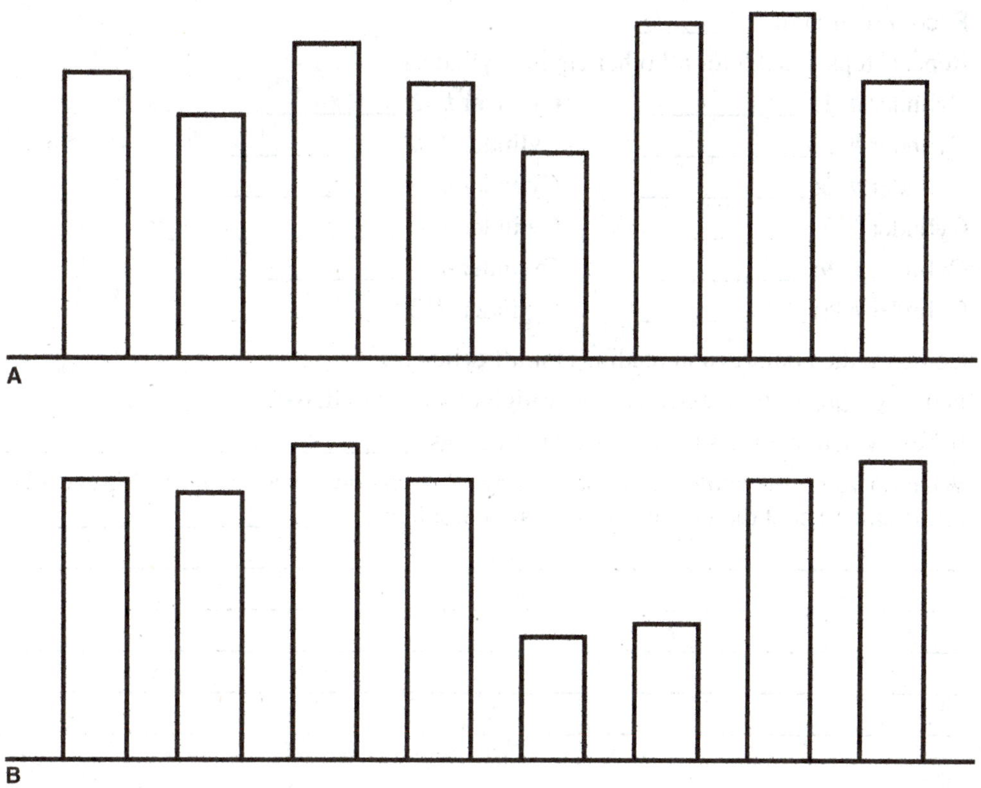

4. Return the engine to its normal idle speed and turn it off.
5. Compare the rpm drops for all cylinders.

   Did the rpm fail to drop when any cylinder was disabled? Yes ___ No ___

   If Yes, what was the number of the cylinder(s) that did not drop?_____

   What do you think could cause the readings that you observed? ____________________

6. Remove the test equipment leads from the engine.

Static Compression Test

1. Remove all spark plugs.
2. Disable the fuel system by removing the fuel pump relay or relay control fuse, or by unplugging the pump.

Tech Tip

It is not necessary to disable the fuel system on engines with carburetors.

3. Block the throttle valve in the open position.
4. Install the compression tester in first spark plug opening.
5. Crank the engine through four compression strokes.

   Record the reading:__________

6. Repeat steps 4 and 5 for all other engine cylinders.

   Cylinder # 1: __________ Cylinder # 2: __________
   Cylinder # 3: __________ Cylinder # 4: __________
   Cylinder # 5: __________ Cylinder # 6: __________
   Cylinder # 7: __________ Cylinder # 8: __________
   Cylinder # 9: __________ Cylinder #10: __________
   Cylinder #11: __________ Cylinder #12: __________

7. Compare the compression readings for all cylinders.

   Is the compression excessively low or high on any cylinder(s)? Yes ___ No ___

   If Yes, which cylinders have abnormal readings? ____________________

   What do you think could cause the readings that you observed? Refer to **Figure 12-3** for information about diagnosing compression problems. ____________________

Name ____

Figure 12-3. The causes of the these compression readings apply to any engine. Consult the manufacturer's service information for any special problem.

Compression Gauge Readings		
Compression Test Results	**Cause**	**Wet Test Results**
All cylinders at normal pressure (no more than 15% difference between cylinders)	Engine is in good shape, no problems.	No wet test needed.
All cylinders low (more than 20%)	Burned valve or valve seat, blown head gasket, worn rings or cylinder, valves misadjusted, jumped timing chain or belt, physical damage to engine.	If compression increases, cylinder or rings are worn. No increase, problem caused by valve train. Near zero compression caused by engine damage.
One or more cylinders low (more than 20% difference)	Burned valve, valve seat, damage or wear on affected cylinder(s).	If compression increases, cylinder or rings are worn. No increase, problem caused by valve train. Near zero compression caused by engine damage.
Two adjacent cylinders low (more than 20% difference)	Blown head gasket, cracked block or head.	Little or no increase in pressure.
Compression high (more than 20% difference)	Carbon build-up in cylinder.	Do not wet test for high compression.

☐ 8. If any cylinder had a low compression reading, perform a wet test. Pour approximately one teaspoon (one milliliter) of engine oil into the cylinder and retest the compression.

Did the compression improve? Yes ___ No ___

What is a possible cause? ____

____

____

____

☐ 9. Return the throttle valve to the closed position and replace the fuel pump relay or relay control fuse if it was removed.

☐ 10. Reinstall the spark plugs and remove the test equipment leads from the engine.

Running (Dynamic) Compression Test

Caution

Allow the engine to cool before performing this task, and between individual cylinder tests. A hot cylinder may fire spontaneously, destroying the compression gauge.

☐ 1. After the static test is complete, reinstall all spark plugs except number one.

☐ 2. Install the compression gauge in place of the spark plug in the number one cylinder.

☐ 3. Ground the number one plug wire.

☐ 4. If the system uses ported fuel injection, disconnect the fuel injector of the number one cylinder.

☐ 5. Start the engine and note the compression reading at idle on the following chart:

	Idle	Throttle Snapped		Idle	Throttle Snapped
Cylinder # 1:	________	________	Cylinder # 2:	________	________
Cylinder # 3:	________	________	Cylinder # 4:	________	________
Cylinder # 5:	________	________	Cylinder # 6:	________	________
Cylinder # 7:	________	________	Cylinder # 8:	________	________
Cylinder # 9:	________	________	Cylinder #10:	________	________
Cylinder #11:	________	________	Cylinder #12:	________	________

☐ 6. Snap (quickly open and close) the throttle and record the compression reading on the chart.

☐ 7. Repeat steps 2 through 6 for all cylinders. Remember to reconnect each cylinder's plug wire and injector after testing it.

☐ 8. Compare the compression readings for all cylinders. At idle, running compression will be much lower than static compression. When the throttle is snapped, pressure should reach about 4/5 of the static compression.

Is the compression excessively low or high on any cylinder(s)? Yes ___ No ___

Do the static and running tests show defects in the same cylinders? Yes ___ No ___

What do you think could cause the readings that you observed? ____________________

____

____

____

Relative Compression Test

Tech Tip

If this is the first time you are performing a relative compression test, practice on a 4-cylinder engine. The fewer cylinders the engine has, the easier the test results will be to interpret.

☐ 1. Disable the fuel delivery system by removing the fuel pump relay, removing the fuel pump fuse, or unplugging the fuel pump.

☐ 2. Turn on the scope (or scanner with a scope feature).

☐ 3. Connect a high-amp clamp to the scope.

☐ 4. Turn on the high-amp clamp and zero it.

☐ 5. Place the high-amp clamp around either the positive or negative battery cable that connects to the starter, but not both. (Remember that with current, the current that leaves the battery returns to the battery. This is not the case with voltage.)

☐ 6. Hold the throttle plate open.

☐ 7. Crank the engine while the scope is recording. This may need to be done several times to get the right settings on the scope. Turn the engine over enough to have a few screens' worth of waveforms. If the amp clamp is installed in the correct direction, the current will spike upward when the engine is cranked as shown in **Figure 12-4**.

☐ 8. The scope waveform should contain a series of peaks and valleys. The peaks and valleys should all be alike.

☐ 9. Are any of the peaks and valleys unlike the rest? Yes ___ No ___

Name ____

Project 2: Job 12 *(continued)*

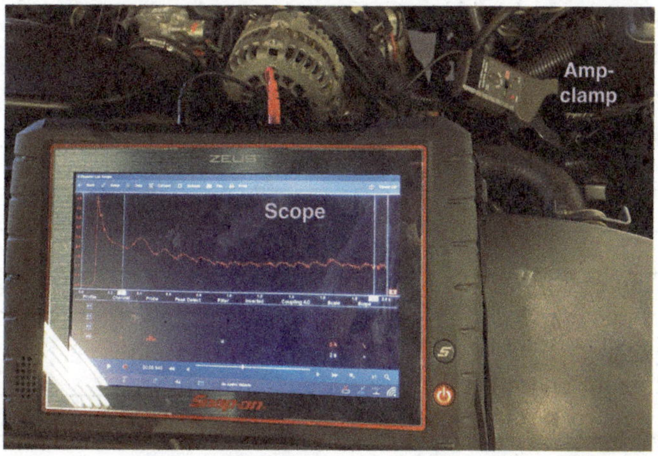

Figure 12-4. A scope with a high-amp clamp connected to the positive battery cable.

☐ 10. If Yes, add another channel to your scope and put the ignition pick-up on that channel. Use the ignition pick-up clamp on cylinder #1. Consult your service data to determine which cylinder is #1 and what the ignition firing order is.

☐ 11. Crank the engine again. The spark event for cylinder #1 will line up with the compression event for cylinder #1. Each of the waveforms afterward represents the firing order for compression events. This is how you will determine which cylinder has low compression.

> **Tech Tip**
>
> If the engine is a diesel, use a voltage lead on the electronic injector instead of the ignition pick-up as the injection event occurs on the compression stroke.

☐ 12. Which cylinder has lower compression than the others?

Cylinder Leakage Test

> **Tech Tip**
>
> A cylinder leakage test is usually performed when a compression test indicates low compression on a cylinder. Your instructor may direct you to perform this test on a randomly selected cylinder in good condition.

☐ 1. Disable the fuel system to prevent accidental starting.

☐ 2. Attach a shop air hose to the leak tester.

☐ 3. Adjust the tester pressure to the recommended setting. This is usually about 5–10 psi (35–70 kPa).
Manufacturer's pressure setting: __________ psi or kPa (circle one).

☐ 4. Remove the spark plug from the suspect cylinder.

☐ 5. Bring the suspect cylinder to the top of its compression stroke by feeling for compression as the piston comes up. Some technicians use a whistle to indicate when the compression stroke is occurring.

☐ 6. Install the leak tester hose in the spark plug opening.

Project 2: Job 12—Perform a Vacuum Test, Power Balance Test, Compression Test, and Cylinder Leakage Test *(continued)*

☐ 7. Open the valve allowing regulated pressure into the cylinder.

☐ 8. Observe the pressure. It should be at or near the regulated pressure.

Pressure reading: __________ psi or kPa (circle one).

Does this pressure match the regulated pressure? Yes ___ No ___

If No, what is a possible cause? ____

____

____

____

____

☐ 9. If the pressure is low, refer to the chart in **Figure 12-5**.

After consulting the chart, list the possible engine problem: ____________________

____

____

____

____

☐ 10. Remove the tester hose and reinstall the spark plug.

☐ 11. Repeat steps 4 through 10 on all suspect cylinders.

Figure 12-5. The engine cylinder is supposed to be almost airtight on the top of its compression stroke. Air escaping anywhere is caused by a defect.

Cylinder Leakage Test Results

Condition	Possible Causes
No air escapes from any of the cylinders.	Normal condition, no leakage.
Air escapes from carburetor or throttle body.	Intake valve not seated or damaged. Incorrect valve timing. Possible jumped timing chain or belt. Broken or damaged valve train part.
Air escapes from tailpipe.	Exhaust valve not seated or damaged. Incorrect valve timing. Broken or damaged valve train part.
Air escapes from dipstick tube or oil fill opening.	Worn piston rings. Worn cylinder walls. Damaged piston. Blown head gasket.
Air escapes from adjacent cylinder.	Blown head gasket. Cracked head or block.
Air bubbles in radiator coolant.	Blown head gasket. Cracked head or block.
Air heard around outside of cylinder.	Cracked or warped head or block. Blown head gasket.

Name ____

Project 2: Job 12 *(continued)*

☐ 12. Analyze the readings of all tested cylinders.
What conclusions can you make? ____
____
____
____

☐ 13. Remove the shop air hose from the tester.

☐ 14. Reconnect the ignition system connectors.

Job Wrap-Up

☐ 1. Clean the work area and return any equipment to storage.

☐ 2. Did you encounter any problems during this procedure? Yes ___ No ___
If Yes, describe the problems: ____
____
What did you do to correct the problems? ____
____

☐ 3. Have your instructor check your work and sign this job sheet.

Performance Evaluation—Instructor Use Only

How would you rate this student's overall performance on this task/job?

4 Competent/Proficient. Able to perform all elements of the task/job successfully and independently.

3 Satisfactory performance of the task/job. Able to perform elements of the task/job with minimal instructor assistance.

2 Completed the task/job with significant instructor assistance.

1 Unsuccessfully attempted the task/job.

0 No exposure. Note reason below (absence, skill not covered, etc.).

Comments:
____
____
____
____

Instructor's Signature: ____

Notes

Name ____

Date ______________________ Class ______________________

Project 2: Job 13—Inspect and Test a Cooling System

After completing this job, you will be able to inspect a cooling system and diagnose cooling system problems.

Instructions

As you read the job instructions, answer the questions and perform the tasks. Record your answers using complete sentences. Consult the proper service information and ask your instructor for help as needed.

Warning

Before performing this job, review all pertinent safety information in the text and discuss safety procedures with your instructor.

Procedures

☐ 1. Obtain a vehicle on which cooling system service can be performed. Your instructor may direct you to perform this job on a shop vehicle.

☐ 2. Gather the tools needed to perform the following job. Refer to the tools and materials list at the beginning of the project.

☐ 3. Determine the type of antifreeze to be used in the vehicle cooling system.

Antifreeze type: ____

Inspect Belts and Hoses

☐ 1. Open the hood and visually inspect the condition of the cooling system hoses. Examine the hoses for bulges, leaks, or deterioration (such as frayed areas). Ensure that the hoses do not contact any moving parts. Squeeze the hoses to check for hardness, cracks, or softness, **Figure 13-1**.

Are any problems found? Yes ___ No ___

If Yes, describe the problems: ____

____

Figure 13-1. Squeeze the hose to determine whether it is excessively soft. Be careful when doing this on a warmed up engine; the hose will be hot.

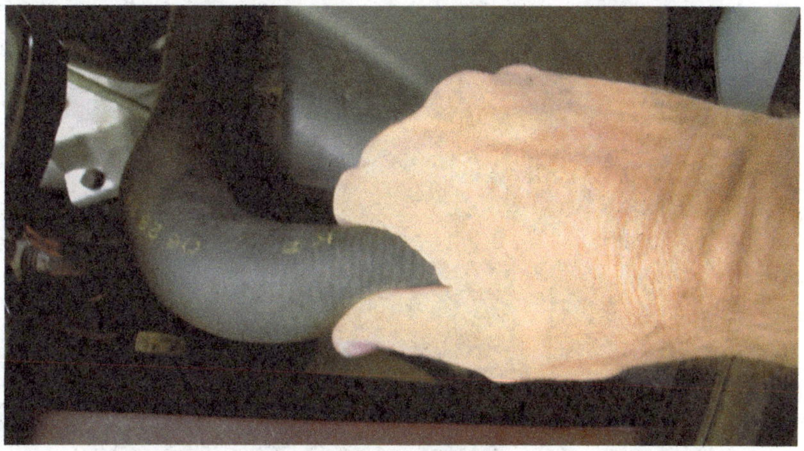

☐ 2. Determine the condition of the vehicle's belts. Examine the belts for glazing, fraying, or oil contamination. Note whether the belts are loose by attempting to turn the pulley on one of the accessories with the engine off. If applicable, note the condition of the belt tensioner.

Are any problems found? Yes ___ No ___

If Yes, describe the problems: ______________________________

____

☐ 3. Inspect the belt tensioner for the following defects:

- Weak tensioner spring resistance.
- Worn pulley grooves.
- Worn bearings (roughness when turning the tensioner).

Can the tensioner be reused? Yes ___ No ___

If No, explain: ______________________________

____

☐ 4. Check the pulley alignment of the belt system(s). Sight along the pulleys to ensure that they are properly aligned, as shown in **Figure 13-2**.

Are the pulleys and belts aligned? Yes ___ No ___

If No, describe the relative positions of the pulleys: ______________________________

____

Inspect Other Cooling System Components

☐ 1. Visually check the radiator's condition. Make sure the radiator fins are free of leaves or other debris and are not damaged. Also, check for obvious leaks.

Are any problems found? Yes ___ No ___

If Yes, describe the problems: ______________________________

____

Figure 13-2. The easiest way to determine whether the pulleys and belts are aligned is to make a visual check. Note the alignment of the various pulleys and the belt in this figure.

Name____

Project 2: Job 13 *(continued)*

☐ 2. Check the condition of the coolant recovery system. Inspect the coolant recovery tank, cap, and hoses for damage. Inspect the coolant in the tank for excessive rust and discoloration. This can be done visually, as shown in **Figure 13-3**.

Are any problems found? Yes ___ No ___

If Yes, describe the problems: ____

____

☐ 3. Ensure that the engine and cooling system are sufficiently cool (cooling system not under pressure) to allow the radiator cap to be safely removed.

☐ 4. Remove the radiator cap and check its condition. Replace the cap if it is corroded or if the rubber seal is hard, cracked, or otherwise damaged.

Is the cap in good condition? Yes ___ No ___

☐ 5. Check the coolant level in the radiator. If the cooling system has a coolant recovery system, the coolant level should be at the top of the filler neck. If the vehicle does not have a coolant recovery system, the coolant level should be about 3″ (77 mm) below the filler neck.

Is the coolant level correct? Yes ___ No ___

☐ 6. Visually check the coolant for rust.

Is the coolant rusty? Yes ___ No ___

☐ 7. Check the degree of freeze protection (antifreeze percentage) with a coolant tester. Follow the directions provided by the tester manufacturer.

Antifreeze will protect to __________ °F or °C (circle one).

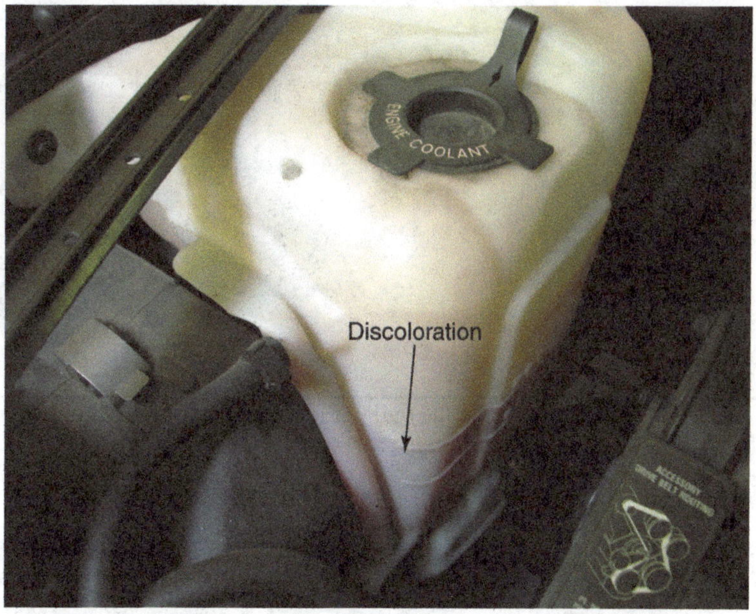

Figure 13-3. Visually check the reservoir for discoloration. Rust will stain the reservoir and discolor the coolant.

Pressure Test the Cooling System

☐ 1. Obtain a cooling system pressure tester.

☐ 2. Check the condition of the radiator cap. Install the cap on the tester, **Figure 13-4**. Adapters may be needed to properly test the cap. Pump up the tester pressure until it levels off. A pressure specification should be printed somewhere on the cap. The radiator cap should hold this pressure without allowing it to drop.

Does the radiator cap pass the pressure test? Yes ___ No ___

If No, replace the radiator cap.

☐ 3. Remove the radiator cap from the pressure tester and install the pressure tester on the radiator filler neck. See **Figure 13-5**. If the system is very low on coolant, first add coolant to make the job of pressurizing easier.

☐ 4. Pump up the pressure tester until the cooling system has been pressurized to the rating on the radiator cap. Carefully observe the cooling system for leaks. If no leaks are visible and the pressure holds for two minutes, the system is not leaking.

Does the cooling system pass the pressure test? Yes ___ No ___

If No, explain why the cooling system failed: ____

____

____

____

Figure 13-4. Install the pressure cap on the pressure tester. Adapters may be needed, as shown here. (Jack Klasey)

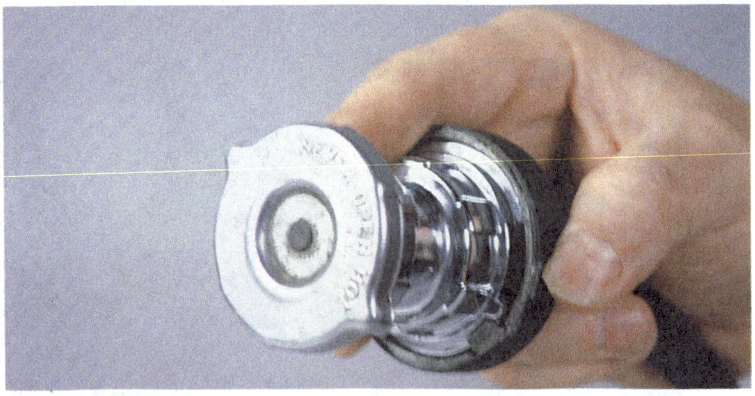

Figure 13-5. Install the pressure tester on the radiator filler neck. (Jack Klasey)

Name ____

Caution

If you add water to the cooling system for diagnostic testing, make sure you drain and refill the system with the proper antifreeze-water mixture before releasing the vehicle to its owner.

Make Visual Checks for Leaks

☐ 1. Check all visible gaskets, fittings, and freeze plugs for the presence of coolant.

Describe any leaks or suspicious areas: ____

____

____

☐ 2. Check all engine surfaces for pools of coolant.

Are there pools of coolant on any of the engine surfaces? Yes ___ No ___

If Yes, describe the location: ____

____

Based on your visual inspection, does the engine have leaks that must be corrected?
Yes ___ No ___

If Yes, consult your instructor about the needed repairs.

Check the Coolant Pump

☐ 1. Check the coolant pump for leaks at the gaskets and weep hole. The weep hole is usually located on the housing between the pulley flange and the rear of the pump.

Do you find any leaks? Yes ___ No ___

If Yes, consult your instructor about the needed repairs.

Tech Tip

It is normal for a slight amount of coolant to be present at the weep hole.

Belt-Driven Pump

☐ 1. Check the pump bearings for wear by attempting to move the pump shaft up and down and back and forth. There should be almost no movement.

Do you detect excessive movement? Yes ___ No ___

If Yes, consult your instructor about the needed repairs.

Electric Motor-Driven Pump

☐ 1. Check to determine if electric coolant pump runs while the engine is running.

Does the pump run while the engine is running? Yes ___ No ___

☐ 2. If the pump does not run when the engine is running, does it have power and ground supplied to it while the engine is running? Yes ___ No ___

☐ 3. If Yes, skip down to step 7. If No, which one is missing?

☐ 4. If power or ground is missing, identify the problem as a broken wire, a corroded connection, or blown fuse.

Cause of missing power or ground: ____

☐ 5. If the problem is a broken wire or a corroded connection, skip to step 6. If the fuse is blown, determine why this occurred. Is it caused by a short to ground or a worn motor?

Cause of blown fuse: ______________________________

☐ 6. How did you repair the cause of missing power or ground?

____

☐ 7. If both power and ground are available to the motor but the motor does not operate, the motor must be replaced. This is true of any component: if both power and ground are available but the component does not operate, the component is the problem.

Do you need to replace the pump? Yes ___ No ___

☐ 8. If Yes, consult your instructor for further instructions.

Check Coolant Temperature and the Operation of a Cooling Fan

☐ 1. Ensure that the vehicle cooling system is full.

☐ 2. Replace the radiator cap if it was removed.

☐ 3. Start the vehicle and allow it to warm up. If the vehicle has an air conditioner, turn it on to shorten the warm-up time.

☐ 4. As the engine warms up, periodically check the engine temperature and record it below. Circle the temperature scale used, °F or °C.

One minute after startup: ________ °F or °C

Three minutes after startup: _______ °F or °C

Five minutes after startup: _______ °F or °C

Ten minutes after startup (if necessary): ________ °F or °C

Electric Cooling Fan

☐ 1. Observe the cooling fans. It should come on shortly after the engine reaches operating temperature and cycle on and off after that.

☐ 2. To ensure that the ECM is capable of turning the fans on, connect the scan tool to the DLC. Use scanner mode (vehicle-specific mode) instead of OBD II.

☐ 3. Go to Functional Tests or Output Controls on the scan tool. Operate the cooling fans at both low and high speeds to verify ECM control.

Did the fans come on with the scan tool? Yes ___ No ___

☐ 4. If both fans came on with the scan tool, the fan system is operational. If not, proceed to step 5.

☐ 5. If the fans did not come on, check for power and ground to the fans while using the scan tool to command the fans on. Note that at low speed, it is normal to find a 6-volt drop across a fan. At low speed, the two fans are usually operated in series with each other. Therefore, it is possible that neither fan will operate at low speed, but both will operate at high speed. Do the fans operate only at high speed? Yes ___ No ___

☐ 6. If the fans only operate at one of the speeds, the next step is to diagnose the relays. Consult a wiring diagram to understand the wiring layout. Be patient, as understanding this for the first time takes time.

Were any of the relays faulty? Yes ___ No ___

☐ 7. Did you jumper from 30 to 87 slot on the relay panel to bypass the relay to diagnose it or them? (Use a wiring diagram to understand this question.) ___

☐ 8. If the relays are found to be in good working order and power or ground is absent for the fans, do a voltage drop on the wires to the fans while the scan tool is still commanding the fans *on*. Use a wiring diagram to verify the starting point of power and ground for the fans.

Name ____

Project 2: Job 13 *(continued)*

What is the voltage drop of the power side of the circuit? ___

What is the voltage drop of the ground side of the circuit? ___

☐ 9. Perform a voltage drop of the command side of the circuit from ECU to relays.

What is the voltage drop of each of the power wires?

____

____

____

What is the voltage drop of each of the ground wires?

____

____

____

☐ 10. What was found to be faulty in this circuit (fan, relay, wires, or ECU)? ____

☐ 11. Consult your instructor for further instructions.

Belt-Driven Fan and Fan Clutch

☐ 1. Observe the cooling fan airflow. It should be pulling air through the radiator when the engine is at operating temperature.

> **Tech Tip**
>
> Consult your instructor if you are not sure whether the fan is pulling enough air through the radiator.

☐ 2. Stop the engine while observing the fan. The fan should stop turning within one revolution.

Does the fan stop within one revolution? Yes ___ No ___

If No, consult your instructor for further instructions.

Check Fan Shroud and Air Dams

☐ 1. Visually inspect the fan shroud for the following:

- Cracks.
- Missing parts.
- Loose or missing shroud fasteners.
- Evidence that the fan is hitting the shroud.

☐ 2. Visually inspect the air dams for the following:

- Tears or cracks.
- Missing dams.
- Loose or missing dam fasteners.

Do you observe any of the above problems? Yes ___ No ___

If Yes, consult your instructor for further instructions.

Check for Combustion Leaks

> **Tech Tip**
>
> Due to the variation in types of combustion testers, the following steps outline only a general method of combustion testing.

☐ 1. Ensure that the vehicle's cooling system is full.

☐ 2. Check that the cooling system is *not* under pressure and then remove the radiator cap.

☐ 3. Install the combustion tester on the filler neck.

☐ 4. Start the engine and follow the manufacturer's directions to test for the presence of combustion gases in the cooling system.

Are combustion gases detected in the cooling system? Yes ___ No ___

If Yes, consult your instructor for further instructions before continuing.

☐ 5. Remove the tester and replace the radiator cap.

Inspect the Engine Oil Cooler

☐ 1. If the vehicle has an auxiliary engine oil cooler, check it for the following:

- Visible leaks.
- Clogged fins.
- Cracked or damaged hoses or lines.

Are any problems found? Yes ___ No ___

If Yes, describe the problems: ____________________

____

____

☐ 2. Clean up any spilled coolant.

Job Wrap-Up

☐ 1. Clean the work area and return any equipment to storage.

☐ 2. Did you encounter any problems during this procedure? Yes ___ No ___

If Yes, describe the problems: ____________________

____

What did you do to correct the problems? ____________________

____

☐ 3. Have your instructor check your work and sign this job sheet.

Name ______________________________

Project 2: Job 13 *(continued)*

Performance Evaluation—Instructor Use Only

How would you rate this student's overall performance on this task/job?

4 Competent/Proficient. Able to perform all elements of the task/job successfully and independently.

3 Satisfactory performance of the task/job. Able to perform elements of the task/job with minimal instructor assistance.

2 Completed the task/job with significant instructor assistance.

1 Unsuccessfully attempted the task/job.

0 No exposure. Note reason below (absence, skill not covered, etc.).

Comments:

____

____

____

____

Instructor's Signature: ______________________________

Notes

Name ____________________

Date ____________________ Class ____________________

Project 2: Job 14—Use a Four- or Five-Gas Analyzer to Check Emission System Operation

After completing this job, you will be able to use a four- or five-gas exhaust gas analyzer to check exhaust gas readings. You will also be able to interpret the readings.

Instructions

As you read the job instructions, answer the questions and perform the tasks. Record your answers using complete sentences. Consult the proper service information and ask your instructor for help as needed.

Warning

Before performing this job, review all pertinent safety information in the text and discuss safety procedures with your instructor.

Procedures

- [ ] 1. Obtain a vehicle to be used in this job. Your instructor may direct you to perform this job on a shop vehicle.
- [ ] 2. Gather the tools needed to perform this job. Refer to the tools and materials list at the beginning of the project.
- [ ] 3. Obtain the exhaust gas analyzer and start it. **Figure 14-1** shows a modern five-gas exhaust analyzer. Many exhaust gas analyzers require several minutes to reach operating temperature. During this time other preparatory steps can be performed.

  Type of analyzer: ____________________

  Number of gases analyzed: ____________________

Figure 14-1. This is a typical exhaust gas analyzer. Connections are made to the vehicle to measure gases, as well as engine temperature and rpm. (Ferret)

Project 2: Job 14—Use a Four- or Five-Gas Analyzer to Check Emission System Operation *(continued)*

☐ 4. Start the engine and allow it to reach operating temperature.

☐ 5. Check engine temperature using a temperature tester. A temperature-measuring device may be part of the analyzer.

Type of tester used: _______________

Caution

Do *not* rely on the vehicle temperature gauge; they are not reliable for exact temperature measurements.

If the engine temperature is below normal, allow the engine to warm further. Ensure that the thermostat is not stuck open or missing.

If the engine temperature is above normal, check cooling system condition. Correct as necessary before proceeding with the test.

☐ 6. Calibrate the exhaust gas analyzer.

☐ 7. Inspect the vehicle for obvious problems that will affect emissions readings, such as disconnected wiring or hoses; damaged or missing components; and fuel, oil, or coolant leaks. Refer to other jobs as needed and correct obvious problems before proceeding.

☐ 8. Place the exhaust gas analyzer hose in the exhaust pipe.

☐ 9. Make other engine connections as needed. Install a tachometer if one isn't incorporated into the analyzer.

☐ 10. Observe exhaust readings at different engine speeds and write the readings in the following chart. Indicate whether each reading is a percentage or a grams per mile figure. Write "NA" in the space if the gas cannot be read by this analyzer.

	Idle	1000 rpm*	2500 rpm*	Other Speed* (list) _________
HC	________	________	________	________
CO	________	________	________	________
NO_X	________	________	________	________
CO_2	________	________	________	________
O_2	________	________	________	________

*The equipment/vehicle manufacturer or state regulations may require a different engine speed for testing.

☐ 11. If the exhaust gas analyzer has a printout feature, print a copy of the exhaust gas readings.

Do the analyzer readings indicate that the emission controls and engine are operating properly? Yes ___ No ___

If No, which readings are incorrect?

What could cause these readings? ____

____

____

☐ 12. Turn off the engine.

☐ 13. Remove the analyzer hose from the tailpipe and remove other engine connections, as applicable.

☐ 14. Make other tests to the engine and emission control systems as necessary.

What are the results of the tests? ____

____

____

Name ____

Project 2: Job 14 *(continued)*

☐ 15. After consulting your instructor, make any needed repairs to the engine and/or emissions control systems.

List the repairs made: ____

____

____

☐ 16. When repairs are complete, repeat steps 5 through 12 to recheck the exhaust gas readings. Record the readings in the following chart. Indicate whether each reading is a percentage or a grams per mile figure. Write "NA" in the space if the gas cannot be read by this analyzer.

	Idle	**1000 rpm***	**2500 rpm***	**Other Speed* (list)** ________
HC	________	________	________	________
CO	________	________	________	________
NO_X	________	________	________	________
CO_2	________	________	________	________
O_2	________	________	________	________

*The equipment/vehicle manufacturer or state regulations may require a different engine speed for testing.

☐ 17. Compare the readings in steps 10 and 16.

Do the readings indicate that any problems have been corrected? Yes ___ No ___

If No, repeat steps 5 through 16 to isolate the problem.

Job Wrap-Up

☐ 1. Clean the work area and return any equipment to storage.

☐ 2. Did you encounter any problems during this procedure? Yes ___ No ___

If Yes, describe the problems: ____

____

What did you do to correct the problems? ____

____

☐ 3. Have your instructor check your work and sign this job sheet.

Performance Evaluation—Instructor Use Only

How would you rate this student's overall performance on this task/job?

4 Competent/Proficient. Able to perform all elements of the task/job successfully and independently.

3 Satisfactory performance of the task/job. Able to perform elements of the task/job with minimal instructor assistance.

2 Completed the task/job with significant instructor assistance.

1 Unsuccessfully attempted the task/job.

0 No exposure. Note reason below (absence, skill not covered, etc.).

Comments:

____

____

____

____

Instructor's Signature: ______________________________

PROJECT 3

Diagnosing and Repairing an Ignition System

Introduction

Modern vehicles use many types of ignition systems. There are still many distributor-equipped engines in use. The pickup coil is usually located in the distributor, although a few systems have a distributor and a crankshaft-mounted pickup.

Engines without a distributor have a crankshaft pickup. Some systems have a second pickup on the camshaft. Many distributorless ignitions use the waste spark system, in which the coil fires two plugs at once, one on the compression stroke and the other on the exhaust stroke. A later variation of this system has two plugs per cylinder.

The latest ignition systems have one ignition coil per cylinder. The coil-near-plug system uses coil wires, while the direct, or coil-on-plug, version places the coil directly over the spark plug. You will inspect and test an ignition system's secondary circuit components in Job 15, and its primary circuit components in Job 16.

Project 3 Jobs

- Job 15—Inspect and Test an Ignition System's Secondary Circuit Components and Wiring
- Job 16—Inspect and Test an Ignition System's Primary Circuit Components and Wiring

Tools and Materials

The following list contains the tools and materials that may be needed to complete the jobs in this project. The items used will depend on the make and model of vehicle being serviced.

- One or more vehicles in need of service.
- Applicable service information.
- Spark tester.
- Equipment capable of reading waveforms.
- Multimeter or ohmmeter.
- Timing light with advance meter (optional).
- Hand tools.
- Safety glasses and other protective equipment.

Safety Notice

Before performing this job, review all pertinent safety information in the text and review safety information with your instructor.

Name ______________________________

Date ____________________ Class ____________________

Project 3: Job 15—Inspect and Test an Ignition System's Secondary Circuit Components and Wiring

After completing this job, you will be able to inspect and service a vehicle's secondary ignition circuit.

Instructions

As you read the job instructions, answer the questions and perform the tasks. Record your answers using complete sentences. Consult the proper service information and ask your instructor for help as needed.

Warning

Before performing this job, review all pertinent safety information in the text and discuss safety procedures with your instructor.

Procedures

☐ 1. Obtain a vehicle to be used in this job. Your instructor may direct you to perform this job on a shop vehicle.

☐ 2. Gather the tools needed to perform this job. Refer to the tools and materials list at the beginning of the project.

☐ 3. Determine the type of ignition system to be tested. See **Figure 15-1** for some typical ignition systems.

- Distributorless (waste spark). ___
- Coil-near-plug (uses coil wires). ___
- Distributor with internal pickup. ___
- Distributorless with two plugs per cylinder. ___
- Coil-on-plug (direct, no plug wires). ___
- Distributor without internal pickup. ___

Figure 15-1. Four common types of ignition systems are shown here. A—Distributorless ignition. B—Coil-on-plug ignition. C—Dual ignition (in this design, a combination of coil-over-plug and coil-near-plug systems. D—Distributor-type ignition.

☐ 4. Locate service information for the ignition system to be tested.

Test for a Spark from the Secondary System

☐ 1. Detach the coil or plug wire or remove one coil from its plug.

☐ 2. Attach a spark tester to the wire or coil, as applicable.

☐ 3. Have an assistant crank the engine as you observe the spark. Describe the spark produced:
- No spark. ___
- Spark is weak. Describe: ______________________________
- Spark is acceptable. Describe: ______________________________

☐ 4. If there is no spark or the spark is weak, make further checks to isolate the problem to the primary or secondary ignition system components, as outlined in the following sections of this job.

Read and Interpret Ignition System Waveforms

☐ 1. Obtain one of the following testers that are capable of reading ignition system waveforms:
- Engine analyzer. ___
- Oscilloscope. ___
- Waveform meter. ___

☐ 2. Attach the tester leads to the ignition system connections.
Attachment method(s): ______________________________
____

☐ 3. Set the tester controls to match the type of ignition system.

☐ 4. Start the engine and observe the oscilloscope patterns.

☐ 5. Draw the secondary oscilloscope pattern.

Name ____

Project 3: Job 15 *(continued)*

☐ 6. Draw the primary oscilloscope pattern.

Do the primary and secondary patterns indicate that the ignition system is operating correctly? Yes ___ No ___

If No, what could be the problem? ____

____

☐ 7. Stop the engine and remove the tester leads.

Check the Spark Plugs

☐ 1. Before removing a spark plug, clean the area around the base of the plug with a compressed air gun to keep debris from falling into the cylinder. This step is particularly important if the plugs are recessed in the valve cover and head at the top of the engine.

Tech Tip

If the plugs were difficult to remove, clean the threads in the cylinder head with a properly sized thread chaser. Place a small amount of grease on the thread chaser to catch any debris and turn the chaser by hand into the plug opening.

☐ 2. Visually inspect the spark plugs for excessive wear, fouling, or other signs of damage. List the defects found by cylinder number.

Plug from Cylinder #	Defect

☐ 3. Determine the cause of the plug's condition, replace defective plugs, and retest the ignition system.

Tech Tip

Before plug installation or reinstallation, check and set the plug gaps. Use anti-seize on the plug threads only if recommended by the manufacturer. Thread the plugs into the head by hand. If the plug opening is difficult to access, use a small section of hose to hold the plug. Be careful not to cross thread the plugs. Many manufacturers recommend using a torque wrench to finish tightening the plugs.

Check the Spark Plug Wires

☐ 1. Visually inspect the wires for the following:

- Chafing or other damage. ___
- Cracked or split wire insulation. ___
- Evidence of flashover or shorting. ___
- Damaged boots. ___

Describe any defects: ____________________

☐ 2. Use an ohmmeter to check wire resistance. List any defects found by cylinder number.

Wire from Cylinder #	Defect
________	____________________
________	____________________
________	____________________
________	____________________
________	____________________
________	____________________
________	____________________
________	____________________
________	____________________
________	____________________
________	____________________
________	____________________

☐ 3. After consulting your instructor, replace defective plug wires and recheck the ignition system.

Check Distributor Components

☐ 1. Label the spark plug wires by cylinder number.

☐ 2. Label the #1 cylinder terminal on the distributor cap. If the firing order is not known, label all cylinder terminals.

☐ 3. Remove all spark plug wires from the distributor cap.

☐ 4. Remove the cap and rotor from the distributor body.

Cap and Rotor

☐ 1. Visually inspect the cap and rotor for carbon tracks and flashover, **Figure 15-2**.

Are any defects found? Yes ___ No ___

If Yes, replace the parts.

☐ 2. Check the cap and rotor for cracks or other evidence of mechanical damage.

Are any defects found? Yes ___ No ___

If Yes, replace the parts.

Ignition Coil

☐ 1. Visually inspect the coil for carbon tracks and flashover, **Figure 15-3**.

Are any defects found? Yes ___ No ___

If Yes, replace the parts.

Name____

Project 3: Job 15 *(continued)*

Figure 15-2. Inspect the cap and rotor for defects. A—The exterior of the cap is normally dusty, but should have no evidence of flashover or carbon tracks. B—The interior of this distributor cap shows normal wear on the contacts and no evidence of carbon tracking. C—The center contact on this rotor is worn and the rotor should be replaced.

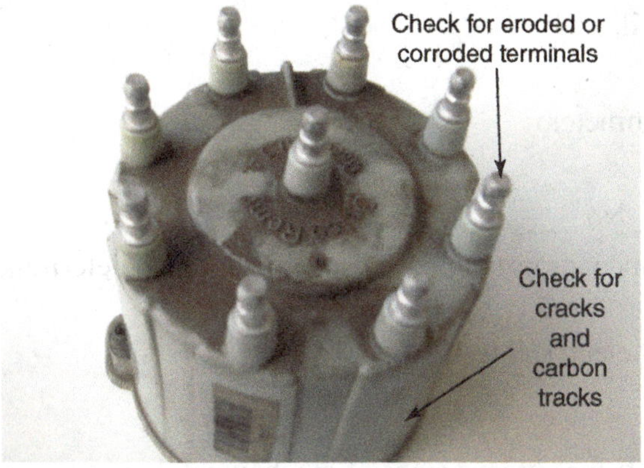

A

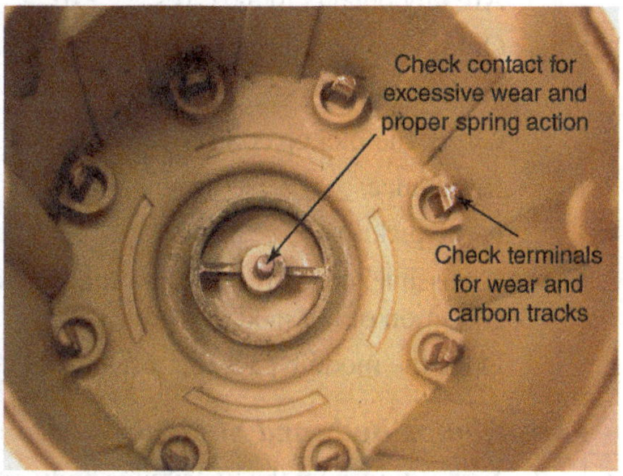

B

C

Figure 15-3. Check the coil towers for flashover where indicated.

Distributor Primary Components

☐ 1. Visually inspect the primary wiring for missing or overheated insulation, missing grommets, and frayed or corroded wires.

Are any defects found? Yes ___ No ___

☐ 2. Obtain the resistance value for the pickup coil.

Resistance: _________ ohms.

☐ 3. Check the pickup coil resistance with an ohmmeter.

Resistance: _________ ohms.

Is the pickup coil resistance correct? Yes ___ No ___

☐ 4. If possible, check the ignition module resistance, or use a module-specific tester to determine the condition of the module.

Does the module pass the resistance or other electrical tests? Yes ___ No ___

Distributor Body and Shaft

☐ 1. Visually inspect the distributor body and shaft for obvious signs of mechanical damage.

Are any defects found? Yes ___ No ___

If Yes, describe the defects: ______________________________

____

☐ 2. Obtain a dial indicator. Using the service information, determine the specifications for distributor shaft side play.

Minimum: __________

Maximum: __________

☐ 3. Check the distributor shaft side play using the following procedure:

a. Attach the dial indicator so the plunger contacts the distributor shaft.

b. Zero the dial indicator.

c. Push the shaft from side to side and note how much the dial indicator moves from zero.

Measured side play: __________

d. Repeat steps a, b, and c at several positions roughly 45° apart and record the readings.

Measured side play: __________

Measured side play: __________

Measured side play: __________

Is the maximum side play within specifications? Yes ___ No ___

If No, consult your instructor, replace defective components as necessary, and recheck the ignition system.

☐ 4. Replace the cap, rotor, and spark plug wires.

Job Wrap-Up

☐ 1. Clean the work area and return any equipment to storage.

☐ 2. Did you encounter any problems during this procedure? Yes ___ No ___

If Yes, describe the problems: ______________________________

____

What did you do to correct the problems? ______________________________

____

☐ 3. Have your instructor check your work and sign this job sheet.

Name ____________________

Project 3: Job 15 *(continued)*

Performance Evaluation—Instructor Use Only

How would you rate this student's overall performance on this task/job?

4 Competent/Proficient. Able to perform all elements of the task/job successfully and independently.

3 Satisfactory performance of the task/job. Able to perform elements of the task/job with minimal instructor assistance.

2 Completed the task/job with significant instructor assistance.

1 Unsuccessfully attempted the task/job.

0 No exposure. Note reason below (absence, skill not covered, etc.).

Comments:

____

____

____

____

Instructor's Signature: ____________________

Notes

Name ______________________________

Date ____________________ Class ____________________

Project 3: Job 16—Inspect and Test an Ignition System's Primary Circuit Components and Wiring

After completing this job, you will be able to inspect and service a vehicle's primary ignition circuit.

Instructions

As you read the job instructions, answer the questions and perform the tasks. Record your answers using complete sentences. Consult the proper service information and ask your instructor for help as needed.

Warning

Before performing this job, review all pertinent safety information in the text and discuss safety procedures with your instructor.

Procedures

☐ 1. Obtain a vehicle to be used in this job. Your instructor may direct you to perform this job on a shop vehicle.

☐ 2. Gather the tools needed to perform this job. Refer to the tools and materials list at the beginning of the project.

☐ 3. Determine the type of ignition system to be tested.

Type of ignition system: ______________________________

Visually Inspect Primary Circuit Wiring

☐ 1. Obtain system wiring diagrams.

☐ 2. Using the wiring diagram as a guide, inspect all ignition system wiring for the following conditions. Indicate any defects found.

Tech Tip

Wiring and connectors are often located in inaccessible locations, such as the ignition primary connectors shown in **Figure 16-1**. It is important to check *all* connections, even when it involves removing other parts to gain access to them.

Figure 16-1. The primary connectors on this coil pack and module assembly are hidden behind vacuum hoses and the automatic transaxle dipstick.

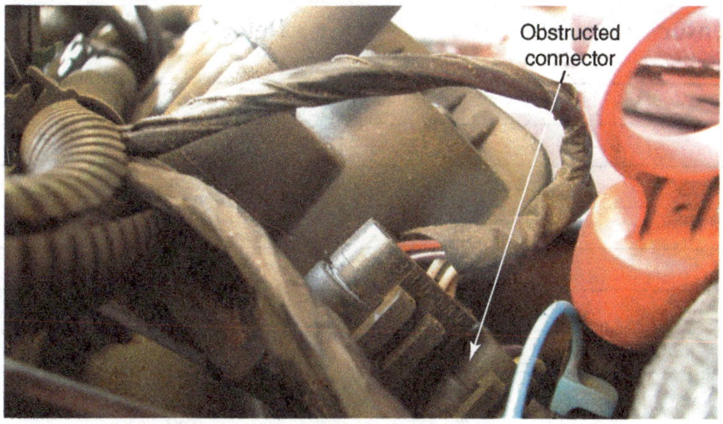

- Insulation discolored and/or swelled (overheating). ___
- White or green deposits on exposed wires (corrosion). ___
- Connectors melted or metal discolored (overheating). ___
- Connectors loose, disconnected. ___

If any problems are found, describe the problems and the actions needed to correct them: ______

______

______

Make Resistance Checks of Wires and/or Connectors

☐ 1. Obtain a multimeter and set it to read resistance.

☐ 2. Locate the wire or connector to be tested and disconnect it from the vehicle's electrical system.

☐ 3. Place the leads of the multimeter on each end of the wire or connector and observe the reading.
Reading: __________ ohms.

☐ 4. Compare this reading to specifications. Most wires and connectors should show very low resistance, usually less than .5 ohm.
Does the wire or connector have excessively high resistance? Yes ___ No ___

______

If Yes, what should be done next? ______

______

☐ 5. After consulting your instructor, make repairs as needed and recheck.

Inspect Solid-State Components

☐ 1. Remove parts as necessary to gain access to the solid state ignition components that are to be inspected.

☐ 2. Inspect and describe the condition of the pickup coils and/or speed sensors and their related toothed wheels or shutters. Look for the following conditions:
- Sensor damaged or disconnected.
- Metal shavings on sensor tip.
- Debris on wheel/shutter.
- Damaged wheel/shutter.
- Improper sensor clearance.

Record the type of sensors being inspected and any defects they may have in the following chart. If an inspected sensor has no defects, write "OK" in the Defects blank.

Type of Sensor	Defects
______	______
______	______
______	______
______	______
______	______
______	______
______	______
______	______

Name ____

Project 3: Job 16 *(continued)*

☐ 3. Locate and note the condition of the following ignition system components. Look for and record damage such as cracks, broken connectors, obvious overheating, disconnected or corroded wires, or other defects.

Ignition module (if separate from the ECM): ____

____

ECM: ____

Relays (when used): ____

Other components (list): ____

____

____

Caution

Perform steps 4 through 8 only when specifically recommended by the applicable service information.

☐ 4. To make resistance checks of a solid-state component, obtain the service information listing the resistance specifications and test terminals for the component.

☐ 5. Obtain a multimeter and set it to read resistance.

☐ 6. Disconnect the component to be tested from the vehicle's electrical system.

☐ 7. Place the leads of the multimeter on the proper terminals of the component and observe the reading.

Reading: __________ ohms.

☐ 8. Compare this reading to specifications.

Does the component show excessively high or low resistance? Yes ___ No ___

If Yes, what should be done next? ____

____

☐ 9. After consulting your instructor, make repairs as necessary and recheck.

Test the Ignition Module and/or ECM

☐ 1. Locate and note the condition of the ignition module (if separate from the ECM) and ECM. Look for, and record, damage such as cracks, damaged connectors, obvious overheating, disconnected or corroded wires, or other defects. ____

____

____

____

____

☐ 2. Turn the vehicle's ignition switch to the *On* position.

☐ 3. Using a test light, ensure that power is available to both sides of all module fuses. Place a check mark next to the results of your tests.

- Test light lights on both sides of all fuses. ___ Go to step 4.
- Test light lights on one side of a fuse. ___ Replace the fuse and recheck module operation.
- Test light does not light on either side of a fuse. ___ Locate and repair the wiring problem between the fuse and ignition switch or battery, then go to step 4.

Caution

If the fuse is blown, you must determine what caused the electrical overload. Do *not* simply replace the fuse and let the vehicle go.

☐ 4. Using a test light, check for power at the module input wire.

Is power available at the module? Yes ___ No ___

If Yes, go to step 5.

If No, repair the wire between the fuse and the module and recheck module operation.

☐ 5. Back probe the system wiring until the reason for the lack of power is determined. Repair the wire or connector between the battery and fuse and recheck operation.

☐ 6. Check the ground at the module.

Is the module properly grounded? Yes ___ No ___

If Yes, go to step 7.

If No, repair the ground wire(s) as needed and recheck module operation.

Caution

Perform steps 7 through 12 only when specifically recommended by the applicable service information.

☐ 7. Obtain service information listing the resistance specifications and test terminals for the module.

☐ 8. Obtain a multimeter and set it to read resistance.

☐ 9. Disconnect the module from the vehicle's electrical system.

Caution

Ensure that the ignition switch is in the *Off* position and the battery negative cable is removed before removing any module electrical connector. Follow all static electricity precautions outlined by the vehicle manufacturer.

☐ 10. Place the leads of the multimeter on the proper terminals of the module and observe the reading.

Reading: ___ ohms

☐ 11. Compare this reading to specifications.

Does the module show excessively high or low resistance? Yes ___ No ___

If Yes, go to step 12.

If No, what should be done next? ______________________________

☐ 12. Replace the module:

Caution

Ensure that the ignition switch is in the *Off* position and the battery negative cable is removed before replacing any module. Follow all static electricity precautions outlined by the vehicle manufacturer.

Name ____

Project 3: Job 16 *(continued)*

a. Remove the module electrical connectors if not already removed.
b. Remove the fasteners holding the module to the engine or body.
c. Place the new module in position and install the fasteners.
d. Install the electrical connectors.

☐ 13. Recheck system operation.

Test Ignition Coil(s)

☐ 1. Make a visual inspection of the suspect coil(s). Indicate any defects found.

- Cracks. ___
- Flashover/carbon tracks. ___
- Damaged terminals. ___

☐ 2. Obtain resistance specifications for the coil(s).

Terminals to check: ______ and ______ Resistance range: ___________ ohms

Terminals to check: ______ and ______ Resistance range: ___________ ohms

Terminals to check: ______ and ______ Resistance range: ___________ ohms

☐ 3. Follow manufacturer's directions to measure the resistance of the coil(s).

Terminals checked: ______ and ______ Resistance range: ___________ ohms

Terminals checked: ______ and ______ Resistance range: ___________ ohms

Terminals checked: ______ and ______ Resistance range: ___________ ohms

☐ 4. Are the resistance readings within specifications? Yes ___ No ___

If No, describe the problem(s) revealed by out-of-specification readings: ___________________

____

____

☐ 5. After consulting your instructor, replace the defective coil(s) and recheck.

Check and Set the Initial Timing—Optional Task

Tech Tip

The following procedure can only be performed on some vehicles with distributor ignition systems. On most modern vehicles, the timing can be read from a scan tool, but not adjusted.

☐ 1. Locate timing procedures and specifications on the underhood emissions label.

Timing specification

Degrees: _______________ before TDC / after TDC (circle one).

☐ 2. Clean and highlight the timing marks as necessary.

☐ 3. Detach electrical connectors or vacuum hoses as directed by the emissions label. See **Figure 16-2**.

Describe the actions taken: ____

____

☐ 4. Attach a timing light to the engine. If the timing light has an advance meter, turn the meter to the 0° position.

Figure 16-2. Many modern vehicles have an electrical connector that must be disengaged to set the initial timing. On older vehicles, a vacuum line may need to be disconnected.

Caution

Make sure the timing light leads will not contact any moving parts, such as belts or pulleys.

- ☐ 5. Start the engine and ensure that the idle speed is correct.
- ☐ 6. Point the timing light at the timing marks and ensure that the marks are illuminated enough to make accurate readings.
- ☐ 7. Observe the ignition timing.

  Degrees: _______________ before TDC / after TDC (circle one).

  Compare the observed timing with the specification. Is the timing correct? Yes ___ No ___

  If No, loosen the distributor hold down bolt and turn the distributor until the timing is correct. Retighten the hold down bolt and recheck the timing.
- ☐ 8. Turn off the engine.
- ☐ 9. Reattach any removed hoses/connectors.

Check the Timing Advance

- ☐ 1. Restart the engine with the timing light attached.
- ☐ 2. Point the timing light at the timing marks.
- ☐ 3. Raise engine speed and observe the ignition timing.

  Does the timing advance as engine speed is increased? Yes ___ No ___

Tech Tip

If exact specifications for timing advance at a specific rpm are not available, as a general rule timing should advance 35° to 45° at 2500 rpm.

If No, what could be the problem? ____

____

Name ______________________________

Project 3: Job 16 *(continued)*

Check Knock Sensor Operation

☐ 1. Strike the engine lightly with a wrench or small hammer and observe ignition timing.
Does the timing retard when the engine is struck? Yes ___ No ___
If No, what could be the problem? ______________________________

☐ 2. Turn off engine.

☐ 3. Disconnect the timing light.

☐ 4. After consulting your instructor, make repairs as necessary and recheck the timing.

Job Wrap-Up

☐ 1. Clean the work area and return any equipment to storage.

☐ 2. Did you encounter any problems during this procedure? Yes ___ No ___
If Yes, describe the problems: ______________________________
____
What did you do to correct the problems? ______________________________
____

☐ 3. Have your instructor check your work and sign this job sheet.

Performance Evaluation—Instructor Use Only

How would you rate this student's overall performance on this task/job?

4 Competent/Proficient. Able to perform all elements of the task/job successfully and independently.

3 Satisfactory performance of the task/job. Able to perform elements of the task/job with minimal instructor assistance.

2 Completed the task/job with significant instructor assistance.

1 Unsuccessfully attempted the task/job.

0 No exposure. Note reason below (absence, skill not covered, etc.).

Comments:
____
____
____
____

Instructor's Signature: ______________________________

Notes

PROJECT 4

Diagnosing and Servicing Fuel and Air Induction Systems

Introduction

Fuel quality is often overlooked as a cause of driveability problems. Low-quality fuel can be the cause of stalling, poor cold engine operation, detonation (pinging) under load, and generally sluggish operation. If a driveability problem cannot be isolated, sometimes switching grades or brands of fuel may solve the problem. In Job 17, you will verify the quality of gasoline and diesel fuel.

Fuel must be supplied to the injectors (or carburetor, on older engines) or the engine will not run. Major components of the fuel supply system are the fuel pump (or pumps), fuel lines and hoses, and fuel filters. Failure in any of these components can cause the engine to run poorly or stop running. In Job 18, you will test and replace fuel supply components.

The throttle body houses the throttle valve, which responds to driver input to regulate the flow of air into the intake manifold. The throttle body also houses the injector(s) in a throttle body injection system. In Job 19, you will inspect and clean a throttle body assembly. Idle speed controls keep the engine idling smoothly despite changes in load and temperature. In Job 20, you will check an idle speed motor or an idle air control valve.

A modern engine may have one of several types of fuel systems. Most modern engines are equipped with multiport, or multipoint, fuel injection. This type of system has an injector for each cylinder. Older vehicles may have central fuel injection with one or two injectors located at top of the intake manifold. There are a variety of tests available to help a technician diagnose a faulty fuel injection system.

Incorrect injector waveforms can alert you to injector failure and help you diagnose the cause of that failure. You will check fuel injector waveforms in Job 21. An injector balance test measures the amount of fuel delivered by the injectors over a specified period of time. This test is useful in detecting clogged injectors or injectors that are failing to fully open. In Job 22, you will perform an injector balance test.

Once the source of the fuel system problem has been determined, it is necessary to correct the problem. This frequently involves replacing worn or faulty injectors. In Job 23, you will replace a faulty fuel injector.

Some vehicles use superchargers or turbochargers to extract extra power from relatively small engines. Superchargers are belt or gear driven from the engine crankshaft. Engine exhaust gases drive turbochargers. Some V-type engines use two turbochargers. Some engines have an intercooler to cool the compressed gases after they have passed through the supercharger or turbocharger. Superchargers and turbochargers are usually replaced as a unit, although the waste gate can sometimes be serviced separately. In Job 24, you will check supercharger and turbocharger operation.

Project 4 Jobs

- Job 17—Verify Fuel Quality
- Job 18—Test and Replace Fuel Supply System Components
- Job 19—Inspect and Service a Throttle Body
- Job 20—Check Idle Speed Motor or Idle Air Control
- Job 21—Check Fuel Injector Waveforms
- Job 22—Perform a Fuel Injector Balance Test
- Job 23—Remove and Replace a Fuel Injector
- Job 24—Check Supercharger and Turbocharger Operation

Tools and Materials

The following list contains the tools and materials that may be needed to complete the jobs in this project. The items used will depend on the make and model of vehicle being serviced.

- Vehicle in need of fuel system service.
- Vehicle in need of exhaust service.
- Vehicle equipped with a supercharger.
- Vehicle equipped with a turbocharger.
- Tachometer or engine analyzer.
- Exhaust gas analyzer.
- Fuel pressure tester.
- Pressure gauge.
- Vacuum gauge.
- Vacuum pump.
- Equipment capable of reading waveforms.
- Dedicated injector tester or scan tool and adapters.
- Scan tool operating instructions.
- Clear glass or plastic container.
- Graduated cylinder.
- Cetane hydrometer.
- Fire extinguisher.
- Hand tools.
- Air-powered tools.
- Safety glasses and other protective equipment.

Safety Notice

Before performing these jobs, review all pertinent safety information in the text and review safety information with your instructor.

Name ____

Date ____________________ Class ____________________

Project 4: Job 17—Verify Fuel Quality

After completing this job, you will be able to verify gasoline and diesel fuel quality.

Instructions

As you read the job instructions, answer the questions and perform the tasks. Record your answers using complete sentences. Consult the proper service information and ask your instructor for help as needed.

Warning

Before performing this job, review all pertinent safety information in the text and discuss safety procedures with your instructor.

Procedures

☐ 1. Obtain a vehicle to be used in this job. Your instructor may direct you to perform this job on a shop vehicle.

☐ 2. Gather the tools needed to perform this job. Refer to the tools and materials list at the beginning of the project.

Warning

Gasoline is extremely flammable and can be ignited by the smallest spark. Even a spark caused by dropping a tool on the shop floor is sufficient to ignite gasoline. Be sure that a fire extinguisher is nearby and that you know how to use it before starting any procedure that requires removing fuel line connections.

Inspect a Gasoline Sample for Contamination

☐ 1. Place a drip pan under the vehicle and have a fire extinguisher handy.

☐ 2. Disconnect the fuel line between the fuel tank and the filter.

Tech Tip

Dirt in the fuel filter is normal. Do *not* decide that the fuel is contaminated based on the contents of the fuel filter.

☐ 3. Drain about 6 oz (180 ml) of gasoline into a glass or fuel-compatible plastic container.

☐ 4. Visually inspect for dirt, rust, or other particles suspended in the gasoline.

Are particles present? Yes ___ No ___

☐ 5. Observe whether the sample is cloudy, indicating water or other contamination.

Is the sample cloudy? Yes ___ No ___

☐ 6. Allow the sample to sit for five to ten minutes. Water will settle to the bottom and be easily observed.

Is any water present? Yes ___ No ___

☐ 7. If the answer to any of the previous questions is Yes, the gasoline is contaminated. After consulting your instructor, clean the fuel tank and related lines. In some cases, a badly contaminated tank must be replaced.

☐ 8. After all tests and necessary repairs are completed, reconnect the fuel line between the tank and the filter.

Check for Excessive Alcohol in Gasoline

Tech Tip

This test checks for excess alcohol (more than 10%) in the gasoline sample. Excess alcohol can cause hard starting, stalling and other performance problems when the engine is fully warmed up.

☐ 1. Obtain a 110 ml (3.5 oz) graduated cylinder.

☐ 2. Pour 90 ml (3 oz) of sample gasoline into the cylinder.

☐ 3. Pour 10 ml (0.3 oz) of water into the cylinder.

☐ 4. Seal the top of the cylinder and vigorously shake it.

☐ 5. Allow the cylinder to sit for five to ten minutes.

☐ 6. Observe the combined water and alcohol in the bottom of the cylinder. If the combined water in the bottom of the cylinder is more than 20 ml (0.6 oz) the sample contains more than 10% alcohol.

Does the sample contain more than 10% alcohol? Yes ___ No ___

If Yes, suggest that the vehicle owner switch gasoline brands.

Tech Tip

Some vehicles are compatible with the E85 blend of gasoline. This gasoline contains 85% ethanol.

Inspect a Diesel Fuel Sample for Contamination

☐ 1. Place a drip pan under the vehicle and have a fire extinguisher handy.

☐ 2. Disconnect the fuel line between the fuel tank and the filter.

Tech Tip

Dirt in the fuel filter is normal. Do *not* decide that the fuel is contaminated based on the contents of the fuel filter.

☐ 3. Drain about 6 oz (180 ml) of diesel fuel into a glass or plastic container.

☐ 4. Visually inspect for particles suspended in the diesel fuel. This is usually evidence of water contamination, which allows microorganisms to grow.

Does the sample contain suspended particles? Yes ___ No ___

☐ 5. Allow the sample to sit for five to ten minutes. Water will settle to the bottom and be easily observed.

Is any water present? Yes ___ No ___

Name ____

Project 4: Job 17 *(continued)*

☐ 6. If the answer to any of the previous questions is Yes, the diesel fuel is contaminated. After consulting your instructor, clean the fuel tank and related lines. In some cases, a badly contaminated tank must be replaced.

☐ 7. After all tests and necessary repairs are completed, reconnect the fuel line between the tank and the filter.

Measure the Diesel Fuel Cetane Rating

☐ 1. Obtain a cetane hydrometer.

> **Tech Tip**
>
> A cetane hydrometer will provide a quick and relatively accurate cetane reading. If your shop uses another type of cetane tester, follow the tester instructions to check cetane.

☐ 2. Ensure that the temperature of the diesel fuel to be sampled is between 75°F (25°C) and 95°F (35°C). If necessary, place the sample in a spot where it can reach this temperature range.

☐ 3. Draw a sample of diesel fuel into the hydrometer.

☐ 4. Be sure that the float is not touching the bottom of the cylinder, then read the number on the float. Diesel fuel should have a minimum cetane number of 40.

Does the fuel have a 40 rating? Yes ___ No ___

If No, suggest that the vehicle owner switch fuel brands.

Check for Diesel Fuel Waxing

> **Tech Tip**
>
> Waxing occurs in cold weather and can clog filters and injectors, keeping the engine from starting or causing it to stall. The temperature at which wax forms in the fuel is known as the *cloud point.*

☐ 1. Place a sample of diesel fuel in a cold place. This can be done by placing the sample outside in temperatures below 32°F (0°C) or placing it in the freezer section of a refrigerator. Record the temperature to which the fuel is cooled.

Temperature: _____°F/°C (circle one)

☐ 2. Wait several hours to allow the sample to completely cool.

☐ 3. Observe the fuel. Wax will form easily observable particles in the fuel.

Are wax particles present? Yes ___ No ___

If Yes, suggest that the vehicle owner switch fuel brands or grades.

> **Tech Tip**
>
> Grade 1D diesel fuel should have a cloud point of –20°F (–30°C). Grade 2D diesel fuel should have a cloud point of 10°F (–10°C).

Job Wrap-Up

☐ 1. Clean the work area and return any equipment to storage.

☐ 2. Did you encounter any problems during this procedure? Yes ___ No ___

If Yes, describe the problems: ______________________________

____

What did you do to correct the problems? ______________________________

____

☐ 3. Have your instructor check your work and sign this job sheet.

Performance Evaluation—Instructor Use Only

How would you rate this student's overall performance on this task/job?

4 Competent/Proficient. Able to perform all elements of the task/job successfully and independently.

3 Satisfactory performance of the task/job. Able to perform elements of the task/job with minimal instructor assistance.

2 Completed the task/job with significant instructor assistance.

1 Unsuccessfully attempted the task/job.

0 No exposure. Note reason below (absence, skill not covered, etc.).

Comments:

____

____

____

____

Instructor's Signature: ______________________________

Name ______________________________

Date ____________________ Class ____________________

Project 4: Job 18—Test and Replace Fuel Supply System Components

After completing this job, you will be able to test and replace fuel supply components.

Instructions

As you read the job instructions, answer the questions and perform the tasks. Record your answers using complete sentences. Consult the proper service information and ask your instructor for help as needed.

Warning

Before performing this job, review all pertinent safety information in the text and discuss safety procedures with your instructor.

Procedures

☐ 1. Obtain a vehicle to be used in this job. Your instructor may direct you to perform this job on a shop vehicle.

☐ 2. Gather the tools needed to perform this job. Refer to the tools and materials list at the beginning of the project.

☐ 3. Verify that your fire extinguisher is handy and properly charged.

Warning

Gasoline is extremely flammable and can be ignited by the smallest spark. Even a spark caused by dropping a tool on the shop floor is sufficient to ignite gasoline. Be sure that a fire extinguisher is nearby and that you know how to use it before starting any procedure that requires removing fuel line connections.

☐ 4. Visually inspect the fuel lines and hoses for the following defects:
- Leaks at connections.
- Kinked lines or hoses.
- Collapsed lines or hoses.
- Swelled hoses.
- Loose or missing clips or brackets.

Describe any fuel line and hose problem(s) found: ______________________________

____

Describe what should be done to correct the problem(s): ______________________________

____

Remove, Check, and Replace Fuel Filters

☐ 1. Locate the fuel filter on the vehicle.

☐ 2. Relieve fuel system pressure.

☐ 3. Remove the fuel filter bracket fasteners.

☐ 4. Place a drip pan under the filter.

☐ 5. Remove the fuel line fittings and allow excess fuel to drip into the pan.

Warning

Some gasoline will spill as the fittings are removed. Be sure to clean up any spilled gasoline before proceeding.

☐ 6. Check the filter condition by one of the following methods:

- Drain the fuel from the inlet side of the filter and observe the fuel's condition. If the fuel is contaminated, the filter must be replaced.
- Attempt to blow through the filter. A restricted filter will be difficult to blow through, indicating that the filter must be replaced.

Warning

Avoid breathing gasoline vapors or ingesting gasoline.

☐ 7. Compare the old and new filters to ensure that the new filter is correct. Check for correct size, fittings, and number of outlets.

Do the filters match? Yes ___ No ___

If No, what could account for the difference? ____

____

☐ 8. Install the new filter.

☐ 9. Tighten the fittings.

☐ 10. Install the bracket fasteners.

☐ 11. Start the engine and check for fuel leaks.

Test Fuel Pressure (Electric Pump)

Tech Tip

This procedure also tests the operation of the fuel pressure regulator.

☐ 1. In the service information, locate the fuel pressure specification.

Fuel pressure: _______________

☐ 2. Attach a fuel pressure gauge to the fuel system. See **Figure 18-1**.

Figure 18-1. Fuel pressure gauge attachment methods are shown here. A—Some systems, especially those using central fuel injectors, require an adapter to attach the gauge to the test port. B—An adapter is *not* needed to connect the pressure gauge to most multiport fuel injection system test ports.

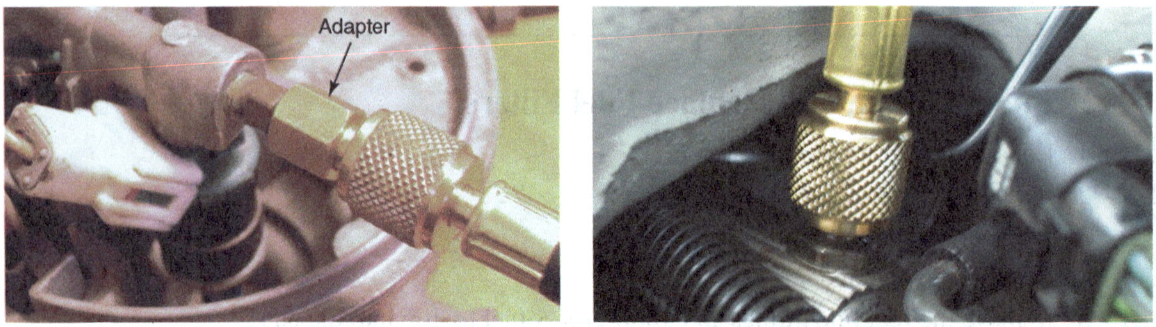

A

B

Name ____

Project 4: Job 18 *(continued)*

Warning

Some gasoline will spill as the test connections are made. Be sure to clean up any spilled gasoline before proceeding.

☐ 3. Turn the ignition switch to the *On* position.

☐ 4. Observe the fuel system pressure.

Is the fuel pressure acceptable? Yes ___ No ___

If No, describe the possible causes: ______________________________

____

____

☐ 5. With the pressure gauge attached, start the engine.

☐ 6. Observe the fuel system pressure.

Does the fuel pressure drop slightly when the engine is started? Yes ___ No ___

Does the pressure remain steady as the engine operates? Yes ___ No ___

If No, describe possible causes: ______________________________

____

____

☐ 7. Consult your instructor for any corrective actions to be taken.

Test Electric Fuel Pump Relays

☐ 1. Allow the engine to stand for at least five minutes.

☐ 2. Locate the fuel pump relay.

☐ 3. Place your hand on the relay and have an assistant turn the ignition switch to the *On* position.

Does the relay click? Yes ___ No ___

If Yes, skip to the *Test the Electric Fuel Pump's Amperage Draw* section of this job.

If No, go to step 4.

☐ 4. Make other electrical checks as necessary to isolate the relay problem.

Test the Electric Fuel Pump's Amperage Draw

☐ 1. Obtain the proper amperage draw specifications from the appropriate service information. If amperage draw specifications are not available, determine the type of fuel system and use these general guidelines:

- **Multiport fuel injection:** 4–6 amps.
- **Throttle body injection:** 3–5 amps.
- **Central point injection:** 8–10 amps.

☐ 2. Obtain an amperage tester or multimeter with amperage testing capabilities and set it to a minimum range of 0–20 amps.

☐ 3. Attach the tester to the fuel pump connectors as necessary. If the tester uses an inductive clamp, place it around the pump's power wire.

☐ 4. Turn the ignition switch to the *On* position and make sure that all other electrical devices are turned off.

☐ 5. Measure pump amperage.

Amperage: _______________

Is the pump amperage within specifications? Yes ___ No ___

If the pump amperage is low, the pump brushes are probably worn and are not properly contacting the armature. If the amperage is high, the pump bearings are worn, allowing the armature to drag against the field windings. In either case, the pump must be replaced.

Test Electric Fuel Pump Waveforms

☐ 1. Obtain a scope and a low-amp clamp. Attach the amp-clamp leads to the scope. Set the probe lead on the scope to amp clamp, turn on the amp clamp, and zero the amp clamp with the button or dial on the clamp.

☐ 2. Using a wiring diagram determine the easiest place to obtain a spot to put the amp clamp around a wire that attaches directly to the pump. If the vehicle uses a fuel pump module, the wire must be power or ground at the pump and not upstream in the wiring from the fuel pump module. If the fuel pump is run from a relay, using a jumper wire in the fuse panel will work, **Figure 18-2**.

Which system type is on this vehicle, fuel pump module or direct?

☐ 3. Start the engine. If the vehicle will not run, crank the engine while recording the waveform. This may need to be done several times to have the right voltage and sweep to capture the entire waveform.

The waveform produced by a healthy fuel pump will have equal peaks and valleys. A fuel pump with a commutator section that is carboned or burnt will show a waveform with a peak or two missing, indicating that the fuel pump should be replaced.

Figure 18-2. Using a jumper in place of the fuse on a vehicle without a fuel pump module will allow the use of an amp clamp. Remember that it doesn't matter whether the power or ground side is used since the current that leaves the battery must return to the battery. Therefore, pick whichever side is easier to get to but don't connect to both wires at the same time, as one field will cancel the other.

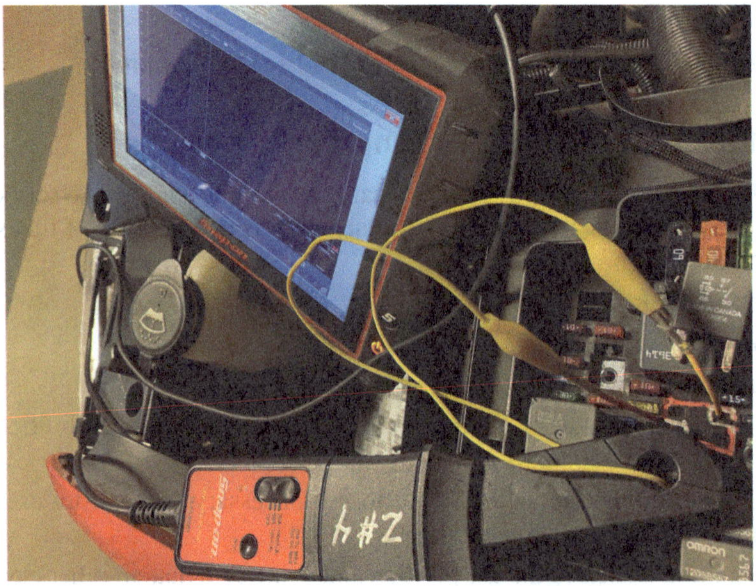

Name ____

Tech Tip

Using a waveform to determine fuel pump health can be used to predict future fuel pump failure. The fuel pump that produced the waveform in **Figure 18-3** failed a few months after the waveform was captured.

Does the fuel pump waveform indicate a fuel pump in good condition? ____

Will you recommend replacing the pump as a preventive measure or has the pump clearly failed and must be replaced?

☐ 4. Consult your instructor for further instruction.

Replace an Inline Electric Fuel Pump

☐ 1. Remove the battery negative cable

☐ 2. Locate the pump on the vehicle, **Figure 18-4**. If the pump is not visible under the hood, raise the vehicle and follow the fuel line.

Where is the pump located? ____

____

Warning

The vehicle must be raised and supported in a safe manner. Always use an approved lift or jacks and jack stands.

Figure 18-3. This waveform was produced by a fuel pump in which the commutator sections of the brushed motor were beginning to wear out. Each hump should be a single peak with no unlevel upslope or downslope.

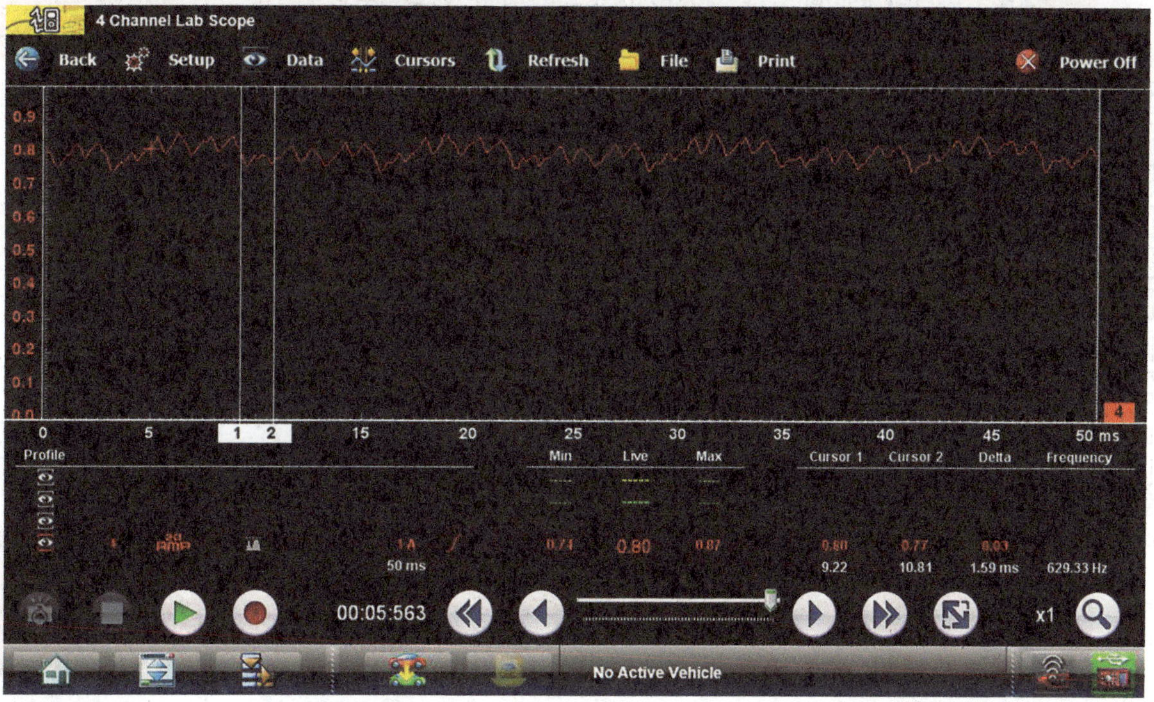

Figure 18-4. A typical location for an inline electric fuel pump is shown here. The bracket holding the pump and filter must be removed to gain access to the pump.

- ☐ 3. Relieve the fuel pressure.
- ☐ 4. Disconnect the electrical connector at the pump.
- ☐ 5. Place a drip pan under the pump.
- ☐ 6. Loosen the pump fittings.
- ☐ 7. Allow excess fuel to drip into the pan, then remove the pump fittings.

Warning

If fuel continues to drip from the lines, plug the lines.

- ☐ 8. Remove the pump bracket fasteners.
- ☐ 9. Remove the pump from the vehicle.
- ☐ 10. Compare the old and new pumps to ensure that the new pump is correct.
- ☐ 11. Place the new pump in position on the vehicle.
- ☐ 12. Install, but do not tighten, the bracket fasteners.
- ☐ 13. Install and tighten the fuel line fittings.
- ☐ 14. Tighten the pump bracket fasteners.
- ☐ 15. Install the electrical connector.
- ☐ 16. Reinstall the battery negative cable.
- ☐ 17. Turn the ignition switch to the *On* position and check pump operation.

Warning

Make sure that the pump fittings do not leak.

Name ____________________

Replace an In-Tank Electric Fuel Pump

- ☐ 1. Remove the battery negative cable.
- ☐ 2. Drain the fuel from the tank into an approved fuel-collecting device. When the fuel is done draining, move the fuel container out of the work area.

Warning

Do *not* allow spilled fuel or vapors to collect. Wipe up spills and ensure that the area is properly ventilated.

- ☐ 3. Disconnect the electrical connectors, fuel lines, and hoses from the tank assembly.
- ☐ 4. Place a transmission jack or other lowering device under the fuel tank. Raise it into position so that it supports the tank.
- ☐ 5. Remove the fuel tank fasteners.

Tech Tip

You may need to disconnect the fuel tank filler neck before lowering the tank from the vehicle.

- ☐ 6. Lower the fuel tank from the vehicle and place it on a bench.
- ☐ 7. Locate the cam lock that holds the fuel pump assembly in place.
- ☐ 8. Locate the tabs that hold the cam lock in place and bend them out enough to allow the cam to be turned.
- ☐ 9. Turn the cam lock using a special tool.

Tech Tip

Some tanks do not require a special tool.

- ☐ 10. Lift the assembly from the tank. See **Figure 18-5**.
- ☐ 11. Remove the tank-to-assembly O-ring and discard it.
- ☐ 12. Wipe up all spilled fuel, and then bring the pump assembly to a clean workbench.
- ☐ 13. Remove the pump from the pickup tube and sender as needed.
- ☐ 14. Remove the strainer (often called the sock) from the pump assembly and inspect it closely. If the strainer appears to be clogged or has any tears or holes, replace it.
- ☐ 15. Compare the old and new pumps to ensure that the new pump is correct.
- ☐ 16. Install the strainer on the new pump.
- ☐ 17. Attach the pickup tube and sender to the new pump, if applicable.
- ☐ 18. Install a new O-ring in the tank's O-ring groove.

Tech Tip

Some manufacturers recommend lubricating O-rings before installation.

- ☐ 19. Lower the pump into the tank opening.

Figure 18-5. A typical tank-mounted electric fuel pump assembly is shown here. Always check the strainer (sock) at the pump inlet for contamination.

Caution

Watch carefully to ensure that the strainer is not damaged or folded over enough to restrict fuel flow.

☐ 20. Install the cam lock.

☐ 21. Tap the lock fully into position and reposition the holding tabs.

☐ 22. Move the tank under the vehicle and raise it into position.

☐ 23. Reinstall the tank in the vehicle. Reconnect any electrical connectors, hoses, and lines that were disconnected during tank removal.

☐ 24. Return the fuel to the tank.

☐ 25. Reinstall the battery negative cable.

☐ 26. Turn the ignition switch to the *On* position and check that the pump operates correctly.

Test Mechanical Fuel Pump Pressure

☐ 1. In the service information, locate the fuel pressure specification.

Fuel pressure: _______________

☐ 2. Attach a fuel pressure gauge to the fuel system.

Warning

Some gasoline will spill as the test connections are made. Be sure to clean up any spilled gasoline before proceeding.

☐ 3. Start the engine.

☐ 4. Record the fuel system pressure.

Fuel system pressure: _______________

Is the system pressure within specifications? Yes ___ No ___

Name ____________________

If No, the fuel pump may be faulty; there may be a leak in the pump's intake line, allowing air to be drawn in; or there may be a restriction in the system, such as a collapsed fuel line or clogged strainer. Consult your instructor for further diagnostic or corrective actions that should be taken.

Replace a Mechanical Fuel Pump

☐ 1. Locate the fuel pump on the engine.

☐ 2. Relieve pressure from the fuel system.

☐ 3. Place a drip pan under the pump.

☐ 4. Remove the fuel line fittings and allow excess fuel to drip into the pan.

Warning

If fuel continues to drip from the lines, plug them as necessary.

☐ 5. Remove the fasteners holding the pump to the engine, **Figure 18-6**.

☐ 6. Remove the pump from the engine.

Tech Tip

Some fuel pumps are operated by a push rod, which could fall free from the block when the pump is removed. If you are replacing a push rod–type pump, remove the pump slowly to avoid dropping the push rod.

Figure 18-6. Most mechanical fuel pumps are attached to the engine with two fasteners. The fasteners can be removed with standard hand tools.

☐ 7. Scrape off all old gasket material from the pump mounting surface.

☐ 8. Compare the old and new pumps.

Do the pumps match? Yes ___ No ___

If No, what could be the reason? ____________________

____

☐ 9. Install a new fuel pump gasket on the engine, using sealer as necessary.

☐ 10. Place the new pump on the engine being sure to align the pump arm (or push rod) with the camshaft.

Tech Tip

If you are installing a push rod–type pump, you can use grease to hold the push rod in position while you install the pump.

☐ 11. Install and tighten the fuel pump fasteners.

☐ 12. Install the fuel line fittings.

☐ 13. Start the engine and check that the pump operates correctly.

Job Wrap-Up

☐ 1. Clean the work area and return any equipment to storage.

☐ 2. Did you encounter any problems during this procedure? Yes ___ No ___

If Yes, describe the problems: ____________________

____

What did you do to correct the problems? ____________________

☐ 3. Have your instructor check your work and sign this job sheet.

Performance Evaluation—Instructor Use Only

How would you rate this student's overall performance on this task/job?

4 Competent/Proficient. Able to perform all elements of the task/job successfully and independently.

3 Satisfactory performance of the task/job. Able to perform elements of the task/job with minimal instructor assistance.

2 Completed the task/job with significant instructor assistance.

1 Unsuccessfully attempted the task/job.

0 No exposure. Note reason below (absence, skill not covered, etc.).

Comments:

____

____

____

____

Instructor's Signature: ____________________

Name ____

Date ____________________ Class ____________________

Project 4: Job 19—Inspect and Service a Throttle Body

After completing this job, you will be able to inspect and service the throttle body in a fuel injection system.

Instructions

As you read the job instructions, answer the questions and perform the tasks. Record your answers using complete sentences. Consult the proper service information and ask your instructor for help as needed.

Warning

Before performing this job, review all pertinent safety information in the text and discuss safety procedures with your instructor.

Procedures

- ☐ 1. Obtain a vehicle to be used in this job. Your instructor may direct you to perform this job on a shop vehicle.
- ☐ 2. Gather the tools needed to perform this job. Refer to the tools and materials list at the beginning of the project.
- ☐ 3. Obtain the proper service information.

Check for Loose or Damaged Air Intake System Ducts or Hoses

- ☐ 1. Open the vehicle hood and remove any air ducts or engine covers as necessary.
- ☐ 2. Locate the air filter housing.
- ☐ 3. Remove the fasteners holding the air filter housing.
- ☐ 4. Remove the housing to gain access to the filter.
- ☐ 5. Remove the filter and inspect the filter element for excessive dirt buildup.
- ☐ 6. Observe the air intake system for obvious damage or missing parts.
- ☐ 7. Remove necessary ductwork to expose the throttle body. Look for broken fittings, damaged gaskets, loose fasteners, and a worn throttle shaft.
- ☐ 8. Check for disconnected, cracked, and split vacuum lines.

  Were any vacuum line problems found? Yes ___ No ___

  If Yes, explain: ____

  ____
- ☐ 9. Inspect the intake manifold for broken fittings and damaged gaskets.
- ☐ 10. Check ductwork for splits, cracks, and loose or missing fittings.

  Were any ductwork problems found? Yes ___ No ___

  If Yes, explain: ____

  ____

Check the Spray Patterns in a Throttle Body Injection (TBI) System

Tech Tip

This section of the job is only applicable for vehicles with throttle body injection (TBI). If the vehicle you are working on does not have throttle body injection, skip to the *Clean the Throttle Body* section of the job.

- [ ] 1. Attach a timing light to any spark plug wire.
- [ ] 2. Remove the air cleaner.
- [ ] 3. Start the engine.
- [ ] 4. Point the timing light at the fuel injector in the throttle body and observe the injector spray pattern, **Figure 19-1**.

   Does the injector spray pattern appear to be steady and evenly cone-shaped? Yes ___ No ___

   If No, what could be the problem? ______________________________

   ____
- [ ] 5. Turn off the engine.
- [ ] 6. Disconnect the timing light.

Inspect and Service a Throttle Body

- [ ] 1. Check for throttle-related diagnostic trouble codes. Codes that relate to range/performance/sync, such as "P0226 Throttle/Pedal Position Sensor/Switch C Circuit Malfunction," may indicate the need for throttle body cleaning.
- [ ] 2. Look at scan tool data. Do the actual and desired throttle positions match?

   Yes ____ No ____

Figure 19-1. Point the timing light at the fuel injector and observe the spray pattern. Raise the idle to get a more consistent flash.

Name ____

Project 4: Job 19 *(continued)*

- ☐ 3. Are there any codes or other data related to the throttle plate misposition?

  Yes ___ No ___

  If Yes, list them here. ____

- ☐ 4. If codes that relate to range/performance/sync or other data related to the throttle plate misposition is present, throttle body cleaning may be necessary. Back out of the scan tool and *turn the ignition switch completely off.*
- ☐ 5. Remove the air cleaner and intake duct as necessary.
- ☐ 6. Inspect the throttle body for deposits.
- ☐ 7. Inspect the throttle plate for smooth movement opening and closing by operating it slowly with your finger.

  Does the throttle body operate smoothly? Yes ___ No ___

  If not, consult your instructor for further corrective actions.

- ☐ 8. If the throttle operates smoothly and there are deposits to clean, spray a lint-free rag with throttle body cleaner. Use gloves so as not to get any cleaner on your skin. Clean the throttle body as shown in **Figure 19-2**.

Tech Tip

Never spray the cleaner directly into the intake, as this may cause code P0172 (System Too Rich, Bank 1) to set and the check engine light to come on once the engine is started. This will also contaminate the catalytic converter.

- ☐ 9. If the throttle body connector was removed while the key was still on, perform a throttle body relearn procedure with the scan tool.
- ☐ 10. Reinstall the air cleaner and ductwork assembly. Ensure that the lip of the ductwork is not folded over on any openings, as this will cause air leaks that will create false MAF sensor readings.
- ☐ 11. Start the engine and check for any leaks and proper operation.

Figure 19-2. Clean the throttle body with a rag sprayed with throttle body cleaner.

Job Wrap-Up

☐ 1. Clean the work area and return any equipment to storage.

☐ 2. Did you encounter any problems during this procedure? Yes ___ No ___

If Yes, describe the problems: ____

____

What did you do to correct the problems? ______________________________________

____

☐ 3. Have your instructor check your work and sign this job sheet.

Performance Evaluation—Instructor Use Only

How would you rate this student's overall performance on this task/job?

4 Competent/Proficient. Able to perform all elements of the task/job successfully and independently.

3 Satisfactory performance of the task/job. Able to perform elements of the task/job with minimal instructor assistance.

2 Completed the task/job with significant instructor assistance.

1 Unsuccessfully attempted the task/job.

0 No exposure. Note reason below (absence, skill not covered, etc.).

Comments:

____

____

____

____

Instructor's Signature: ____

Name ____

Date ____________________________ Class ____________________________

Project 4: Job 20—Check Idle Speed Motor or Idle Air Control

After completing this job, you will be able to check the operation of the idle speed motor or idle air control.

Instructions

As you read the job instructions, answer the questions and perform the tasks. Record your answers using complete sentences. Consult the proper service information and ask your instructor for help as needed.

Warning

Before performing this job, review all pertinent safety information in the text and discuss safety procedures with your instructor.

Procedures

☐ 1. Obtain a vehicle to be used in this job. Your instructor may direct you to perform this job on a shop vehicle.

☐ 2. Gather the tools needed to perform this job. Refer to the tools and materials list at the beginning of the project.

Check Idle Speed Motor or Idle Air Control

Tech Tip

Do *not* move the throttle during this procedure.

☐ 1. Attach a tachometer to the engine.

☐ 2. Start the engine.

☐ 3. Observe the engine speed (engine should be warm).

☐ 4. Place the transmission in gear with the parking brake on or turn on the air conditioner.

Does the idle speed motor compensate for the increased load and maintain idle speed?
Yes ___ No ___

If Yes, skip to step 6.

If No, what could be the problem? ____

____

____

☐ 5. Put the vehicle in *Park* and stop the engine.

☐ 6. Consult your instructor for the corrective action to be taken.

☐ 7. Remove the tachometer.

Remove and Replace an Idle Speed Motor

☐ 1. If necessary, remove the air cleaner to gain access to the idle speed motor.

☐ 2. Determine the idle speed motor design, **Figure 20-1**. Some motors are threaded into the throttle body; others are held in place with fasteners.

☐ 3. Select the proper tools and remove the idle speed motor.

☐ 4. Compare the idle speed motor with the replacement part.

Do the idle speed motor and the replacement match? Yes ___ No ___

If No, consult your instructor.

☐ 5. Install the replacement idle speed motor.

☐ 6. Reinstall the air cleaner if necessary.

☐ 7. Start the engine and ensure that the replacement idle speed motor is operating properly.

Figure 20-1. Two common types of idle speed motors are shown here. A—This idle speed motor is threaded into the throttle body. B—This motor is held in place with fasteners.

A B

Job Wrap-Up

☐ 1. Clean the work area and return any equipment to storage.

☐ 2. Did you encounter any problems during this procedure? Yes ___ No ___

If Yes, describe the problems: ____

____

What did you do to correct the problems: ____

____

☐ 3. Have your instructor check your work and sign this job sheet.

Name ______________________________

Project 4: Job 20 *(continued)*

Performance Evaluation—Instructor Use Only

How would you rate this student's overall performance on this task/job?

4 Competent/Proficient. Able to perform all elements of the task/job successfully and independently.

3 Satisfactory performance of the task/job. Able to perform elements of the task/job with minimal instructor assistance.

2 Completed the task/job with significant instructor assistance.

1 Unsuccessfully attempted the task/job.

0 No exposure. Note reason below (absence, skill not covered, etc.).

Comments:

____

____

____

____

Instructor's Signature: ______________________________

Notes

Name ____

Date ____________________________ Class ____________________________

Project 4: Job 21—Check Fuel Injector Waveforms

After completing this job, you will be able to check injector waveforms for indications of failure.

Instructions

As you read the job instructions, answer the questions and perform the tasks. Record your answers using complete sentences. Consult the proper service information and ask your instructor for help as needed.

Warning

Before performing this job, review all pertinent safety information in the text and discuss safety procedures with your instructor.

Procedures

☐ 1. Obtain a vehicle on which the injectors are visible. The engine may have port or direct injection. If the only vehicle available has the injectors covered, use a wiring diagram to determine which cavity of a bulkhead connector leading to the ECM has all the ground wires to the injectors. The power supply leads to the fuse panel, but the injector circuit is a ground-side switched circuit.

☐ 2. Check voltage using a scope, scope leads, and a T-pin or other device to back probe next to the wire on the injector. The wire to back probe will be the wire that is a different color than the wires at the other injectors. The wire color that is common at all injectors indicates the common power supply. See **Figure 21-1**.

☐ 3. To find almost anything engine-performance related on the scope using voltage, default to 50 volts and 50 ms to begin. Set your trigger slightly below the 14-volt line. Your scope may also have Auto-Find or Guided Component Tests to assist you. Turn the key to the *RUN* position and check voltage on the scope.

Do you show battery voltage? Yes ___ No ___

☐ 4. If battery voltage is displayed on the screen as a straight line at approximately 12.6 volts, proceed to the next step. If not, check for blown fuses and replace as necessary. This positive check tells you that the injector you are working on has no opens in the coil, the wiring supply to that point has no opens, and the fuse is not blown.

☐ 5. Start the engine and allow it to run. Does the voltage rise to approximately 14 volts? Yes ___ No ___

If Yes, the alternator is operating.

☐ 6. Study the waveform displayed on the scope. It should look like the yellow waveform in **Figure 21-1**. The area where the waveform drops is the ECM completing ground to complete the injector circuit. In other words, this is ground-side switched or also called a low-side driver. The voltage spike is the inductive "kick" that occurs when the ground is then opened by the ECM so that the injector closes again.

Does the observed waveform look like the yellow waveform in **Figure 21-1**? Yes ___ No ___

If not, answer the following questions.

a. Does the observed waveform blink from time to time? Yes ___ No ___

If Yes, the trigger is not in the correct spot. Does this fix the observed waveform? Yes ___ No ___

Figure 21-1. Fuel injector waveforms. The yellow waveform represents voltage and the red waveform represents current.

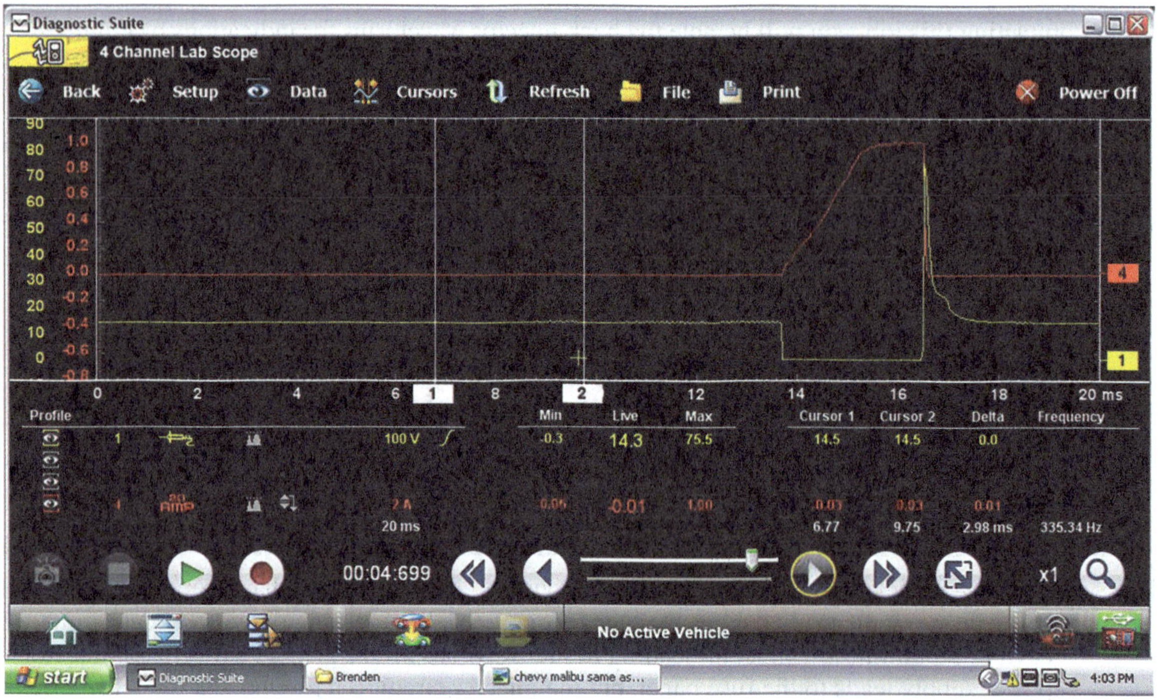

b. Does the observed waveform remain at the approximately 14 volts without wavering?
Yes ___ No ___

If yes, the lead is on the power feed wire for the injector or there is no ECM ground completion for this circuit. Perform a voltage drop of the ground wire from the injector to the ECM.

What is the voltage drop of the ground side of the injector while the engine is running?

What does this voltage drop indicate? ____

____

____

____

c. Is the observed waveform a flat line at 0 volts and does the engine runs well? Yes ___ No ___

If yes, there is either a poor connection or the scope is frozen.

Was it a poor connection or did the scope need a reset? Yes ___ No ___

☐ 7. A better test of an injector is to view the current ramp. Using the low-amp clamp as instructed in Job 10, expose the wires of a working injector and place the low-amp clamp on either of the wires because the current will be the same in both. Adjust the scale of the amp-clamp circuit until the observed waveform looks like the red waveform of **Figure 21-1**.

Does the observed waveform look like the red waveform **Figure 21-1**? Yes ___ No ___

If not, make sure the amp clamp is turned on and the probe function on the scope is set to amp clamp. If necessary, ask your instructor for assistance in adjusting your settings.

☐ 8. Study the waveform displayed on your scope. The slope of the red waveform in **Figure 21-1**, which represents current, shows building of the magnetic field in the coils of the injector. The slight indentation approximately 2/3 of the way up the slope indicates movement of the pintle within the injector. If any of these portions in your waveform are not like those shown in **Figure 21-1**, there may be a fault. Typical faults include a steep upward line where the slope should be, which indicates a short, or a waveform that remains at zero, which is an indication of an open. A slope without the indentation means the injector pintle did not move: the injector did not open to pass fuel.

List any of the injectors indicating any of these faults and which type:____________________

☐ 9. Find the fuse or fuses in the under-hood fuse panel that supply power to a set of injectors on the engine.

☐ 10. Replace the fuse located in step 9 with a fused jumper wire.

☐ 11. Remove the low-amp clamp from the injector and move it to the fused jumper wire just installed.

☐ 12. Start the engine and observe the waveform displayed on the scope. All the injectors that use the fuse that was removed will be displayed on the screen for comparison. Increasing the sweep (time) on the scope may be necessary to see more of the injectors.

Do all the waveforms look alike? Yes ____No ____

☐ 13. The waveforms produced by direct injected engines may look different from those shown in **Figure 21-1**, as some manufacturers use the voltage spike of one injector to initiate the start of the next injector.

If the waveform is different, does the engine have direct injection or is it throttle body injection? Yes ____No ____

☐ 14. Repeat the steps for another injector fuse.

☐ 15. What is the advantage to looking at waveforms for a set of injectors rather than the waveform for an individual injector?

☐ 16. What is an advantage of looking at current instead of voltage on the injectors?

☐ 17. Identify any injector that does not appear to have the proper waveform and list possible causes.

☐ 18. Turn off the engine and disconnect the scope, low-amp clamp, and fused jumper wire.

Job Wrap-Up

☐ 1. Clean the work area and return any equipment to storage.

☐ 2. Did you encounter any problems during this procedure? Yes ___ No ___

If Yes, describe the problems: ____________________

What did you do to correct the problems? ____________________

☐ 3. Have your instructor check your work and sign this job sheet.

Performance Evaluation—Instructor Use Only

How would you rate this student's overall performance on this task/job?

4 Competent/Proficient. Able to perform all elements of the task/job successfully and independently.

3 Satisfactory performance of the task/job. Able to perform elements of the task/job with minimal instructor assistance.

2 Completed the task/job with significant instructor assistance.

1 Unsuccessfully attempted the task/job.

0 No exposure. Note reason below (absence, skill not covered, etc.).

Comments:
____
____
____
____

Instructor's Signature: ______________________________

Name ______________________________

Date ____________________ Class ____________________

Project 4: Job 22—Perform a Fuel Injector Balance Test

After completing this job, you will be able to perform a fuel injector balance test.

Instructions

As you read the job instructions, answer the questions and perform the tasks. Record your answers using complete sentences. Consult the proper service information and ask your instructor for help as needed.

Warning

Before performing this job, review all pertinent safety information in the text and discuss safety procedures with your instructor.

Procedures

☐ 1. Obtain a vehicle to be used in this job. Your instructor may direct you to perform this job on a shop vehicle.

☐ 2. Gather the tools needed to perform this job. Refer to the tools and materials list at the beginning of the project.

☐ 3. Obtain the proper service information.

☐ 4. Ensure that the vehicle ignition switch is in the *Off* position.

☐ 5. Relieve fuel pressure.

☐ 6. Connect a fuel pressure gauge to the fuel rail.

☐ 7. Attach the tester to the first injector, or install the scan tool in the diagnostic connector.

☐ 8. Turn the ignition switch to the *On* position.

☐ 9. Bleed all air from the gauge lines.

☐ 10. After bleeding is finished, wait ten seconds and then record the gauge pressure.

Pressure with the injector closed: ____________

☐ 11. Turn the injector on, using the tester switch or the scan tool.

☐ 12. Note the pressure as soon as the gauge needle reaches its lowest point.

Pressure with the injector open: ____________

☐ 13. Repeat steps 7 through 12 for all injectors and record the readings by injector (cylinder) number.

Injector #	Closed	Open
2	____________	____________
3	____________	____________
4	____________	____________
5	____________	____________
6	____________	____________
7	____________	____________
8	____________	____________
9	____________	____________
10	____________	____________

☐ 14. Retest injectors that appear to be defective.

☐ 15. Once all injectors have been tested, average all of the readings using the following process:

a. Subtract the low reading (injector open) from the high reading (injector closed). This gives the pressure drop for each injector.

b. Add all of the injector pressure drop readings.

c. Divide the above figure by the number of injectors. This gives the average injector pressure drop.

☐ 16. Compare the pressure drop of each injector with the average.

Tech Tip

Any injector with a pressure drop that deviates from the average by 10 psi (70 kPa) or more is suspect.

Do any injectors deviate from the average drop? Yes ___ No ___

What conclusions can you draw from these readings? ______________________________

____

____

____

Job Wrap-Up

☐ 1. Clean the work area and return any equipment to storage.

☐ 2. Did you encounter any problems during this procedure? Yes ___ No ___

If Yes, describe the problems: ______________________________

What did you do to correct the problems? ______________________________

☐ 3. Have your instructor check your work and sign this job sheet.

Performance Evaluation—Instructor Use Only

How would you rate this student's overall performance on this task/job?

4 Competent/Proficient. Able to perform all elements of the task/job successfully and independently.

3 Satisfactory performance of the task/job. Able to perform elements of the task/job with minimal instructor assistance.

2 Completed the task/job with significant instructor assistance.

1 Unsuccessfully attempted the task/job.

0 No exposure. Note reason below (absence, skill not covered, etc.).

Comments:

____

____

____

____

Instructor's Signature: ______________________________

Name ______________________________

Date ____________________ Class ____________________

Project 4: Job 23—Remove and Replace a Fuel Injector

After completing this job, you will be able to remove and replace a fuel injector.

Instructions

As you read the job instructions, answer the questions and perform the tasks. Record your answers using complete sentences. Consult the proper service information and ask your instructor for help as needed.

Warning

Before performing this job, review all pertinent safety information in the text and discuss safety procedures with your instructor.

Procedures

☐ 1. Obtain a vehicle to be used in this job. Your instructor may direct you to perform this job on a shop vehicle.

☐ 2. Gather the tools needed to perform this job. Refer to the tools and materials list at the beginning of the project.

☐ 3. Obtain the proper service information.

☐ 4. Disconnect the battery negative cable.

☐ 5. Relieve fuel system pressure.

☐ 6. Remove the intake plenum (if applicable) or other parts that block access to the fuel rail or injector.

☐ 7. Remove the injector's electrical connector. **Figure 23-1** shows an electrical connector being removed from a throttle body injector.

Figure 23-1. Remove the injector electrical connector carefully. Plastic retainers become brittle over time.

☐ 8. Remove the fuel rail, if applicable. Notice in **Figure 23-2** how the fuel rail is constructed. Attempting to remove any of the injectors without first removing the rail will damage the rail.

Warning

Clean up any spilled gasoline.

Tech Tip

Most injectors are press fit into the fuel rail. Some injectors may have an additional clip holding the rail in place. This clip can be pulled from the injector to release it.

☐ 9. Pull the injector from the manifold or throttle body.

☐ 10. Clean the injector seals or install new ones.

☐ 11. Coat the injector seals with petroleum jelly or transmission gel. This will allow for easier installation and prevent the seals from rolling or ripping.

☐ 12. Install the injectors back in the rail, making sure the electrical connection is pointing the correct direction for the electrical plug.

☐ 13. Install the new injector.

☐ 14. Reinstall the fuel rail, if necessary.

☐ 15. Tighten all fittings.

☐ 16. Reinstall the injector's electrical connector.

☐ 17. Reinstall the intake plenum (if applicable) and any other components that were removed.

☐ 18. Reinstall the battery negative cable.

☐ 19. Start the engine and check for leaks and proper engine operation.

Figure 23-2. The fuel rail (shown here installed in the intake manifold) must be removed before removing any of the injectors. Most fuel rails have an internal coating that will crack and flake off if the rail is bent.

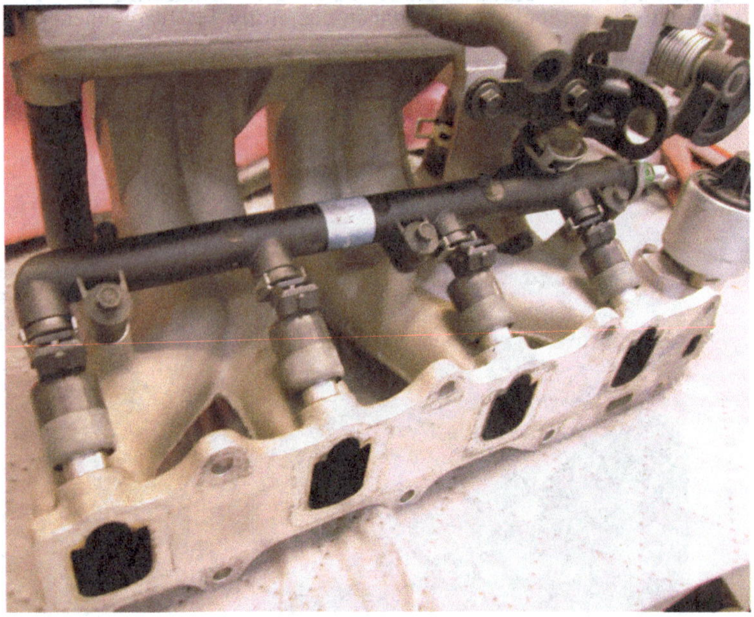

Project 4: Job 23 *(continued)*

Job Wrap-Up

☐ 1. Clean the work area and return any equipment to storage.

☐ 2. Did you encounter any problems during this procedure? Yes ___ No ___

If Yes, describe the problems: ____

____

What did you do to correct the problems? ____

____

☐ 3. Have your instructor check your work and sign this job sheet.

Performance Evaluation—Instructor Use Only

How would you rate this student's overall performance on this task/job?

4 Competent/Proficient. Able to perform all elements of the task/job successfully and independently.

3 Satisfactory performance of the task/job. Able to perform elements of the task/job with minimal instructor assistance.

2 Completed the task/job with significant instructor assistance.

1 Unsuccessfully attempted the task/job.

0 No exposure. Note reason below (absence, skill not covered, etc.).

Comments:

____

____

____

____

Instructor's Signature: ____

Notes

Name ____

Date ____________________________ Class ____________________________

Project 4: Job 24—Check Supercharger and Turbocharger Operation

After completing this job, you will be able to check a supercharger or turbocharger for proper operation.

Instructions

As you read the job instructions, answer the questions and perform the tasks. Record your answers using complete sentences. Consult the proper service information and ask your instructor for help as needed.

Warning

Before performing this job, review all pertinent safety information in the text and discuss safety procedures with your instructor.

Procedures

☐ 1. Obtain a vehicle to be used in this job. Your instructor may direct you to perform this job on a shop vehicle.

☐ 2. Gather the tools needed to perform this job. Refer to the tools and materials list at the beginning of the project.

☐ 3. Obtain the proper supercharger/turbocharger service information. If boost pressures and manifold vacuum specifications are given, list them in the spaces provided. If no specifications are available, go to the next section.

Engine rpm	Boost pressure	Manifold vacuum
________	________ psi/kPa	________ in Hg/mm Hg
________	________ psi/kPa	________ in Hg/mm Hg
________	________ psi/kPa	________ in Hg/mm Hg
________	________ psi/kPa	________ in Hg/mm Hg

☐ 4. Attach pressure and vacuum gauges to the engine.

☐ 5. Measure pressure and vacuum at the correct engine rpm. Record the readings.

Engine rpm	Boost pressure	Manifold vacuum
________	________ psi/kPa	________ in Hg/mm Hg
________	________ psi/kPa	________ in Hg/mm Hg
________	________ psi/kPa	________ in Hg/mm Hg
________	________ psi/kPa	________ in Hg/mm Hg

☐ 6. Compare the actual boost pressures and vacuum readings to the specifications.

Do actual readings match the specifications? Yes ___ No ___

If No, what defects are indicated? ____

____

____

Many external defects can make it appear as if the supercharger or turbocharger is defective:

- A clogged catalytic converter or other exhaust system restriction can cause high supercharger or turbocharger pressures.

- A clogged air filter can cause low supercharger or turbocharger pressures.
- Engine ignition, fuel, and compression problems can appear to be a supercharger or turbocharger problem.

Check the exhaust system, air filter, and general engine condition before condemning the supercharger or turbocharger.

Check a Supercharger

☐ 1. Visually check the supercharger, **Figure 24-1**, for the following:

- Oil leaks. ___
- Disconnected linkage or hoses. ___
- Loose fasteners or damaged gaskets. ___
- Obvious mechanical damage, such as a cracked case. ___

Are any problems found? Yes ___ No ___

If Yes, list: ____

____

☐ 2. If internal damage is suspected, remove the belt and turn the supercharger by hand. The rotors should freely turn with no bearing roughness or scraping sounds.

Are any defects present? Yes ___ No ___

If Yes, explain: ____

____

☐ 3. Check the condition of the belt and pulley.

Are the belt and pulley in good condition? Yes ___ No ___

If No, explain: ____

____

☐ 4. When used, check that the supercharger magnetic clutch engages when boost is needed.

Does the clutch engage when the throttle plate is quickly opened beyond half throttle?
Yes ___ No ___

Figure 24-1. Check the supercharger at all points. It may be necessary to remove engine covers to observe all parts of the supercharger. Many superchargers develop oil leaks at the pulley end seals. This can be spotted by the presence of oil on the pulley and under the vehicle hood directly over the pulley.

Name ____

Project 4: Job 24 *(continued)*

Check a Turbocharger

☐ 1. Remove the air inlet hose from the turbocharger.

☐ 2. Visually check the impeller blades for problems, **Figure 24-2**. Identify any problems found.

- Cracks. ___
- Bent or broken blades. ___
- Blade wear. ___

Are defects found? Yes ___ No ___

If Yes, explain: ____

____

☐ 3. Check the inlet for excessive oil, which indicates a leaking compressor seal.

Is excessive oil found? Yes ___ No ___

☐ 4. Carefully turn the compressor wheel (impeller). There should be no bearing roughness or scraping sounds.

Are any defects noted? Yes ___ No ___

If Yes, explain: ____

____

☐ 5. Push and pull on the impeller while turning. There will be a minimal amount of radial (back-and-forth) and axial (in-and-out) play, but there should be no contact between the impeller/turbine wheels and the turbocharger housing.

Does there appear to be excessive radial or axial play? Yes ___ No ___

If Yes, explain: ____

____

Tech Tip

Some manufacturers specify maximum radial or axial play. This check can be made with a dial indicator.

Figure 24-2. Carefully inspect the impeller blades for damage.

☐ 6. If steps 4 and 5 indicate the possibility of damage to the turbine blades, remove exhaust components as needed and check the turbine blades for cracks, bent or broken blades, and wear. Also, check the turbine and chamber for excessive carbon buildup, which indicates a leaking compressor seal.

Are any defects present? Yes ___ No ___

If Yes, explain: ____

____

☐ 7. If the engine uses two turbochargers, repeat steps 1 through 6 on the other turbocharger.

☐ 8. When inspection is finished, replace the exhaust system components and the air inlet hose(s).

Check Turbocharger Waste Gate and Actuator Diaphragm Operation

Caution

Some waste gates can be adjusted to vary boost pressure. Do *not* raise the boost pressure over the manufacturer's established maximums. Severe engine damage can result.

☐ 1. With the engine off, attempt to move the waste gate linkage. The linkage should freely move. It should move toward the closed position when the linkage is released.

Does the waste gate operate properly? Yes ___ No ___

Tech Tip

The linkage may not fully move to the closed position when the linkage is released. This is acceptable as long as the linkage freely moves.

☐ 2. Check the condition of the vacuum actuator by one of the following methods:

- Connect a vacuum pump to the waste gate actuator diaphragm and apply 5–10 inches of vacuum to the diaphragm.
- Start the engine with the manifold hose connected to the waste gate actuator diaphragm.

Does the waste gate close? Yes ___ No ___

If No, the diaphragm is defective.

☐ 3. If the engine uses two turbochargers, repeat steps 1 and 2 on the other turbocharger.

Check an Intercooler

Tech Tip

Not all supercharged and turbocharged engines have an intercooler.

☐ 1. Remove any shrouds or vehicle parts covering the intercooler.

☐ 2. Check the intercooler for leaks, especially at any seals.

☐ 3. Check for dirt buildup on the outer and inner fins.

☐ 4. Check for mechanical damage, such as cracks and broken tubing.

☐ 5. Replace the shrouds and parts covering the intercooler.

Name ____________________

Project 4: Job 24 *(continued)*

- [ ] 6. After consulting your instructor, decide what repairs are necessary.
  Needed repairs: ____________________

Job Wrap-Up

- [ ] 1. Clean the work area and return any equipment to storage.
- [ ] 2. Did you encounter any problems during this procedure? Yes ___ No ___
  If Yes, describe the problems: ____________________
  What did you do to correct the problems? ____________________
- [ ] 3. Have your instructor check your work and sign this job sheet.

Performance Evaluation—Instructor Use Only

How would you rate this student's overall performance on this task/job?

4 Competent/Proficient. Able to perform all elements of the task/job successfully and independently.

3 Satisfactory performance of the task/job. Able to perform elements of the task/job with minimal instructor assistance.

2 Completed the task/job with significant instructor assistance.

1 Unsuccessfully attempted the task/job.

0 No exposure. Note reason below (absence, skill not covered, etc.).

Comments: ____________________

Instructor's Signature: ____________________

Notes

PROJECT 5

Diagnosing and Servicing an Exhaust System

Introduction

Every technician will eventually have to diagnose and correct an exhaust system problem. Most exhaust system problems consist of leaks and restrictions. All modern exhaust systems have one or more catalytic converters and are connected to other emission control devices, such as exhaust gas recirculation (EGR) systems and oxygen sensors. In Job 25, you will troubleshoot an exhaust system.

Most exhaust system repairs consist of replacing rusted out or damaged parts. Exhaust systems replacement procedures remain relatively simple. However, the technician must therefore be careful when replacing exhaust system parts so that components such as catalytic converters, exhaust gas recirculation (EGR) systems, and oxygen sensors are not damaged. In Job 26, you will replace exhaust system components.

Project 5 Jobs

- Job 25—Inspect and Test an Exhaust System
- Job 26—Replace Exhaust System Components

Tools and Materials

The following list contains the tools and materials that may be needed to complete the jobs in this project. The items used will depend on the make and model of vehicle being serviced.

- Vehicle in need of exhaust system service.
- Air chisel with adapters.
- Pipe cone.
- Pipe expander.
- Vacuum gauge or pressure gauge.
- Hand tools.
- Air-powered tools.
- Safety glasses and other protective equipment.

Safety Notice

Before performing these jobs, review all pertinent safety information in the text and review safety information with your instructor.

Name ____

Date ____________________ Class ____________________

Project 5: Job 25—Inspect and Test an Exhaust System

After completing this job, you will be able to examine and test exhaust systems.

Instructions

As you read the job instructions, answer the questions and perform the tasks. Record your answers using complete sentences. Consult the proper service information and ask your instructor for help as needed.

Warning

Before performing this job, review all pertinent safety information in the text and discuss safety procedures with your instructor.

Procedures

☐ 1. Obtain a vehicle to be used in this job. Your instructor may direct you to perform this job on a shop vehicle.

☐ 2. Gather the tools needed to perform this job. Refer to the tools and materials list at the beginning of the project.

Warning

Exhaust system parts become hot quickly. Do *not* touch any exhaust parts with your bare hands.

Check and Refill Diesel Exhaust Fluid (Diesel Vehicles Only)

☐ 1. If a diesel vehicle is being serviced, check the diesel exhaust fluid (DEF) tank level. Some tanks have a gauge, while others require that the cap be removed and the level observed.

Is the level adequate? Yes ___ No ___

☐ 2. If DEF is needed, remove the filler cap if not already removed, and pour DEF into the tank as needed.

☐ 3. Ensure that the instrument panel LOW DEF warning light goes off when the engine is started.

Tech Tip

DEF is not dangerous. Small amounts of DEF, if spilled, can be washed away.

Visually Inspect the Exhaust System and Check for Exhaust Leaks

☐ 1. Start the engine and set the speed to fast idle.

☐ 2. Raise the vehicle on a lift and determine the exhaust system configuration.

Which type of exhaust system does the vehicle have? Single ___ Dual ___

How many catalytic converters does the vehicle have? __________

Does the vehicle have one or more resonators? Yes ___ No ___

Warning

The vehicle must be raised and supported in a safe manner. Always use an approved lift or jack and jack stands.

☐ 3. Look and listen for leaks. Leaks can be heard, and rusted out components are usually visible. Were any leaks found? Yes ___ No ___

If Yes, describe: ______________________________

____

☐ 4. Turn off the engine. If necessary, lower the vehicle to turn the engine off and then raise the vehicle again.

☐ 5. Visually inspect the exhaust system.

- Are there broken, missing, or corroded hangers? Yes ___ No ___

If Yes, describe: ______________________________

____

- Are there bent or disconnected hangers? Yes ___ No ___

If Yes, describe: ______________________________

____

- Is exhaust hanger or bracket attaching hardware loose or missing? Yes ___ No ___

If Yes, describe: ______________________________

____

- Are there missing, loose, or badly corroded heat shields? (Some corrosion is acceptable, but there must be no missing sections or holes in the shields.) Yes ___ No ___

If Yes, describe: ______________________________

____

- Are any heat shield–attaching fasteners loose or missing? Yes ___ No ___

If Yes, describe: ______________________________

____

☐ 6. Lower the vehicle.

☐ 7. Return the engine to its normal idle speed and turn it off.

Perform a Backpressure Test to Check for Exhaust Restriction

Tech Tip

Your instructor will direct you to use one or both of the following methods to check for exhaust restriction. If your instructor directs you to use only one of the following methods, skip the procedure that does not apply.

Method(s) used: ______________________________

Vacuum Gauge Method

☐ 1. Attach a vacuum gauge to the intake manifold, **Figure 25-1**, and a tachometer to the engine ignition system.

☐ 2. Start the engine.

Name ____

Figure 25-1. Most intake manifolds will have at least one vacuum port that can be disconnected to attach the vacuum gauge. Be sure that the gauge is attached to manifold vacuum and not ported (above the throttle plate) vacuum.

☐ 3. Record manifold vacuum as the engine idles.

Vacuum: ____________

☐ 4. Raise the engine speed to 2500 rpm to check for low vacuum at high engine speed.

Vacuum: ____________

If the vacuum reading at 2500 rpm is about the same or higher than at idle, the exhaust system is not restricted. If the vacuum reading at 2500 rpm is less than the reading at idle, the system is restricted. Many manufacturers consider a 3 psi (20 kPa) drop to be grounds for further investigation and part replacement.

Does the exhaust appear to be restricted? Yes ___ No ___

If Yes, what could be the cause? ____

____

____

☐ 5. Return the engine to its normal idle speed and turn it off.

☐ 6. Remove the vacuum gauge from the intake manifold and the tachometer from the ignition system.

Pressure Gauge Method

☐ 1. Attach a back pressure gauge to the exhaust manifold by removing an oxygen sensor and threading the pressure gauge into the opening. If the engine uses an air injection pump, the check valve can be removed and the pressure gauge installed in the opening.

Tech Tip

If you are testing for a clogged catalytic converter, remove the oxygen sensor nearest to the front of the converter and install the pressure gauge in the opening.

☐ 2. Attach a tachometer to the engine ignition system. Then, start the engine.

☐ 3. Raise engine speed to 2500 rpm and record the exhaust pressure.

Pressure: ____________

☐ 4. Compare the back pressure to specifications. If back pressure specifications are not available, the back pressure should be no more than 4 to 5 psi (27 to 34 kPa) on a single exhaust system or 0.5 to 2 psi (3 to 14 kPa) on one side of a dual exhaust system.

Does the exhaust appear to be restricted? Yes ___ No ___

If Yes, what could be the cause? ______________________________

____

____

Tech Tip

If you are testing for a clogged converter on a system with multiple converters, repeat steps 1 through 4 for the other converter(s).

Scan Tool Method

☐ 1. Connect a scan tool to the DLC and use the OBD II mode to look at intake manifold pressure (MAP).

Tech Tip

Scanner mode can be inaccurate enough to lead the diagnosis in the wrong direction; therefore, OBD mode must be used for this job.

☐ 2. When the engine is fully warmed up and the idle stabilized, read the MAP value on the scan tool. It should be approximately 35 kPa or 10" Hg.

What is the MAP reading? ______________________________

☐ 3. Raise the rpm to approximately 2500 and observe the MAP reading.

What is the MAP reading at 2500 rpm? ______________________________

☐ 4. Was there a vacuum drop (this is an indication of pressure buildup)? Yes ___ No ___

☐ 5. If yes, there is an exhaust restriction. To find the exhaust restriction, remove the most upstream (closest to the cylinder head) oxygen sensor/AFR. If there is more than one head, perform this procedure one head at a time to isolate the exhaust restriction.

☐ 6. Perform step #3 again.

Was there a change in the reading when there was no intake manifold pressure build (upstream oxygen sensor/AFR removed)? Yes ___ No ___

If Yes, then the bank with the exhaust restriction was found.

☐ 7. To determine where the exhaust restriction is after that, reinstall the upstream oxygen sensor/AFR and remove the downstream oxygen sensor/AFR or the exhaust connection after the catalytic converter to reduce pressure at that point. Perform step #3 again. Did pressure decrease compared to the first attempt? Yes ___ No ___

If so, then the restriction is past the catalytic converter. If not, the catalytic converter is the restriction.

Name ____

Tech Tip

This job can be done using MAF sensor readings rather than MAP sensor readings, but the MAF sensor readings should continue to increase with throttle opening. If they do not, perform the same tests listed above to pinpoint the location of the exhaust restriction.

Tech Tip

While MAF or MAP codes may be set in response to an exhaust restriction, these sensors can fail independently of the exhaust. Therefore, check the health of these sensors before using this method.

☐ 8. Consult your instructor for recommendations.

Job Wrap-Up

☐ 1. Clean the work area and return any equipment to storage.

☐ 2. Did you encounter any problems during this procedure? Yes ___ No ___

If Yes, describe the problems: ____

____

What did you do to correct the problems? ____

____

☐ 3. Have your instructor check your work and sign this job sheet.

Performance Evaluation—Instructor Use Only

How would you rate this student's overall performance on this task/job?

4 Competent/Proficient. Able to perform all elements of the task/job successfully and independently.

3 Satisfactory performance of the task/job. Able to perform elements of the task/job with minimal instructor assistance.

2 Completed the task/job with significant instructor assistance.

1 Unsuccessfully attempted the task/job.

0 No exposure. Note reason below (absence, skill not covered, etc.).

Comments:

____

____

____

____

Instructor's Signature: ____

Notes

Name ______________________________

Date ____________________ Class ____________________

Project 5: Job 26—Replace Exhaust System Components

After completing this job, you will be able to replace exhaust system components, such as mufflers, exhaust pipes, and catalytic converters.

Instructions

As you read the job instructions, answer the questions and perform the tasks. Record your answers using complete sentences. Consult the proper service information and ask your instructor for help as needed.

Warning

Before performing this job, review all pertinent safety information in the text and discuss safety procedures with your instructor.

Procedures

☐ 1. Obtain a vehicle to be used in this job. Your instructor may direct you to perform this job on a shop vehicle.

☐ 2. Gather the tools needed to perform this job. Refer to the tools and materials list at the beginning of the project.

Remove and Replace Exhaust Components

Warning

The vehicle must be raised and supported in a safe manner. Always use an approved lift or jack and jack stands.

Exhaust system parts become hot quickly. Do *not* touch any exhaust parts with your bare hands. Also, do *not* spray penetrating oil onto hot exhaust parts or a fire may result.

☐ 1. Raise the vehicle.

☐ 2. Remove any heat shields or skid plates that prevent access to the exhaust system component to be replaced.

☐ 3. Apply penetrating oil to all of the pipe bracket fasteners and joint clamps. If an exhaust manifold is being replaced, apply penetrating oil to the manifold-to-engine fasteners.

☐ 4. Remove any parts that are attached to the exhaust component, such as oxygen sensors or EGR tubes.

☐ 5. Remove the clamps and bracket fasteners.

☐ 6. Loosen the outlet joint and pull the pipe free with a chain wrench. If the parts are welded together, cut off the pipe where necessary ensuring that the remaining pipe can engage the new parts.

Tech Tip

If any parts will be removed using an oxyacetylene cutting torch, refer to the procedures in the next section.

Tech Tip

Carefully remove and handle any pipe or parts that will be reused, such as exhaust doughnuts.

- [ ] 7. If any parts are joined at flanges, remove the fasteners and separate the flanges.
- [ ] 8. Remove the components from the vehicle.
- [ ] 9. After removal, use a pipe-end straightening cone or a pipe expander to straighten the ends of all pipes that will be reused. See **Figure 26-1**.
- [ ] 10. Clean the inside or outside of the nipples that will be reused. If a nipple is distorted, use a pipe expander to restore it to a perfectly round state.
- [ ] 11. Inspect all bell-mouth connectors, **Figure 26-2**, and replace any that are damaged.
- [ ] 12. Determine what parts will be needed to finish the job.

List the parts: ______________________________

____

____

Figure 26-1. Carefully straighten the ends of exhaust components that will be reused.

Figure 26-2. Check all bell-mouth connectors for distortion and replace as necessary.

Name____

Project 5: Job 26 *(continued)*

☐ 13. Compare the old and new exhaust system parts.

Do the parts match? Yes ___ No ___

If No, explain why: ____

____

____

☐ 14. Scrape old gasket material off of any flanged connectors that will be reused, such as the one in **Figure 26-3**.

☐ 15. Apply a coating of exhaust system sealant to any section of a component that will be installed inside of another pipe.

☐ 16. Slide the pipes and nipples together.

Caution

Make certain that the depth is correct.

☐ 17. Slide the clamps into position and lightly tighten them.

☐ 18. Install and tighten any flanged connections, making sure that gaskets are used where necessary.

Caution

Make sure that all parts are installed in the correct position and facing in the proper direction. Make sure that the exhaust system parts are aligned with each other and do not contact any other part of the vehicle.

☐ 19. Tighten all clamps and brackets.

Caution

Do *not* overtighten the clamps.

Figure 26-3. A typical flanged connector is shown here. Scrape off any old gasket material before reusing the connector.

☐ 20. Install any related parts, such as oxygen sensors, EGR tubes, or heat shields.

☐ 21. Start the engine and check for exhaust leaks.

Use an Oxyacetylene Cutting Torch

☐ 1. Put on all needed safety equipment, including leather gauntlet-style gloves, welding helmet or goggles with proper shaded lens(es), leather jacket buttoned to the collar, and leather high-top shoes or boots.

☐ 2. Inspect the cutting equipment for damage and make sure all cylinder, regulator, and torch valves are closed, **Figure 26-4**.

Figure 26-4. Familiarize yourself with the different valves and gauges on this typical oxygen acetylene cutting rig. (Thermadyne Industries, Inc.)

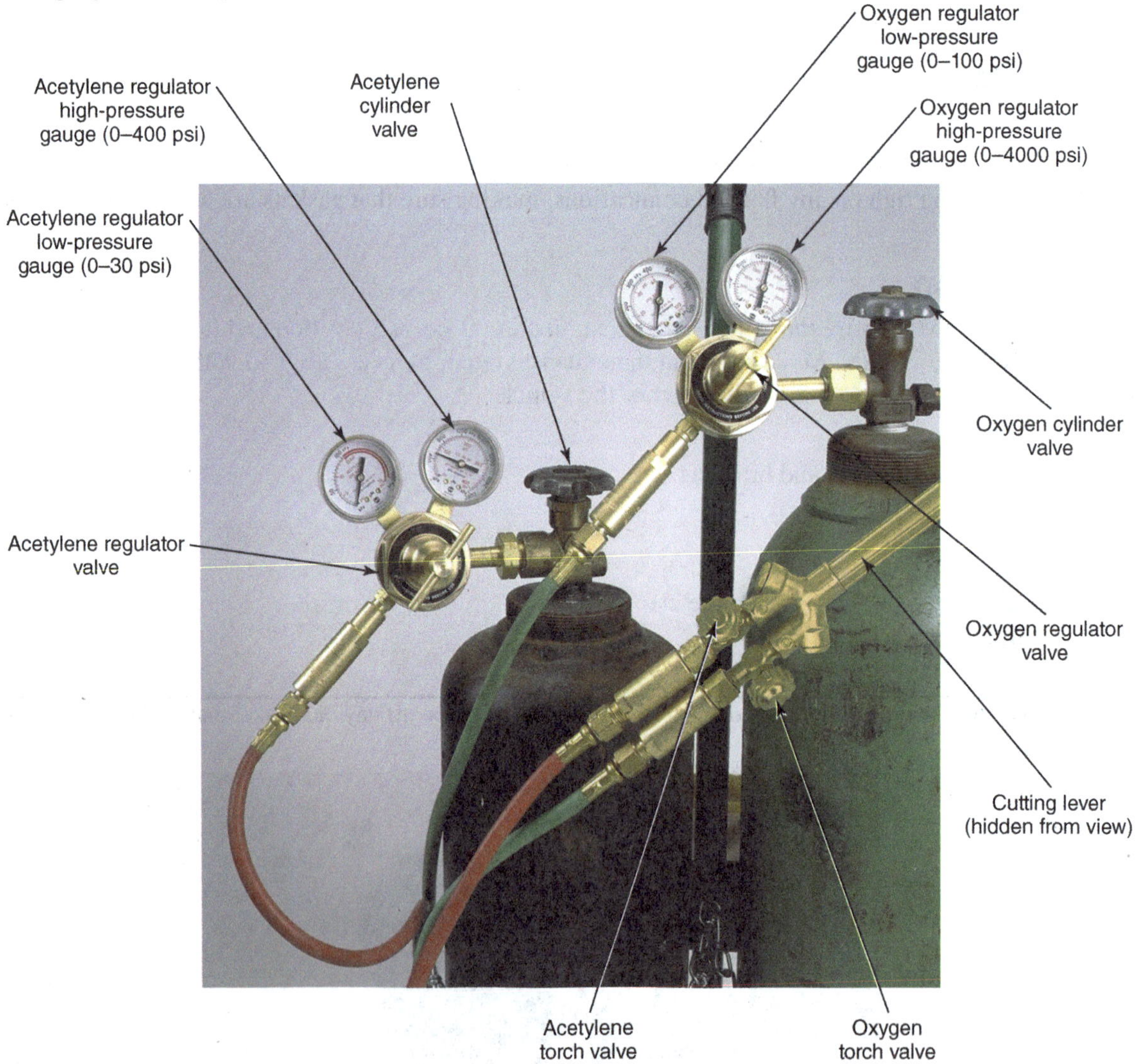

Warning

Regulator valves are loose when they are closed. If the regulator valve is not loose, it is open. Be careful not to back off the regulator valves too much once they are loose or they will fall out of the regulator.

Name ____________________

☐ 3. Install the proper cutting tip on the torch.

☐ 4. Stand so you are not in front of the regulators and slowly open the acetylene cylinder valve approximately 1/2 turn. Then, very slowly open the oxygen cylinder valve until the pressure displayed on the regulator's high pressure gauge no longer increases. When the pressure has stabilized, open the cylinder valve all of the way.

Warning

The oxygen cylinder contains gas under very high pressure. If the oxygen cylinder valve is opened too quickly, a sudden rush of gas could cause the regulator diaphragm or gauges to rupture.

☐ 5. Open the acetylene torch valve 1/2 to one full turn.

☐ 6. Set the proper working pressure on the acetylene regulator by turning the regulator valve clockwise until the proper pressure is shown on the regulator's low pressure gauge. When the proper working pressure is set, close the acetylene torch valve.

Tech Tip

Proper working pressure depends on the size of the cutting torch tip being used. Refer to the manufacturer's specifications for the proper pressure.

☐ 7. Open the oxygen torch valve 1/2 to one full turn. Open the cutting oxygen valve on the torch by pressing the cutting lever.

☐ 8. Set the proper working pressure on the oxygen regulator by turning the regulator valve clockwise until the proper pressure is shown on the regulator's low pressure gauge. When the proper working pressure is set, release the cutting lever and close the oxygen torch valve.

☐ 9. Open the acetylene torch valve approximately 1/16 of a turn. Use a striker to ignite the preheating flames.

Tech Tip

Flames should light at all preheating orifices at the same time. If flames do not light at one or more of the preheating orifices, shut down the torch and clean the tip. After cleaning the tip, open the oxygen torch valve briefly to blow any debris from the tip.

☐ 10. Continue opening the acetylene torch valve until smoke clears from the flame. Make sure that the visible flame stays in contact with the tip. If the flame moves away from the tip, the valve is opened too far.

☐ 11. Open the oxygen torch valve until a neutral flame appears. Two distinct flame areas can be seen in a neutral flame: a smooth, white, bullet-shaped inner cone and blue outer flame.

- If three flame areas are seen—an inner cone, an intermediate cone, and an outer flame—open the oxygen valve until a neutral flame appears.
- If there are only two flame areas visible, but the inner cone is sharply pointed and the flame hisses excessively, close the oxygen valve until a neutral flame appears.

☐ 12. When the torch is adjusted to provide a neutral flame, press the cutting lever and recheck the flame. With the cutting lever pressed, adjust the torch valves so a neutral flame is produced.

☐ 13. Hold the preheating flame to the spot on the exhaust system where the cut is to begin.

Tech Tip

The torch should be held at a 90° angle to the work.

- [ ] 14. Wait until the spot is cherry red.

Warning

Make sure that there are no flammable materials near the cutting area. Do *not* cut near a gas tank or fuel line.

- [ ] 15. Depress the cutting lever. This will begin the cut.
- [ ] 16. While holding down the cutting lever, move the torch as quickly as possible along the area to be cut.
- [ ] 17. When the cut is complete, release the cutting lever.
- [ ] 18. Turn off the acetylene torch valve.
- [ ] 19. Turn off the oxygen torch valve.
- [ ] 20. Tightly close the valves on the oxygen and acetylene cylinders.
- [ ] 21. Open the oxygen and acetylene torch valves. Wait until the high-pressure and low-pressure gauges on both the oxygen and acetylene regulators reach zero, and then close the oxygen and acetylene torch valves.
- [ ] 22. Close the valves on the oxygen and acetylene regulators. Regulator valves are closed by turning them counterclockwise until the handles are loose in the regulator.

Job Wrap-Up

- [ ] 1. Clean the work area and return any equipment to storage.
- [ ] 2. Did you encounter any problems during this procedure? Yes ___ No ___

   If Yes, describe the problems: ______________________________

   ____

   What did you do to correct the problems? ______________________________

   ____
- [ ] 3. Have your instructor check your work and sign this job sheet.

Name ____

Project 5: Job 26 *(continued)*

Performance Evaluation—Instructor Use Only

How would you rate this student's overall performance on this task/job?

4 Competent/Proficient. Able to perform all elements of the task/job successfully and independently.

3 Satisfactory performance of the task/job. Able to perform elements of the task/job with minimal instructor assistance.

2 Completed the task/job with significant instructor assistance.

1 Unsuccessfully attempted the task/job.

0 No exposure. Note reason below (absence, skill not covered, etc.).

Comments:

____

____

____

____

Instructor's Signature: ______________________________________

Notes

PROJECT 6

Diagnosing and Servicing Emission Control Systems

Introduction

This project covers diagnosis and service of the exhaust gas recirculation (EGR), evaporative emissions, and exhaust treatment (air injection and catalytic converter) systems. Any of the three systems can develop problems that affect emissions, engine performance, and driveability. Some of these systems, such as the air injection system and catalytic converter, work together to clean the exhaust gases. A problem in one can cause a malfunction in the other. A defect in the EGR system can cause an apparently unrelated problem, such as detonation or engine missing. As with the other two types of emission control systems covered in this project, an inoperative PCV or evaporative emissions system can cause driveability and emissions problems. Lack of crankcase ventilation can also damage the engine.

You will test and service an EGR valve in Job 27 and an air pump and air injection system in Job 28. In Job 29, you will inspect, test, and replace a catalytic converter. Finally, you will inspect and service positive crankcase ventilation systems in Job 30 and evaporative emission control systems in Job 31.

Project 6 Jobs

- Job 27—Test and Service an EGR Valve
- Job 28—Test and Service an Air Pump and Air Injection System
- Job 29—Test and Service a Catalytic Converter
- Job 30—Test and Service Positive Crankcase Ventilation (PCV) Systems
- Job 31—Test and Service Evaporative Emissions Control Systems

Tools and Materials

The following list contains the tools and materials that may be needed to complete the jobs in this project. The items used will depend on the make and model of vehicle being serviced.

- A vehicle requiring emissions service.
- Applicable service information.
- Scan tool.
- Rubber hammer.
- Pressure gauge.

- Smoke generating machine.
- Infrared thermometer.
- Drill motor and cleaning attachments.
- Hand tools.
- Air-operated tools.
- Safety glasses and other protective equipment.

Safety Notice

Before performing these jobs, review all pertinent safety information in the text and review safety information with your instructor.

Name ____________________

Date ____________________ Class ____________________

Project 6: Job 27—Test and Service an EGR Valve

After completing this job, you will be able to test, clean, and remove and replace an EGR valve.

Instructions

As you read the job instructions, answer the questions and perform the tasks. Record your answers using complete sentences. Consult the proper service information and ask your instructor for help as needed.

Warning

Before performing this job, review all pertinent safety information in the text and discuss safety procedures with your instructor.

Procedures

☐ 1. Obtain a vehicle to be used in this job. Your instructor may direct you to perform this job on a shop vehicle.

☐ 2. Gather the tools needed to perform this job. Refer to the tools and materials list at the beginning of the project.

☐ 3. Obtain the proper service information for the vehicle being serviced.

☐ 4. Locate the EGR valve.

Describe the location of EGR control devices: ____________________

Where is the EGR valve located on the engine? ____________________

____

Is the EGR valve solenoid operated or vacuum operated? See **Figure 27-1**. ____________________

____

Figure 27-1. Vacuum-operated and solenoid-operated EGR valves can be distinguished by whether they have vacuum or electrical connections. A—Solenoid-operated EGR valve. B—Vacuum-operated EGR valve.

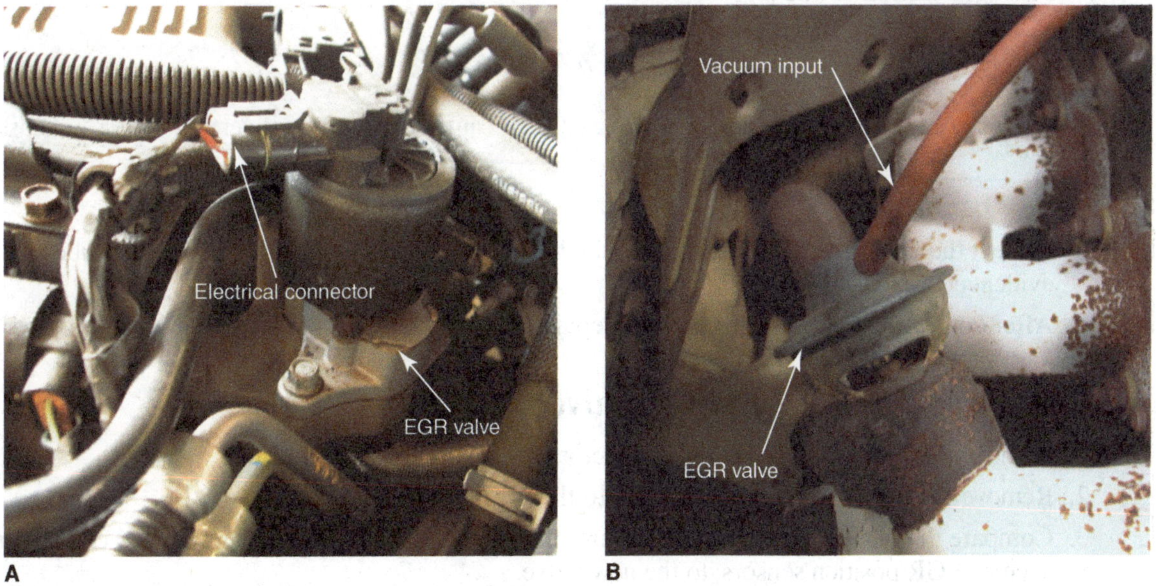

☐ 5. If the EGR valve is vacuum-operated, make sure the vacuum lines are properly routed. Refer to vacuum routing diagrams in the service information or on the emission certification label as needed.

Are the vacuum hoses properly routed? Yes ___ No ___

If No, reroute the vacuum lines properly.

Are the vacuum hoses in good condition? Yes ___ No ___

If Yes, proceed to step 6.

If No, replace the hoses as needed.

☐ 6. Check EGR valve operation using the procedures for the type of EGR valve being tested.

Solenoid-Operated EGR Valve

Use one of the following procedures:

- Attach a scan tool and check EGR solenoid and position sensor operation. If possible, open and close the solenoid using the scan tool.
- Use a test light or multimeter to check EGR power supply and solenoid operation.

Vacuum-Operated EGR Valve

Use one of the following procedures:

- Observe that the valve moves when the engine is accelerated.
- Apply vacuum to the diaphragm and note valve movement. Check any vacuum control solenoids or thermostatic EGR controls, especially if the EGR valve itself appears to be working properly.

☐ 7. Determine the EGR valve and control system condition from the tests made in steps 5 and 6.

Is the EGR valve operating properly? Yes ___ No ___

If No, what could be causing the problem? ______________________________

____

____

☐ 8. Remove the EGR valve from the engine. See the *Remove and Replace an EGR Valve* section of this job.

☐ 9. Visually inspect the EGR passages.

Are any passages blocked? Yes ___ No ___

If Yes, the passages must be cleaned using the procedures in the *Clean an EGR Valve and Passages* section of this job.

Tech Tip

One or more clogged EGR passages can cause misfiring by diverting excess exhaust gases into one or two cylinders.

☐ 10. Inspect the EGR transfer tube(s), if used. Check for obvious cracks or breaks in the tube or evidence of exhaust leakage.

☐ 11. After consulting your instructor, make repairs as needed and recheck system operation.

Remove and Replace an EGR Valve

☐ 1. Remove the EGR valve electrical connector or vacuum line, as applicable.

☐ 2. Remove the fasteners holding the valve to the engine.

☐ 3. Compare the old and new valves to ensure that they match and transfer any related components, such as EGR position sensors, to the new valve.

Name______________________________________

Project 6: Job 27 *(continued)*

☐ 4. Clean the EGR valve mounting surfaces on the engine.

☐ 5. Install the new EGR valve and tighten the fasteners.

☐ 6. Reinstall the electrical connector or vacuum line.

☐ 7. Start the engine and test the EGR valve operation.

Clean an EGR Valve and Passages

☐ 1. Remove the EGR valve as described in the previous section.

☐ 2. If necessary, clean the valve passages with a wire brush. You can use solvent, but it usually has no effect on hardened carbon deposits. Some EGR valves can be partially disassembled for thorough cleaning, **Figure 27-2**. Use one of the following techniques, depending on the condition of the passages.

Caution

Do *not* allow solvent to contact any rubber or electrical parts on the EGR valve.

- **If the passage is not entirely clogged,** attach a circular wire brush, a length of old speedometer cable, or stranded wire to an electric drill. Run the brush or wire into the passage while operating the drill at low speed. It is not necessary to remove every fragment of soot. Some soot formation is normal; however, all major deposits should be removed. All loose deposits should be removed from the EGR passages and surrounding area. Do not allow the debris to enter the intake manifold.
- **If the passage is completely clogged,** create an opening by hand turning a drill bit into the passage. Once an opening has been created, finish cleaning the passage as explained in the previous paragraph.

☐ 3. Reinstall the EGR valve.

☐ 4. Start the engine and check EGR and engine operation.

Figure 27-2. On some EGR valves, the pintle seat can be removed to allow a more thorough cleaning.

Job Wrap-Up

☐ 1. Clean the work area and return any equipment to storage.

☐ 2. Did you encounter any problems during this procedure? Yes ___ No ___

If Yes, describe the problems: ______________________________

____

What did you do to correct the problems? ______________________________

____

☐ 3. Have your instructor check your work and sign this job sheet.

Performance Evaluation—Instructor Use Only

How would you rate this student's overall performance on this task/job?

4 Competent/Proficient. Able to perform all elements of the task/job successfully and independently.

3 Satisfactory performance of the task/job. Able to perform elements of the task/job with minimal instructor assistance.

2 Completed the task/job with significant instructor assistance.

1 Unsuccessfully attempted the task/job.

0 No exposure. Note reason below (absence, skill not covered, etc.).

Comments:

____

____

____

____

Instructor's Signature: ______________________________

Name ______________________________

Date ____________________ Class ____________________

Project 6: Job 28—Test and Service an Air Pump and Air Injection System

After completing this job, you will be able to test an air injection system and replace faulty components.

Instructions

As you read the job instructions, answer the questions and perform the tasks. Record your answers using complete sentences. Consult the proper service information and ask your instructor for help as needed.

Warning

Before performing this job, review all pertinent safety information in the text and discuss safety procedures with your instructor.

Procedures

- [ ] 1. Obtain a vehicle to be used in this job. Your instructor may direct you to perform this job on a shop vehicle.
- [ ] 2. Gather the tools needed to perform this job. Refer to the tools and materials list at the beginning of the project.
- [ ] 3. Obtain the proper service information for the vehicle being serviced.

Test Air Pump and Air Injection System Valve Operation

Tech Tip

When present, the air injection systems on most newer vehicles are controlled by the on-board computer and can be checked with a scan tool. Many newer vehicles no longer use an air injection system. Not all systems use the parts described below.

- [ ] 1. Open the vehicle hood and visually check for damaged or disconnected hoses and a missing or loose drive belt.
- [ ] 2. Start the engine. The engine should be cold if possible.

Tech Tip

Perform steps 3 and 4 quickly before the engine reaches normal operating temperature.

- [ ] 3. Observe the pump output with the engine running.
- [ ] 4. Observe the operation of the switching valve as the engine warms up.
- [ ] 5. Place your hand near the diverter valve outlet as an assistant opens and closes the throttle valve, **Figure 28-1**. You should feel air blowing out of the outlet as the engine is quickly accelerated and decelerated. This tells you that the diverter valve is operating properly.
- [ ] 6. Check the condition of the check valve(s) by removing the inlet hose and starting the engine. There should be little or no exhaust flow from the check valve.

Figure 28-1. Hold your hand near the diverter valve outlet and feel for exhausting air as the throttle is opened and then closed.

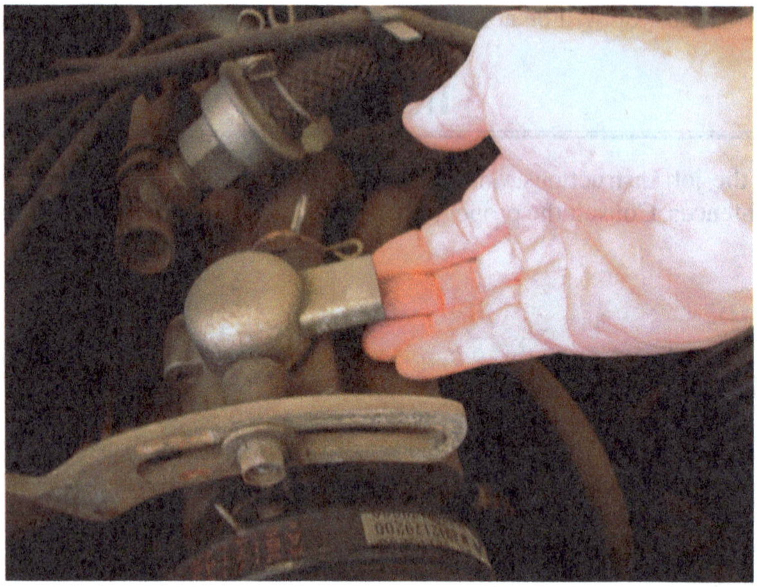

Tech Tip

The check valve can also be tested by removing it from the engine and attempting to blow through it. If you can blow through the inlet side but not the outlet side, the valve is OK. If you can blow through both sides, the valve is not sealing against exhaust gases and should be replaced.

☐ 7. Use a scan tool to obtain trouble codes and other air injection system information.

a. Ensure that the ignition switch is in the Off position.

b. Attach the scan tool connector cable and power lead, if applicable.

c. Turn the ignition switch to the On position.

d. Ensure that the scan tool is working properly. If the scan tool does not appear to be working, locate and correct any problems before proceeding.

e. If necessary, enter vehicle information as needed to program the scan tool. Most modern scan tools can read the VIN from the vehicle computer.

f. Use the scan tool to check for trouble codes.

Are any codes found? Yes ___ No ___

If Yes, are the codes related to the air injection system? Yes ___ No ___

If the answer to both questions is Yes, list the codes and their descriptions.

Code	Defect
____________	______________________________
____________	______________________________
____________	______________________________
____________	______________________________
____________	______________________________

Name ____________________

Project 6: Job 28 *(continued)*

☐ 8. From the information gathered in steps 3 through 7, determine whether the air injection system is working properly.

Is the system working properly? Yes ___ No ___

If No, what could be the problem? ____________________

☐ 9. After consulting your instructor, make repairs as needed and recheck system operation.

Replace an Air Injection Pump

☐ 1. Remove the pump drive belt.

☐ 2. Remove any hoses attached to the pump.

☐ 3. Remove the fasteners holding the pump to the engine and remove the pump.

☐ 4. Compare the old and new pumps.

☐ 5. Transfer parts from the old pump to the new pump as needed.

☐ 6. Place the new pump in position.

☐ 7. Install the pump fasteners.

☐ 8. Install the hoses.

☐ 9. Reinstall and tighten the pump drive belt.

☐ 10. Start the engine and check pump operation.

Replace a Vacuum Switching or Diverter Valve

☐ 1. Remove air and vacuum hoses attached to the valve.

☐ 2. If necessary, remove the fasteners holding the valve to the pump.

☐ 3. Compare the old and new valves.

☐ 4. Place the new valve in position.

☐ 5. Install the valve fasteners.

☐ 6. Install the hoses.

☐ 7. Start the engine and check the valve and system operation.

Replace an Electrical Switching or Diverter Valve

☐ 1. Disconnect the battery negative cable.

☐ 2. Remove any parts that block access to the valve and electrical connector(s).

☐ 3. Remove the valve electrical connector(s).

☐ 4. Remove the valve fasteners.

☐ 5. Remove the valve from the vehicle.

☐ 6. Compare the old and new valves.

☐ 7. Place the new valve in position.

☐ 8. Reinstall the valve and electrical connector(s).

☐ 9. Replace any other parts that were removed.

☐ 10. Reconnect the battery negative cable.

☐ 11. Check valve and system operation.

Replace a Check Valve

☐ 1. Remove the hose from the inlet side of the check valve.
☐ 2. Loosen the fitting holding the check valve to the injector tube assembly.

Tech Tip

Use two wrenches to avoid damaging the injector tube assembly. See **Figure 28-2**.

☐ 3. Remove the check valve from the injector tube assembly.
☐ 4. Compare the old and new check valves to ensure that the fittings are correct, **Figure 28-3**.
☐ 5. Install the replacement check valve on the injector tube assembly, **Figure 28-4**.
☐ 6. Reinstall the hose on the check valve and tighten the hose clamp, if necessary.

Figure 28-2. Loosen the check valve using two wrenches to avoid damaging the tubing.

Figure 28-3. Compare the old and replacement check valves. The replacement may not look exactly the same as the original, but it should fit and function like the original.

Name ____

Figure 28-4. Carefully thread the new check valve onto the discharge tubing.

Replace an Injector Tube Assembly

☐ 1. Allow the engine to cool.

☐ 2. Remove the hose from the check valve at the injector tube assembly.

Tech Tip

If the check valve must be removed from the tube assembly, loosen it now while the assembly is firmly attached to the engine.

☐ 3. Remove the fittings holding the injector tube assembly to the exhaust manifold.

☐ 4. Carefully pull the injector tube assembly out of the exhaust manifold.

☐ 5. Remove the check valve from the injector tube assembly.

☐ 6. Install the check valve on the replacement injector tube assembly.

☐ 7. Place the injector tube assembly into position on the exhaust manifold.

☐ 8. Tighten the injector tube fittings to the exhaust manifold.

☐ 9. Reinstall the hose on the check valve.

Job Wrap-Up

☐ 1. Clean the work area and return any equipment to storage.

☐ 2. Did you encounter any problems during this procedure? Yes ___ No ___

If Yes, describe the problems: ____

____

What did you do to correct the problems? ____

____

☐ 3. Have your instructor check your work and sign this job sheet.

Performance Evaluation—Instructor Use Only

How would you rate this student's overall performance on this task/job?

4 Competent/Proficient. Able to perform all elements of the task/job successfully and independently.

3 Satisfactory performance of the task/job. Able to perform elements of the task/job with minimal instructor assistance.

2 Completed the task/job with significant instructor assistance.

1 Unsuccessfully attempted the task/job.

0 No exposure. Note reason below (absence, skill not covered, etc.).

Comments:

____

____

____

____

Instructor's Signature: ______________________________

Name ______________________________

Date ______________________ Class ______________________

Project 6: Job 29—Test and Service a Catalytic Converter

After completing this job, you will be able to test a catalytic converter for physical damage and correct operation. You will also be able to replace a faulty catalytic converter.

Instructions

As you read the job instructions, answer the questions and perform the tasks. Record your answers using complete sentences. Consult the proper service information and ask your instructor for help as needed.

Warning

Before performing this job, review all pertinent safety information in the text and discuss safety procedures with your instructor.

Related Trouble Codes

Trouble codes are not specifically addressed in this job. For background information, some common OBD II evaporative emissions trouble codes are listed below.

P0420 Catalyst System Efficiency Below Threshold (Bank 1)
P0421 Warm Up Catalyst Efficiency Below Threshold (Bank 1)
P0422 Main Catalyst Efficiency Below Threshold (Bank 1)
P0423 Heated Catalyst Efficiency Below Threshold (Bank 1)
P0424 Heated Catalyst Temperature Below Threshold (Bank 1)
P0430 Catalyst System Efficiency Below Threshold (Bank 2)
P0431 Warm Up Catalyst Efficiency Below Threshold (Bank 2)
P0432 Main Catalyst Efficiency Below Threshold (Bank 2)
P0433 Heated Catalyst Efficiency Below Threshold (Bank 2)
P0434 Heated Catalyst Temperature Below Threshold (Bank 2)

Procedures

☐ 1. Obtain a vehicle to be used in this job. Your instructor may direct you to perform this job on a shop vehicle.

☐ 2. Gather the tools needed to perform this job. Refer to the tools and materials list at the beginning of the project.

☐ 3. Obtain the proper service information for the vehicle being serviced.

Test Catalytic Converter Operation

Tech Tip

Catalytic converter operation can be tested with a four- or five-gas analyzer. Excessive CO may indicate a defective converter. Note also that a defect in the air injection system can cause improper catalytic converter operation.

In addition to the tests described in this job, a back pressure test can also be performed to check for a clogged catalytic converter. Refer to Job 25 for procedures for performing a backpressure test.

Mechanical Damage Test

☐ 1. Ensure that the catalytic converter is cool.

☐ 2. Strike the converter housing with a rubber hammer.

Does the converter rattle when it is pounded? Yes ___ No ___

If Yes, the converter has internal damage, such as loose catalyst, screens, or baffles. Refer to the *Replace a Catalytic Converter* section in this job.

Tech Tip

The following procedure can be performed only on OBD II–equipped vehicles. The scan tool test may uncover other engine and emission control problems.

Scan Tool Test

☐ 1. Obtain a scan tool that is compatible with the vehicle being tested.

☐ 2. Attach the scan tool to the vehicle diagnostic connector.

☐ 3. Retrieve any trouble codes that are set.

☐ 4. Operate the engine and observe the waveform readings from the oxygen sensors upstream and downstream of the converter.

☐ 5. Determine whether the oxygen sensor inputs indicate that the converter is operating properly.

Is the converter working properly? Yes ___ No ___

Explain: ____

What could be the cause? ____

____

____

Temperature Test

☐ 1. Obtain an infrared thermometer.

Type of thermometer: ____

☐ 2. Run the vehicle at a high engine speed (about 2500 rpm) for two minutes. This needs to be done to ensure that the catalytic converter begins to operate.

Tech Tip

If the engine is started cold, a longer run time may be needed. Leave the engine running during steps 3 and 4.

Name ____

Project 6: Job 29 *(continued)*

☐ 3. Quickly aim the thermometer at the front of the converter and note the temperature. See **Figure 29-1**.

Temperature: __________ °F or °C (circle one)

☐ 4. Quickly aim the thermometer at the rear of the converter and note the temperature. See **Figure 29-2**.

Temperature: __________ °F or °C (circle one)

Figure 29-1. Aim the thermometer at the front of the converter body. Be sure to aim at the body of the converter, not any attached heat shields.

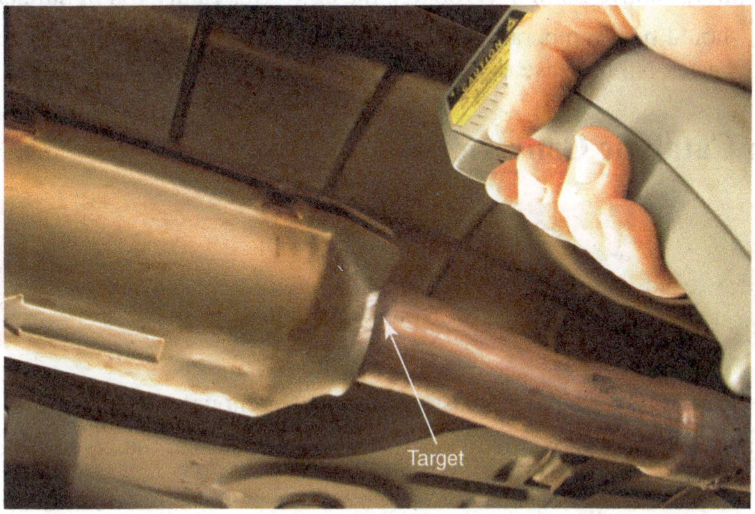

Figure 29-2. Aim the thermometer at the rear of the catalytic converter. Be sure to aim at the body of the converter, not any attached heat shields.

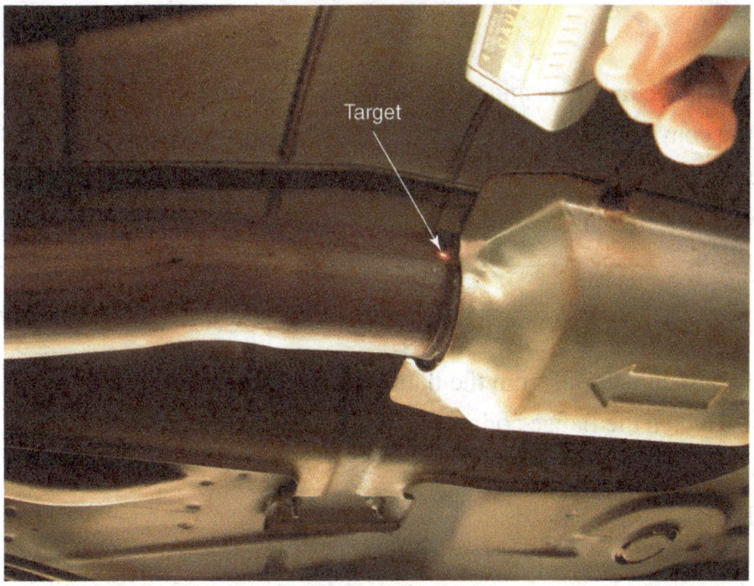

☐ 5. Turn off the engine and compare the readings taken in steps 3 and 4.

Is there a substantial difference between the two temperatures? Yes ___ No ___

Is the rear temperature greater? Yes ___ No ___

If the answer to either question is No, the converter is not working properly.

☐ 6. Consult the manufacturer's service information for exact temperature specifications. If specifications are not available, use the following general guidelines:

- The converter must reach 500–600°F (250–300°C) to begin working. If converter temperatures are below this when the engine is fully warmed up, the catalyst is coated or worn out.
- Normal converter operating temperatures are 750–1200°F (400–650°C). A temperature higher than this indicates that the converter is overheating, usually because of a rich fuel mixture. At temperatures above 2000°F (1100°C), the converter catalyst is in danger of melting.
- There should be a temperature increase of 40–100°F (5–40°C) between the front and rear of the converter. No increase or a small increase indicates that the catalyst is coated or worn out.

Replace a Catalytic Converter

Warning

Raise and support the vehicle in a safe manner. Always use an approved lift or jack and jack stands.

☐ 1. Raise the vehicle. Ensure the exhaust system is cool enough to allow work.

☐ 2. Remove any heat shields or skid plates that prevent access to the converter.

☐ 3. Remove the air inlet tube from the converter.

☐ 4. Remove any clamps and bracket fasteners.

Tech Tip

Carefully handle any pipes or other parts that will be reused.

☐ 5. Remove the flange fasteners and separate the flanges.

☐ 6. Remove the converter from the vehicle.

☐ 7. Compare the old and new converters.

Do the converters match? Yes ___ No ___

If No, explain: ____

____

____

☐ 8. Scrape old gasket material from the flanged connectors that will be reused.

☐ 9. Install and tighten the flange connections; use gaskets where necessary.

Caution

Make sure that all parts are installed in the correct position and facing in the proper direction. Also, make sure that all exhaust system parts are aligned with each other and do not contact any other part of the vehicle.

Name ____

Project 6: Job 29 *(continued)*

- [ ] 10. Install and tighten all clamps and brackets.
- [ ] 11. Install the air inlet tube.
- [ ] 12. Start the engine and check for exhaust leaks.

Job Wrap-Up

- [ ] 1. Clean the work area and return any equipment to storage.
- [ ] 2. Did you encounter any problems during this procedure? Yes ___ No ___

  If Yes, describe the problems: ____

  ____

  What did you do to correct the problems? ____

  ____

- [ ] 3. Have your instructor check your work and sign this job sheet.

Performance Evaluation—Instructor Use Only

How would you rate this student's overall performance on this task/job?

4 Competent/Proficient. Able to perform all elements of the task/job successfully and independently.

3 Satisfactory performance of the task/job. Able to perform elements of the task/job with minimal instructor assistance.

2 Completed the task/job with significant instructor assistance.

1 Unsuccessfully attempted the task/job.

0 No exposure. Note reason below (absence, skill not covered, etc.).

Comments:

____

____

____

____

Instructor's Signature: ____

Notes

Name ____________________

Date ____________________ Class ____________________

Project 6: Job 30—Test and Service Positive Crankcase Ventilation (PCV) Systems

After completing this job, you will be able to diagnose and service a PCV system.

Instructions

As you read the job instructions, answer the questions and perform the tasks. Record your answers using complete sentences. Consult the proper service information and ask your instructor for help as needed.

Warning

Before performing this job, review all pertinent safety information in the text and discuss safety procedures with your instructor.

Procedures

☐ 1. Obtain a vehicle to be used in this job. Your instructor may direct you to perform this job on a shop vehicle.

☐ 2. Gather the tools needed to perform this job. Refer to the tools and materials list at the beginning of the project.

☐ 3. Obtain the proper service information for the vehicle being serviced.

Test and Service a PCV System

☐ 1. Symptoms of a plugged PCV usually start with a customer complaint of an oil leak.

Does this engine have an oil leak? Yes ___ No ___

If so, where is the oil leak? ____________________

____

____

☐ 2. Remove the intake ductwork. Is there any oil residue in the intake? Yes ___ No ___

Oil in the intake is another indication of a plugged PCV, as the crankcase pressure will push into the intake tube if the PCV does not have enough flow to handle the pressure.

☐ 3. Check manifold vacuum either through the MAP sensor or by using a pressure gauge. Is the manifold vacuum less than normal at idle when the engine is fully warmed up? Yes ___ No ___

☐ 4. If the manifold vacuum is less than normal and there is oil in the intake, perform a compression or leak-down test to determine if there is excessive blow-by in the engine.

Is there excessive blow-by? Yes ___ No ___

If there is excessive blow-by, replacing the PCV will not fix the problem of excessive oil vapor in the intake. Consult your instructor for engine mechanical recommendations.

☐ 5. If the engine vacuum is normal, locate the PCV valve on the engine. It may be located on a valve cover or between the cylinder heads. The PCV hose will be attached to the intake manifold after the throttle plate for manifold vacuum. The fresh air supply for the PCV system will have a hose attached to the intake ductwork before the throttle plate.

Are there any cracks or broken connections for any of these hoses? Yes ___ No ___

If yes, where are the cracks or broken connections? ______________________________

What can be done to fix these problems? ______________________________

☐ 6. Remove the oil fill cap and place a PCV tester over the opening. Run the engine to warm it up. After the engine is warm, read the PCV tester.

Does the engine pass the PCV test? Yes ___ No ___

☐ 7. Remove the PCV valve from the grommet while the engine idles. Does the engine rpm increase slightly with the valve removed from the crankcase but still attached to the tubing?

Yes ___ No ___

It should increase slightly, as now the PCV is pulling in air instead of crankcase vapors. If there is no change, there is a good possibility that the valve is plugged.

☐ 8. Shut down the engine. Remove the PCV valve from the hose and shake the valve.

Did the valve rattle? Yes ___ No ___

If it does not rattle, it is likely plugged with carbon.

☐ 9. These tests may not apply to all manufacturers. European vehicles often have different systems used to remove crankcase vapors. Many do not have a valve because they have calibrated passages that allow vapor without allowing oil into the intake. Many have rubber in their PCV systems that degrades over time and, therefore, they still have problems.

Does this engine have a PCV system without a valve? Yes ___ No ___

☐ 10. What is the manufacturer's recommended procedure for repairing a failed PCV system?

☐ 11. One recommendation with oil leaks is to replace the PCV valve as a preventive measure.

Will the fix for this vehicle be to replace a gasket for an oil leak and to replace the PCV?
Yes ___ No ___

☐ 12. Return all the hoses and components to their original position.

Job Wrap-Up

☐ 1. Clean the work area and return any equipment to storage.

☐ 2. Did you encounter any problems during this procedure? Yes ___ No ___

If Yes, what did you do to correct the problem? ______________________________

____

☐ 3. Have your instructor check your work and sign this job sheet.

Name ____

Project 6: Job 30 *(continued)*

Performance Evaluation—Instructor Use Only

How would you rate this student's overall performance on this task/job?

4 Competent/Proficient. Able to perform all elements of the task/job successfully and independently.

3 Satisfactory performance of the task/job. Able to perform elements of the task/job with minimal instructor assistance.

2 Completed the task/job with significant instructor assistance.

1 Unsuccessfully attempted the task/job.

0 No exposure. Note reason below (absence, skill not covered, etc.).

Comments:

____

____

____

____

Instructor's Signature: ______________________________

Notes

Name ______________________________

Date ____________________ Class ____________________

Project 6: Job 31—Test and Service Evaporative Emissions Control Systems

Instructions

As you read the job instructions, answer the questions and perform the tasks. Record your answers using complete sentences. Consult the proper service information and ask your instructor for help as needed.

Warning

Before performing this job, review all pertinent safety information in the text and discuss safety procedures with your instructor.

Related Trouble Codes

Trouble codes are not specifically addressed in this job. For background information, some common OBD II evaporative emissions trouble codes are listed in the following chart.

P0440 Evaporative emissions system (general).
P0442 Small leak detected.
P0446 System performance.
P0455 Large leak detected.
P0496 Flow during non-purge.
P1441 Flow during non-purge.

Procedures

Tech Tip

The year and type of test vehicle and the available test equipment will determine which of the following tests can be performed. Consult your instructor to determine which tests will be performed.

☐ 1. Customer complaints that may indicate a problem in the EVAP system include the following:
- Check engine light is on, but no other symptoms.
- Fuel vapors are smelled.
- Trouble getting fuel into the tank (nozzle shuts off).
- Extended crank time or hard start after refueling.

Which complaint fits the vehicle being used for this job? ______________________________

____

☐ 2. If the check engine light is illuminated, connect the scan tool to the DLC. Read codes in OBD II first and then in scanner mode.

Are there any codes that are different in OBD II than in scanner mode? Yes ___ No ___

If Yes, list them here. ____

____

____

____

Which code(s) turned the check engine light on? ____

____

____

____

Describe what the code(s) mean: ____

☐ 3. Most EVAP codes are associated with a leakage or blockage. Does the customer smell fuel? Yes ___ No ___

If so, when—all the time or just after refueling? ____

____

Smelling fuel all the time means there is a leak. Smelling fuel near the engine right after refueling and hard start means that the purge valve is leaking.

Warning

Escaping fuel vapors are extremely flammable. Keep the test area well-ventilated and make sure that open flames, sparking devices, or any other ignition sources are kept well away from the area.

Using the Scan Tool to Give Direction to the Diagnosis on Vacuum-Based Systems

☐ 1. First, perform a visual inspection of the EVAP system. Be sure to include the wiring, hoses, and tightness of the gas cap.

What faults were found with the visual inspection? ____

____

☐ 2. With the scan tool still connected, start the engine and allow it to run. Look at PIDS (data) for purge valve commanded position. If the scan tool has the capability, compare the actual position to the commanded position. This is usually displayed as a percentage.

Do the commanded position and actual position agree? Yes ___ No ___

If not, turn off the engine, remove the purge valve, and blow through it. Since the purge valve is normally closed, no air should pass through it.

Will air pass through the purge valve while out of the vehicle? Yes ___ No ___

If so, replace it.

☐ 3. To check if the purge valve operates, reinstall it in the system. Start the engine and allow it to run. Use a scan tool with output controls to operate the purge valve. If the purge valve works, it will introduce fuel vapors into the intake, making a rich mixture. The vehicle will correct for this

Name ____

when the upstream oxygen sensor/AFR detects the rich mixture. Other PIDS that can be use to verify purge operation include the following:

- MAP sensor will show an increase in pressure/loss of vacuum momentarily.
- MAF sensor will show an increase in airflow to add oxygen to the correct the rich condition.
- IAC or TPS will show a momentary increase to allow the extra oxygen.
- Pulse width of the injectors will show a decrease to account for the rich condition.
- RPM will decrease the moment the valve is opened more but will recover once the rest of the conditions correct themselves to account for the rich condition.
- Tank pressure sensor will show an increase in vacuum/loss of pressure.
- Fuel trim will show negative until the correction to air-fuel ratio is made. This is the best method to check for many conditions.

Which method was used to verify purge operation? ______________________________

____

____

☐ 4. Run the engine and make sure it is fully warmed up.

☐ 5. With the engine fully warmed up, the ECM will command the purge to open slightly, normally around 20% at idle. Confirm in PIDs/data that the purge is operating. While in PIDs/data, look at the tank pressure sensor. There should be a slight vacuum in the tank. If there is no point of comparison, turn the engine off and keep the key on to look at tank pressure again. KOEO should show no vacuum or pressure because there will be atmospheric pressure in the tank.

Is there a slight vacuum in the tank when the engine is running? Yes ___ No ___

If not, the purge is not operating. Fix the purge first before the next step.

☐ 6. With the engine running and using Functional Tests or Output Controls on the scan tool, knowing that the purge is working, close the vent valve.

Did the vacuum increase in the tank when the vent valve was closed? Yes ___ No ___

If the vacuum increased, both the purge and vent are working.

If the vacuum did not increase, either the vent valve does not work or there is a leak large enough to prevent from increasing.

☐ 7. If there is a code for EVAP, it is usually related to a leak. There is also the service bay EVAP test in Functional Tests or Output Controls. Use of the service bay test provides a "scripted test," where a set of directions are provided that you follow in order. In this test the vent will be commanded closed while the purge is open. Next, the purge will be closed while the vent is still held closed. Observe the tank pressure sensor.

Did the vehicle pass the EVAP service bay test? Yes ___ No ___

If not, the next step is to locate the leak using the smoke-generating machine.

Tech Tip

Some manufacturers use more solenoids than just a purge and vent and may require further diagnosis to determine if a solenoid is at fault. Remember that all of them are normally open or normally closed. Therefore, they can be tested by removing them from the vehicle. When 12 volts and ground are applied to them, the valve will either open or close. Blowing air through them in either of these two states (power and ground applied, or not) will reveal if they work or leak.

Using the Scan Tool to Give Direction to the Diagnosis on Pressure-Based Systems

☐ 1. First, perform a visual inspection. Be sure to include the wiring, hoses, and tightness of the gas cap.

What faults were found during the visual inspection of the EVAP system? ______________________

____

☐ 2. With the scan tool still connected, start the engine. Look at PIDS (data) for purge commanded position. If the scan tool has it, compare the actual position to the commanded position. This is usually expressed as a percentage.

Is the actual position the same as the commanded position? Yes ___ No ___

If not, turn off the engine and remove purge. Since the purge is normally closed, no air should pass through it. Blow through the purge to see if air will pass through it.

Does air pass through the purge while it is out of the vehicle? Yes ___ No ___

If so, replace it.

☐ 3. To check if the purge operates, reinstall it in the system. Run the engine. Use a scan tool with output controls to operate the purge valve. If the purge valve works, the valve will introduce fuel vapors into the intake, making a rich mixture. The vehicle will correct for this when the upstream oxygen sensor/AFR detects this condition. Other PIDS that can be used to verify purge operation include:

- MAP sensor will show an increase in pressure/loss of vacuum momentarily.
- MAF sensor will show an increase in airflow to add oxygen to the correct the rich condition.
- IAC or TPS will show a momentary increase to allow the extra oxygen.
- Pulse width of the injectors will show a decrease to account for the rich condition.
- RPM will decrease the moment the valve is opened more but will recover once all the rest of the conditions correct themselves to account for the rich condition.
- Tank pressure sensor will show an increase in vacuum/loss of pressure.
- Fuel Trim will show negative until the correction to air-fuel ratio is corrected. Best method for many conditions.

Which method was used to verify purge operation? ______________________________

____

____

☐ 4. Run the engine and make sure it is fully warmed up.

☐ 5. With the engine fully warmed up, the ECM will command the purge to open slightly, normally around 20% at idle. Confirm in PIDs/data that the purge is operating. While in PIDs/data, look at the tank pressure sensor. There should be a slight vacuum in the tank. If there is no point of comparison, turn the engine off and keep the key on to look at tank pressure again. KOEO should show no vacuum or pressure because there will be atmospheric pressure in the tank.

Is there a slight vacuum in the tank when the engine is running? Yes ___ No ___

If not, the purge is not operating. Fix the purge first before the next step.

☐ 6. With the engine running and using functional tests or output controls on the scan tool, close the vent valve. On pressure systems, the sound of the pressure pump will be heard. The pump is either a pulsing solenoid or an electric motor. It may be located in the front of the vehicle (pulsing solenoid) or the rear (electric motor). Many European vehicles have the electric motor and measure motor current to detect system leakage.

Did the *pressure* increase in the tank when the vent valve was closed? Yes ___ No ___

If the pressure increased, both the purge and vent are working.

If the pressure did not increase, either the vent valve does not work or there is a system leak that is large enough to prevent pressure buildup.

☐ 7. If there is a code for EVAP, it will usually be caused by a leak. There is also the service bay EVAP test in functional tests or output controls. Use of the service bay test provides a "scripted test," where a set of directions are provided that you must follow in order. In this test, the vent will be commanded closed and the pressure generator run. Observe the tank pressure sensor.

Did the vehicle pass the EVAP service bay test? Yes ___ No ___

If not, the next step is to locate the leak using the smoke-generating machine.

Locate Evaporative Emissions System Leaks with a Smoke-Generating Machine

☐ 1. With the key on and the engine off (KOEO), use a scan tool to set the vent valve to the closed position, **Figure 31-1**. The purge valve is normally closed. Therefore, there is no need to focus on anything other than the vent valve.

Tech Tip

Not every manufacturer allows access to the vent valve on the scan tool. Therefore, it may be necessary to crimp the vent tube to or from the vent valve. Another option is to apply 12 volts and ground to the vent valve to force it to close.

Figure 31-1. A scan tool can be used to set the vent valve to the closed position.

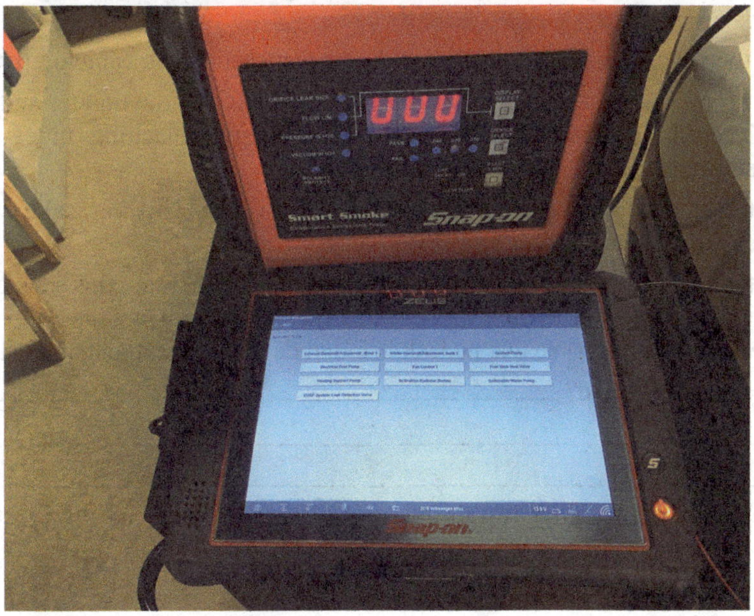

☐ 2. Find an easy access spot to insert the smoke nozzle. Usually, the hose that connects to the purge valve at the engine is an easy spot. Use service data to determine where the purge is located. Remember that it connects to engine vacuum, **Figure 31-2**.

Figure 31-2. Access points for the smoke machine nozzle.

Tech Tip

To locate the vent valve faster, leave the vent valve open but still apply the smoke. The smoke will become visible near the vent valve.

☐ 3. Connect the smoke machine to shop air or a nitrogen source. Connecting it to nitrogen is safer, but it may create an engine stumble when the purge opens when the engine is running again since nitrogen is an inert gas.

☐ 4. Connect the smoke machine to a 12-volt dc source, such as the vehicle's battery.

☐ 5. On older smoke-generating machines, set the flow gauge so the pointer and floating ball are aligned. There is no need to change settings on the digital machines unless you are changing the leak settings.

☐ 6. Operate the smoke machine to fill the system with smoke. This may take a few minutes. The larger the system, the longer it will take.

☐ 7. Observe the ball or digital readout to determine the leak rate. From this smoke location (from the hose that connects the purge valve to the rest of the vent system, not the hose between the engine and the purge valve), it is possible that no leak is found depending on the manufacturer's style of EVAP.

How much leak is found? ____

____

____

☐ 8. Turn off the smoke machine. Install the smoke nozzle in the opposite direction to test the purge valve.

Turn the smoke back on.

How much leak is found? ____

____

____

Name ______________________________

Project 6: Job 31 *(continued)*

☐ 9. Turn off the smoke machine. Remove the vehicle's gas cap. (This is done because some systems isolate areas of the EVAP system, especially those with multiple solenoids.). Install the smoke nozzle where the gas cap was using the cap adapter or other method to seal the system. Turn the smoke machine back on. The scan tool may have timed out on closing the vent valve and may need to be reset.

How much leak is found? ______________________________

____

____

Tech Tip

Some manufacturers mount the vent valve to the charcoal canister. Only if the leak is before the charcoal canister will the smoke be seen. Any smoke that passes through the charcoal canister will be absorbed by the charcoal, but the pressure will not be absorbed. Use a spray bottle of soap and water in this case to locate the leak by looking for bubbles around the vent and charcoal canister, **Figure 31-3**.

Figure 31-3. The vent valve is mounted on the charcoal canister on this vehicle.

☐ 10. Consult your instructor for instructions on how to repair the leaks or leaks. Note that there may be more than one leak. Therefore, you should smoke the system again after repairing a leak to check for other leaks.

☐ 11. Disconnect the smoke machine connections from pressure and the 12-volt source.

☐ 12. Return all applied conditions on the scan tool and back out of engine controls. Make sure the scan tool is no longer communicating with the vehicle before disconnecting it from the DLC. Power down the scan tool.

Job Wrap-Up

☐ 1. Clean the work area and return any equipment to storage.

☐ 2. Did you encounter any problems during this procedure? Yes ___ No ___
If Yes, what did you do to correct the problem? ______________________________

____

☐ 3. Have your instructor check your work and sign this job sheet.

Performance Evaluation—Instructor Use Only

How would you rate this student's overall performance on this task/job?

4 Competent/Proficient. Able to perform all elements of the task/job successfully and independently.

3 Satisfactory performance of the task/job. Able to perform elements of the task/job with minimal instructor assistance.

2 Completed the task/job with significant instructor assistance.

1 Unsuccessfully attempted the task/job.

0 No exposure. Note reason below (absence, skill not covered, etc.).

Comments:

____

____

____

____

Instructor's Signature: ____

PROJECT 7

Performing Engine-Related Service

Introduction

Periodic oil and filter changes can greatly prolong the life of an engine. Oil and filter changes are relatively simple, but must be done correctly. It is also vital that any oil or coolant leaks be found and promptly fixed. In Job 32, you will drain and replace the engine oil and change the oil filter.

In Job 33, you will repair damaged threads. This requires special tools that can restore external threads or replace internal threads with a threaded insert. These may seem like simple jobs that are beneath the driveability technician, but eventually they will need to be done, and you will be called upon to perform them.

As a technician, you will likely be required to perform cylinder head service, usually called a "valve job." Cylinder heads can be made of cast iron, aluminum, or magnesium with two, three, or four valves per cylinder. A variety of camshaft placements and valve train designs can be used to open and close the valves. In Job 34, you will test and service variable valve timing or variable valve lift components. In Job 35, you will inspect camshaft drives and other valve timing components. You will adjust the engine's valves in Job 36.

In Job 37, you will remove and replace a vehicle's thermostat. The thermostat controls engine temperature for maximum driveability and mileage, and lowest emissions and engine wear. A thermostat that sticks closed will cause obvious overheating. One that sticks open will be harder to spot, although it will greatly effect engine efficiency.

Project 7 Jobs

- Job 32—Change Oil and Filter
- Job 33—Repair Damaged Threads
- Job 34—Test and Service Variable Valve Timing or Lift Components
- Job 35—Service Valve Timing Components
- Job 36—Adjust Valves
- Job 37—Remove and Replace Thermostat and Gasket

Tools and Materials

The following list contains the tools and materials that may be needed to complete the jobs in this project. The items used will depend on the make and model of vehicle being serviced.

- A vehicle requiring service.
- Applicable service information.
- Drain pan.
- Hand tools.
- Air-operated tools.
- Safety glasses and other protective equipment.

Safety Notice

Before performing these jobs, review all pertinent safety information in the text and review safety information with your instructor.

Name ______________________________

Date ____________________ Class ____________________

Project 7: Job 32—Change Oil and Filter

After completing this job, you will be able to perform an engine oil and filter change.

Instructions

As you read the job instructions, answer the questions and perform the tasks. Record your answers using complete sentences. Consult the proper service information and ask your instructor for help as needed.

Warning

Before performing this job, review all pertinent safety information in the text and discuss safety procedures with your instructor.

Procedures

☐ 1. Obtain a vehicle to be used in this job. Your instructor may direct you to perform this job on a shop vehicle or engine.

☐ 2. Gather the tools needed to perform the following job. Refer to the tools and materials list at the beginning of the project.

☐ 3. Obtain the correct oil filter and type and grade of motor oil.

Brand, grade, and weight of oil: ______________________________

Brand and stock number of oil filter: ______________________________

☐ 4. Run the engine until it reaches operating temperature.

☐ 5. Raise the vehicle on a lift or raise it with a jack and secure it on jack stands. The vehicle should be level when raised to allow all of the oil to drain from the pan.

Warning

The vehicle must be raised and supported in a safe manner. Always use approved lifts or jacks and jack stands.

☐ 6. Place the oil drain pan under the engine oil pan. **Figure 32-1** shows a typical oil drain pan.

Figure 32-1. The oil pan should be large enough to fit under both the oil drain and the oil filter.

☐ 7. Remove the oil drain plug. A few engines have two drain plugs.

Warning

Avoid contact with hot oil. You could be severely burned.

☐ 8. Inspect the drain plug. The seal should be undamaged to prevent leaks. Check the drain plug's threads for damage. If the drain plug is damaged, replace it.

Are the drain plug threads and seal OK? Yes ___ No ___

☐ 9. Loosen the oil filter using a filter wrench and remove the filter from the engine. If necessary, reposition the oil drain pan under the filter or use a second drain pan.

☐ 10. Wipe off the oil filter mounting base and check that the old filter seal is not stuck on the base.

☐ 11. Check the new filter to ensure that it is the correct replacement.

☐ 12. Fill the new filter with the correct grade of motor oil. If the oil filter is mounted with the opening down, skip this step.

☐ 13. Smear a thin film of clean engine oil on to the new oil filter rubber seal as shown in **Figure 32-2**.

☐ 14. Screw on the new oil filter and hand tighten it.

☐ 15. Turn the filter an additional 1/2 to 3/4 turn.

☐ 16. Install and tighten the oil drain plug.

☐ 17. Remove the oil filler cap from the engine.

☐ 18. Open the first oil container and pour the oil into the filler opening in the engine. Carefully monitor the filler opening to ensure that oil does not spill out.

☐ 19. Repeat step 18 until the engine is filled to the proper level.

☐ 20. Replace the filler cap and wipe any spilled oil from the engine.

☐ 21. Start the engine and watch the oil pressure light or gauge. The light should go out or the gauge should begin to register within 10 to 20 seconds. If it does not, stop the engine immediately and locate the problem.

☐ 22. Raise the vehicle and check for leaks from the oil filter and drain plug.

Are there any leaks? Yes ___ No ___

Figure 32-2. Use clean oil to lightly lubricate the filter seal.

Name ______________________________

Project 7: Job 32 *(continued)*

If you found leaks, what did you do to correct them? ______________________________

____

____

____

☐ 23. Lower the vehicle and stop the engine.

☐ 24. Allow the engine to sit for several minutes.

☐ 25. Recheck the oil level.

Is the level correct? Yes ___ No ___

If the level is low, add oil until the dipstick reads full.

Job Wrap-Up

☐ 1. Clean the work area and return any equipment to storage. Dispose of the old oil filter properly, **Figure 32-3**.

☐ 2. Did you encounter any problems during this procedure? Yes ___ No ___

If Yes, describe the problems: ______________________________

____

What did you do to correct the problems? ______________________________

____

☐ 3. Have your instructor check your work and sign this job sheet.

Figure 32-3. Always dispose of the old oil filter in special oil filter containers. Care should be taken to dispose of the oil filters without damaging the environment.

Performance Evaluation—Instructor Use Only

How would you rate this student's overall performance on this task/job?

4 Competent/Proficient. Able to perform all elements of the task/job successfully and independently.

3 Satisfactory performance of the task/job. Able to perform elements of the task/job with minimal instructor assistance.

2 Completed the task/job with significant instructor assistance.

1 Unsuccessfully attempted the task/job.

0 No exposure. Note reason below (absence, skill not covered, etc.).

Comments:

____

____

____

____

Instructor's Signature: ____

Name ____________________

Date ____________________ Class ____________________

Project 7: Job 33—Repair Damaged Threads

After completing this job, you will be able to repair a variety of damaged threads and chase threads in a bore.

Instructions

As you read the job instructions, answer the questions and perform the tasks. Record your answers using complete sentences. Consult the proper service information and ask your instructor for help as needed.

Warning

Before performing this job, review all pertinent safety information in the text and discuss safety procedures with your instructor.

Procedures

☐ 1. Obtain a piece of metal or a part with a threaded bore that has stripped threads.

☐ 2. Gather the tools needed to perform the following job. Refer to the tools and materials list at the beginning of the project.

Repair External Threads

Tech Tip

Most stripped external threads occur on cap screws, bolts, or other parts that are usually replaced when damaged. Occasionally, the technician will be asked to repair damaged external threads. The usual reason for repairing an external thread is to remove burrs. External threads may also be repaired if hammering or cross-threading has damaged the beginning thread.

☐ 1. Carefully inspect the external threads and determine whether they can be repaired.

- Are large sections of the threads missing? Yes ___ No ___
- Have large sections of the thread been cross-threaded? Yes ___ No ___
- Are the threads badly damaged throughout their length? Yes ___ No ___
- Are the threads badly damaged at the spot where they will be under the most tension? Yes ___ No ___

A Yes answer to any of these questions usually means that the part must be replaced.

Can the threads be repaired? Yes ___ No ___

Warning

Do *not* attempt to repair badly damaged external threads, or damaged threads on critical parts. Part failure and possible injury could result.

☐ 2. Use one of the following methods to repair an external thread.

Die Method

a. Install the correct size die in the die stock.

b. Place the die and die stock over the external threads to be repaired.

c. Lubricate the external threads.

d. Begin turning the die stock over the threads to remove burrs or straighten a cross-threaded or damaged beginning thread.

e. After the damaged threads are repaired, remove the die and die stock by turning it in the opposite direction.

f. Thoroughly clean and reinspect the threads.

Can the part be reused? Yes ___ No ___

Die-Type Thread Chaser

a. Install the correct size thread chaser over the external threads to be repaired. See **Figure 33-1**.

b. Lubricate the external threads.

c. Use a wrench to turn the thread chaser over the threads, **Figure 33-2**.

d. After the threads are repaired, remove the die and die stock by turning it in the opposite direction.

e. Thoroughly clean and inspect the threads.

Can the part be reused? Yes ___ No ___

Figure 33-1. Install the correct thread chaser over the damaged stud. (Heli-Coil)

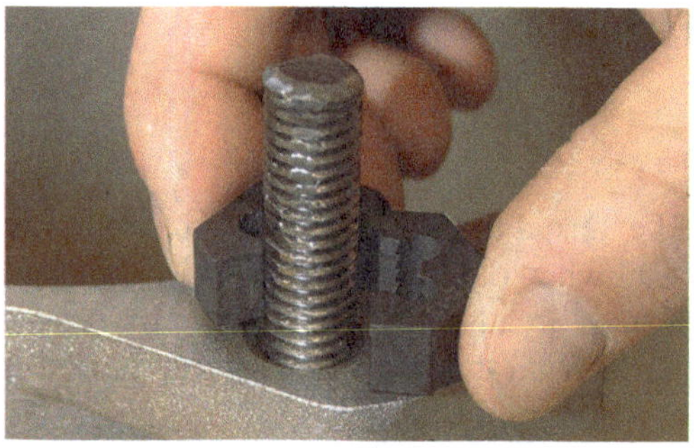

Figure 33-2. Turn the thread chaser with a wrench or socket as necessary to clean up the threads. This particular thread chaser can be turned in either direction. (Heli-Coil)

File-Type Thread Chaser

a. Lubricate the external threads.

b. Select the proper size thread chaser. Most file-type thread chasers will be four-sided, with a different thread on each side of one end, and four other thread sizes on the other end.

Name____

c. Place the thread chaser on the damaged threads. Make sure that the high points of the chaser rest over the low points of the thread.

d. Slowly draw the thread chaser over the damaged threads, stopping frequently to inspect the work.

e. Thoroughly clean the threads and reinspect.

Can the part be reused? Yes ___ No ___

Repair Internal Threads

Tech Tip

Stripped threads are usually found in aluminum assemblies, but can occur in any type of metal. Thread repair kits contain the needed drills, taps, thread repair inserts, and special mandrels for installing the inserts.

☐ 1. Determine the size and pitch of the stripped thread.

☐ 2. If necessary, place rags around the stripped thread to catch metal chips.

☐ 3. Select the proper drill bit according to the instructions of the thread repair kit.

☐ 4. Drill out the stripped threads and clean the metal chips from the hole, **Figure 33-3**.

☐ 5. Tap the hole with the appropriate tap from the thread repair kit. See **Figure 33-4**. Be sure to lubricate the tap with cutting oil before beginning the tapping operation.

☐ 6. Clean the threads to remove any remaining chips.

☐ 7. Thread the repair insert onto the correct mandrel. The insert tang should be engaged with the matching slot on the mandrel.

Figure 33-3. Drill out the stripped thread with the correct size drill bit. (Heli-Coil)

Figure 33-4. Tap the drilled hole with the proper tap. Be sure to generously lubricate the tap and hole with cutting oil. (Heli-Coil)

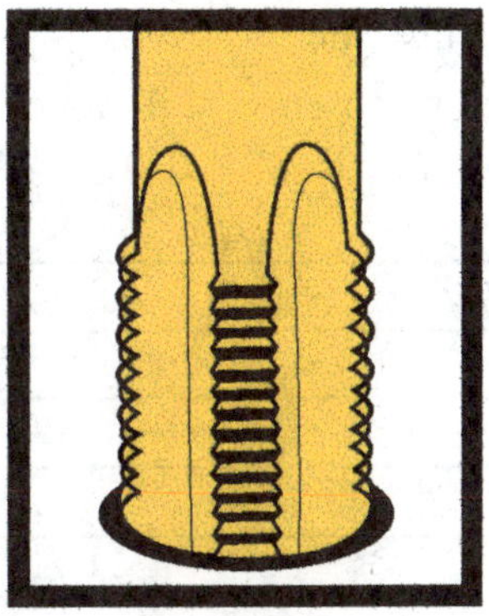

Figure 33-5. Install the thread insert with the proper tool. (Heli-Coil)

- ☐ 8. If installing the insert into an iron or steel part, lubricate it with engine oil. Do not lubricate the insert if it is to be installed in an aluminum part.
- ☐ 9. Turn the mandrel to advance it into the tapped hole, **Figure 33-5**.
- ☐ 10. Back the mandrel out of the hole when the insert reaches the bottom.
- ☐ 11. If the tang did not break off when the mandrel was removed, lightly tap it with a drift punch and hammer to remove the tang.

Job Wrap-Up

- ☐ 1. Clean and return all of the tools, and clean the work area.
- ☐ 2. Did you encounter any problems during this procedure? Yes ___ No ___

  If Yes, describe the problems: ____________________

  ____

  What did you do to correct the problems? ____________________

  ____
- ☐ 3. Have your instructor check your work and sign this job sheet.

Performance Evaluation—Instructor Use Only

How would you rate this student's overall performance on this task/job?

4 Competent/Proficient. Able to perform all elements of the task/job successfully and independently.

3 Satisfactory performance of the task/job. Able to perform elements of the task/job with minimal instructor assistance.

2 Completed the task/job with significant instructor assistance.

1 Unsuccessfully attempted the task/job.

0 No exposure. Note reason below (absence, skill not covered, etc.).

Comments:

____

____

____

____

Instructor's Signature: ____________________

Name ______________________________

Date ______________________ Class ______________________

Project 7: Job 34—Test and Service Variable Valve Timing or Lift Components

Instructions

As you read the job instructions, answer the questions and perform the tasks. Record your answers using complete sentences. Consult the proper service information and ask your instructor for help as needed.

Warning

Before performing this job, review all pertinent safety information in the text and discuss safety procedures with your instructor.

Related Trouble Codes

Trouble codes are not addressed in every job, but the following codes are examples associated with VVT and VVL:

P0010 Camshaft Position Actuator Circuit/Open

P0011 Camshaft Position A-Timing Over Advanced or System Performance Bank 1

P0012 Camshaft Position A-Timing Over Retarded or System Performance

P0013 Exhaust B Camshaft Position Actuator Circuit/Open Bank 1

P0014 Camshaft Position B-Timing Over-Advanced or System Performance Bank 1

Procedures

Caution

Perform the following test only if it is specifically mentioned in the manufacturer's service information. Do not ground any computer control system wire without checking the service information.

☐ 1. Locate the variable valve timing (VVT) solenoids, which control the flow of oil to the variable valve timing mechanisms. Use service data to locate them if you are unfamiliar with the engine being serviced. Some are small solenoids located in the camshaft area, **Figure 34-1**. Others are mounted in the front cover, **Figure 34-2**. All have two wires, as they are actuators, not sensors.

☐ 2. Perform a visual inspection. Are there any broken wires or damaged solenoids? Yes ___ No ___

☐ 3. Fix any broken wires or replace damaged solenoids.

Using a scan tool, check for diagnostic trouble codes. Are there camshaft timing–related codes? Yes ___ No ___

If Yes, list any camshaft timing codes and identify which bank of cylinders they pertain to:

____

____

____

☐ 4. Use service data to determine which bank is which so that the correct solenoids are diagnosed.

Figure 34-1. These VVT solenoids on a V-type engine are mounted through the top of the valve covers.

Figure 34-2. VVT solenoids mounted on the front of a horizontally opposed piston engine.

☐ 5. Warm up the engine. Use the scan tool in either the special functions or output controls mode to vary the variable valve timing to verify that the system operates.

Does the engine rpm change when the scan tool is used to vary the valve timing? Yes ___ No ___

If Yes, the VVT system is working. If not, the VVT system is not working.

Another way to test the system is to drive the vehicle under different loads while another technician views PIDs/data. Does cam timing change under different load conditions?
Yes ___ No ___

If yes, the cam phaser is working. If not, the cam phaser is not working.

☐ 6. A way to test the system without a scan tool is use a wiring diagram to determine which of the two wires is the control side of the circuit. While the engine is running, ground the control wire by back probing next to the wire.

Name ____

Does the engine speed change when the control wire is grounded? Yes ___ No ___

If yes, the cam phaser is working. If not, the cam phaser is not working.

☐ 7. With a meter, check voltage drops of the wires for the solenoids. (Remember that the solenoid must be in use to check voltage drops. Refer to Step 7.)

Are the voltage drops close to zero? Yes ___ No ___

If not, repair the wires.

☐ 8. Double check that the correct viscosity oil has been used and that the oil has been changed regularly. The incorrect viscosity will affect the solenoids.

Is the correct viscosity used? Yes ___ No ___

If not, perform an oil and filter change and install the correct viscosity oil.

☐ 9. Refer to service data to determine if any resets or relearns must be performed after replacing a VVT or VVL solenoid. The same procedures above apply to diagnosis of a variable valve lift solenoid.

☐ 10. Clear codes if monitors are not needed for a state inspection.

☐ 11. Back out of output controls and back out of scanner completely before removing the connection to the DLC.

☐ 12. Verify proper engine operation.

Job Wrap-Up

☐ 1. Clean the work area, including coolant spills, and return any equipment to storage.

☐ 2. Did you encounter any problems during this procedure? Yes _____ No _____

If Yes, describe the problems: ____

What did you do to correct the problem? ____________________________________

____

☐ 3. Have your instructor check your work and sign this job sheet.

Performance Evaluation—Instructor Use Only

How would you rate this student's overall performance on this task/job?

4 Competent/Proficient. Able to perform all elements of the task/job successfully and independently.

3 Satisfactory performance of the task/job. Able to perform elements of the task/job with minimal instructor assistance.

2 Completed the task/job with significant instructor assistance.

1 Unsuccessfully attempted the task/job.

0 No exposure. Note reason below (absence, skill not covered, etc.).

Comments:

____

____

____

____

Instructor's Signature: ____

Notes

Name ____

Date ______________________________ Class ______________________________

Project 7: Job 35—Service Valve Timing Components

After completing this job, you will be able to service valve timing components.

Instructions

As you read the job instructions, answer the questions and perform the tasks. Record your answers using complete sentences. Consult the proper service information and ask your instructor for help as needed.

Warning

Before performing this job, review all pertinent safety information in the text and discuss safety procedures with your instructor.

Procedures

☐ 1. Obtain an engine to be used in this job. Your instructor may direct you to perform this job on a shop engine.
- Make of engine: ____________________
- Number of cylinders: ____________________
- Cylinder arrangement (V-type, inline, etc.): ____________________
- Cooling system: Liquid ___ Air ___

☐ 2. Gather the tools needed to perform the following tasks. Refer to the tools and materials list at the beginning of the project.

☐ 3. Look up the following torque specifications in the vehicle's service information. Record the information in the appropriate spaces.

Intake manifold/plenum fasteners: ______ ft-lb ______ N·m

Rocker arm fasteners (if applicable): ______ ft-lb ______ N·m

Valve cover fasteners: ______ ft-lb ______ N·m

Timing mechanism fasteners: ______ ft-lb ______ N·m

Front cover fasteners: ______ ft-lb ______ N·m

Check Operation of a Variable Valve Timing Mechanism

Caution

Perform the following test only if it is specifically mentioned in the manufacturer's service information. Do *not* ground any computer control system wire without checking the service information.

☐ 1. Locate the solenoid that controls the flow of oil to the variable valve timing mechanism. The solenoid may be installed on the valve cover, on the side of the engine, or in the head under the valve cover.

☐ 2. Determine which solenoid wire receives a ground signal from the ECM by consulting the appropriate wiring diagram.

☐ 3. Start the engine and raise the engine speed to about 2500 rpm.

☐ 4. Ground the solenoid signal wire and observe engine operation. There should be a noticeable change in engine speed and sound as the valve timing changes.

Does the engine speed change? Yes ___ No ___

Does the sound of the engine change? Yes ___ No ___

If the engine speed or sound does not change, the solenoid is defective, the internal advance mechanism is stuck or leaking, or the engine's oil pressure is low. Make further checks according to the manufacturer's service information.

Check Camshaft Drive Parts

Tech Tip

Figure 35-1 illustrates the three types of timing mechanisms. Placement of sprockets and belts or chains varies greatly by design. Some overhead camshaft engines may have as many as four camshaft sprockets.

Figure 35-1. Three types of timing mechanisms are shown here. A—Gear-driven timing mechanism. B—Chain-driven timing mechanism. C—Belt-driven timing mechanism. (DaimlerChrysler, Ford)

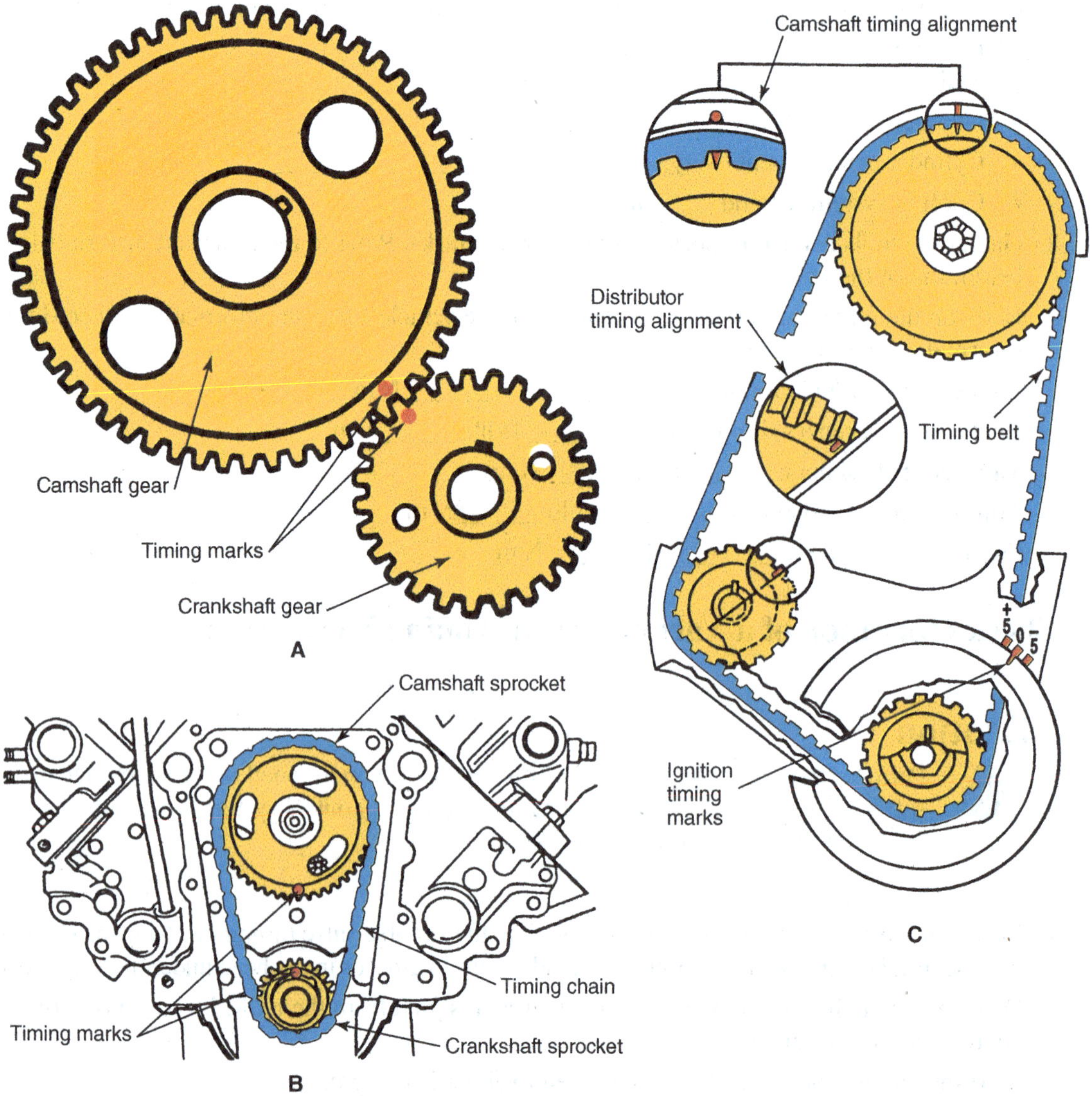

Name ______________________________

Project 7: Job 35 *(continued)*

☐ 1. Remove the camshaft drive parts from the engine as necessary.

☐ 2. Visually inspect the condition of gears and drive sprockets.

☐ 3. Check the condition of the timing chain or belt. Most checks can be made visually. A worn chain will have excessive slack. A worn belt will have cracks and possible missing teeth.

☐ 4. Check the condition of the chain or belt tensioner.
   a. Check the tensioner for obvious physical damage.
   b. When possible, check the tensioner spring pressure with the proper special tool.
   c. Check hydraulic tensioners for leaks, lack of oil, or other damage.

Install Valve Timing Components

> **Tech Tip**
>
> Not all of the following steps will apply to every engine. This procedure assumes that if the engine has an in-block camshaft, the camshaft has been previously installed.

☐ 1. Install the lifters, push rods, and rocker arms in their original locations.

☐ 2. If a rocker shaft is used, start the rocker shaft fasteners by hand. Then, tighten the fasteners, starting with the middle bolts and turning each bolt one-half turn at a time. This will prevent a strain on any one bolt. Remember, the pressure of the compressed valve springs will be pushing against the rocker shaft assembly.

> **Tech Tip**
>
> On some engines, the valves may need adjusting at this time. See Job 36.

☐ 3. Loosely place the timing gears or sprockets on the crankshaft and camshaft and rotate the crankshaft and camshaft until the timing marks are aligned. **Figure 35-2** shows common alignment marks for chain- and belt-type timing gears.

Figure 35-2. Make sure that the timing gears are correctly aligned before completing assembly. A—This is a chain and timing gear assembly with the timing marks correctly aligned. B—Mark the timing belt sprockets with a tire crayon or other durable marker before installing them.

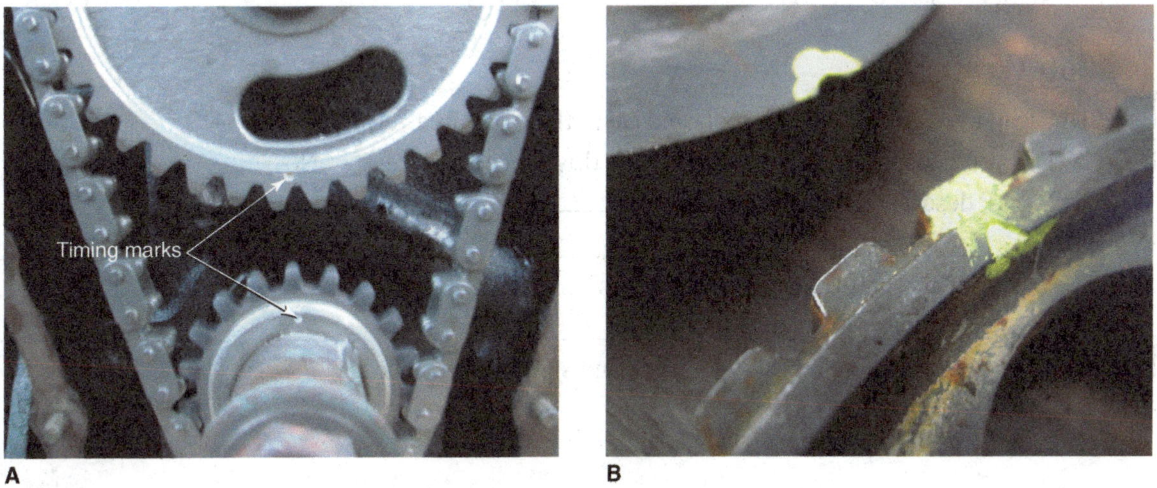

☐ 4. Carefully remove the sprockets or gears, ensuring the crankshaft and camshaft do not turn.

☐ 5. Place the timing chain or belt in position over the sprockets. Be careful to maintain the alignment of the timing marks.

☐ 6. Install the sprockets and chain or belt into position on the camshaft and crankshaft. Be careful not to allow the crankshaft or camshaft to rotate.

☐ 7. Install and tighten the timing device fasteners.

☐ 8. Check and adjust belt/chain tension using one of the following methods, as outlined by the manufacturer's instructions:

> **Tech Tip**
>
> On many engines, belt or chain tension is not adjustable.

- Measure belt deflection with a special tool and adjust the tensioner as required. Adjustment devices include slotted holes in the tensioner, adjusting screws, or shims.
- Adjust the tensioner until the belt can be twisted to a 90° angle.
- Use a torque wrench to adjust the tensioner to the proper torque value.
- Align marks on the tensioner with marks on the engine block or head.
- Method used: ______________________________

☐ 9. After all parts are installed, recheck the timing marks to ensure that they are in position.

☐ 10. Index the camshaft position sensor using manufacturer's procedures. On most engines, the camshaft and crankshaft position sensors are indexed by the following procedure:

a. Place the sensor in position on the engine block or timing cover and lightly attach the fasteners.

b. Ensure that the marks on the camshaft position sensor are aligned with the marks on the engine block or timing cover.

c. Tighten the fasteners, being sure that the marks remain in alignment.

☐ 11. Scrape the timing cover, coolant pump, and block mating surfaces to remove old gasket material.

☐ 12. Place the timing cover gaskets and seals on the engine block. Use the proper type of sealant, if required.

☐ 13. Place the timing cover on the block.

☐ 14. Install and tighten the timing cover fasteners. Tighten the fasteners to the proper torque in the correct sequence.

Job Wrap-Up

☐ 1. Clean and return all of the tools and clean the work area.

☐ 2. Did you encounter any problems during this procedure? Yes ___ No ___

If Yes, describe the problems: ______________________________

____

What did you do to correct the problems? ______________________________

____

☐ 3. Have your instructor check your work and sign this job sheet.

Name ____________________

Project 7: Job 35 *(continued)*

Performance Evaluation—Instructor Use Only

How would you rate this student's overall performance on this task/job?

4 Competent/Proficient. Able to perform all elements of the task/job successfully and independently.

3 Satisfactory performance of the task/job. Able to perform elements of the task/job with minimal instructor assistance.

2 Completed the task/job with significant instructor assistance.

1 Unsuccessfully attempted the task/job.

0 No exposure. Note reason below (absence, skill not covered, etc.).

Comments:

____

____

____

____

Instructor's Signature: ____________________

Notes

Name ____

Date ______________________ Class ______________________

Project 7: Job 36—Adjust Valves

After completing this job, you will be able to adjust mechanical and hydraulic valve lifters to provide proper valve clearance.

Instructions

As you read the job instructions, answer the questions and perform the tasks. Record your answers using complete sentences. Consult the proper service literature and ask your instructor for help as needed.

Warning

Before performing this job, review all pertinent safety information in the text and discuss safety procedures with your instructor.

Procedures

☐ 1. Obtain a vehicle to be used in this job. Your instructor may direct you to perform this job on a shop vehicle or engine.

☐ 2. Gather the tools needed to perform the following job. Refer to the tools and materials list at the beginning of the project.

☐ 3. Remove the engine valve cover(s) to reveal the valve adjustment device.

Tech Tip

On some overhead camshaft engines, clearance is adjusted by changing lifters or adding shims at the lifters. Consult the manufacturer's service information for these procedures.

☐ 4. Determine whether the engine uses mechanical or hydraulic valve lifters.

Mechanical ___ Hydraulic ___

Tech Tip

The following sections provide instructions for adjusting valves with mechanical lifters and adjusting valves with hydraulic lifters. Use the procedure that is appropriate for the type of lifters used in your vehicle. Skip the procedure that does not apply.

Adjust Valves—Mechanical Valve Lifters

☐ 1. Obtain the proper specification for valve clearance.

Specification for intake valve: ____________ inches or millimeters (circle one).

Does the specification call for the engine to be warmed up? Yes ___ No ___

Specification for exhaust valve: ____________ inches or millimeters (circle one).

Does the specification call for the engine to be warmed up? Yes ___ No ___

☐ 2. By hand, turn the crankshaft until the camshaft lobe for the valve to be adjusted points away from the lifter.

☐ 3. Loosen the adjuster locknut.

- [ ] 4. Insert the proper thickness feeler gauge between the valve and the rocker arm. See **Figure 36-1**.
- [ ] 5. Turn the adjuster while moving the feeler gauge between the valve and rocker arm. When there is a light drag on the feeler gauge, clearance is correct.
- [ ] 6. Tighten the adjuster locknut while holding the adjuster in position.
- [ ] 7. Recheck the adjustment to ensure that the adjuster did not move when the locknut was tightened.
- [ ] 8. Repeat steps 2 through 7 for the other valves.
- [ ] 9. Start the engine and recheck the adjustment by inserting a feeler gauge between the valve and rocker arm.

Does the feeler gauge fit between the valve and rocker arm? Yes ___ No ___

Are any valves noisy (clattering or tapping sounds)? Yes ___ No ___

Does the noise stop when the feeler gauge is inserted between the valve and rocker arm? Yes ___ No ___

Adjust Valves—Hydraulic Valve Lifters

- [ ] 1. Place shielding around the valve assemblies to reduce oil spray.
- [ ] 2. Start the engine.
- [ ] 3. Loosen the valve adjuster locknut on the first valve to be adjusted. Note that not all rocker assemblies are equipped with valve adjuster locknuts.
- [ ] 4. Back off the valve adjuster until the valve begins to make a clattering noise. See **Figure 36-2**.
- [ ] 5. Tighten the adjuster until the noise just stops.
- [ ] 6. Tighten the adjuster an additional number of turns as specified by the service information. If the rocker assembly is equipped with a valve adjuster locknut, retighten it. Be careful not to allow the valve adjuster to rotate.
- [ ] 7. Repeat steps 3 through 6 for all other engine valves.
- [ ] 8. Shut off the engine.
- [ ] 9. Remove all splash shields from the valve assemblies.
- [ ] 10. Replace the valve cover(s) using a new gasket as necessary.

Figure 36-1. Insert the feeler gauge between the rocker arm and the valve stem. The cam lobe must be at its lowest point (putting no pressure on the valve train).

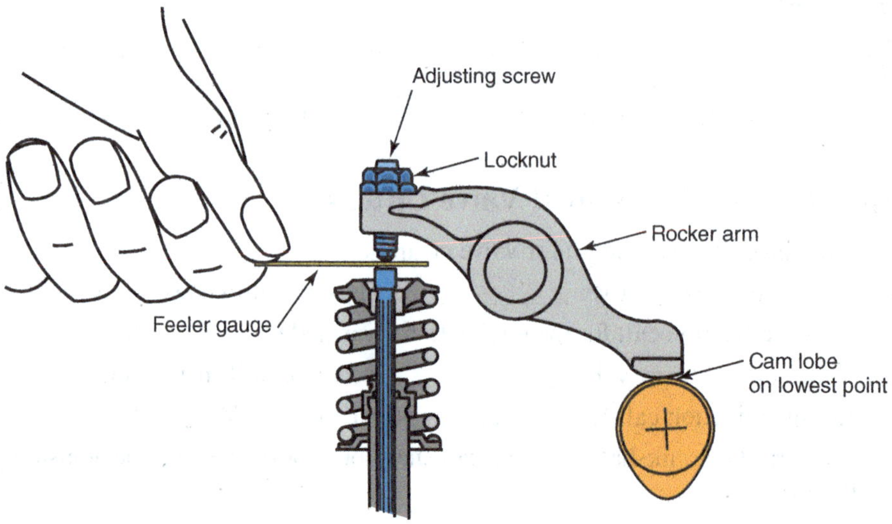

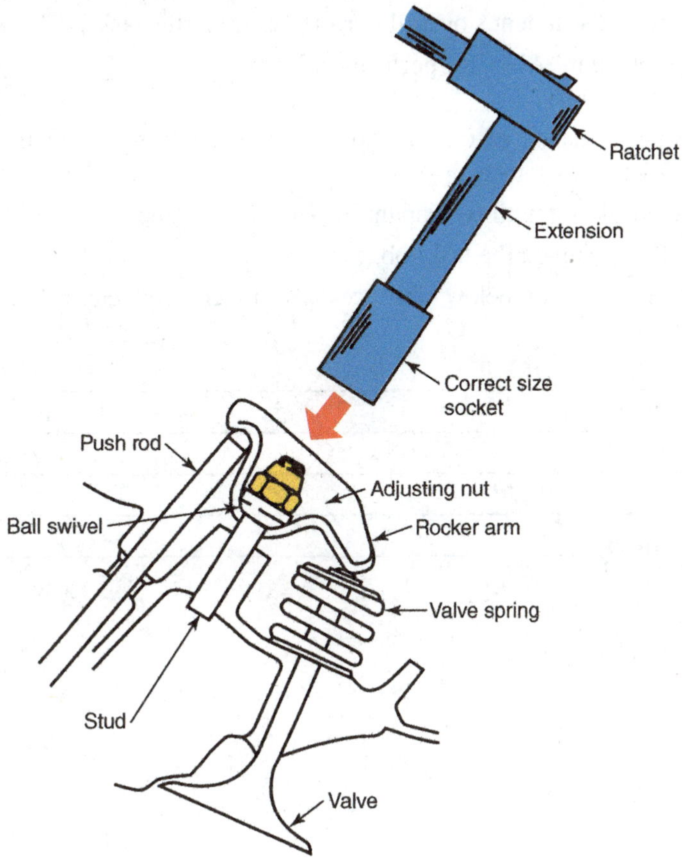

Figure 36-2. Adjust the valve until it just stops clattering, then turn the adjuster in an additional specified number of turns. The adjusting nut shown here has an interference fit and does not use a locknut.

Job Wrap-Up

☐ 1. Clean the work area and return any equipment to storage.

☐ 2. Did you encounter any problems during this procedure? Yes ___ No ___

If Yes, describe the problems: ____________________

____

What did you do to correct the problems? ____________________

____

☐ 3. Have your instructor check your work and sign this job sheet.

Performance Evaluation—Instructor Use Only

How would you rate this student's overall performance on this task/job?

4 Competent/Proficient. Able to perform all elements of the task/job successfully and independently.

3 Satisfactory performance of the task/job. Able to perform elements of the task/job with minimal instructor assistance.

2 Completed the task/job with significant instructor assistance.

1 Unsuccessfully attempted the task/job.

0 No exposure. Note reason below (absence, skill not covered, etc.).

Comments:

____

____

____

____

Instructor's Signature: ______________________________

Name ______________________________

Date ____________________ Class ____________________

Project 7: Job 37—Remove and Replace a Thermostat

After completing this job, you will be able to remove and replace a thermostat.

Instructions

As you read the job instructions, answer the questions and perform the tasks. Record your answers using complete sentences. Consult the proper service information and ask your instructor for help as needed.

Warning

Before performing this job, review all pertinent safety information in the text and discuss safety procedures with your instructor.

Procedures

☐ 1. Obtain a vehicle to be used in this job. Your instructor may direct you to perform this job on a shop vehicle.

☐ 2. Gather the tools needed to perform the following job. Refer to the tools and materials list at the beginning of the project.

☐ 3. Ensure that the engine and cooling system are sufficiently cool (cooling system not under pressure) to allow the radiator cap to be safely removed.

☐ 4. Remove the radiator cap, then locate the radiator drain plug.

☐ 5. Place a suitable container under the drain plug.

☐ 6. Open the radiator drain plug. Ensure that coolant drains into the container.

Warning

Clean up any coolant spills. Antifreeze is poisonous to people and animals.

☐ 7. Allow coolant to drain out so that the level of coolant in the engine is below the level of the thermostat. It is not necessary to remove all of the coolant.

☐ 8. Loosen the upper radiator hose clamp and remove the hose from the thermostat housing.

☐ 9. Remove the fasteners holding the thermostat housing to the engine and remove the housing. The thermostat should now be visible. See **Figure 37-1**.

Figure 37-1. On V-type engines, the thermostat is usually located at the front of the engine between the cylinder banks. On inline engines, thermostats are usually near the upper radiator hose at the front of the engine.

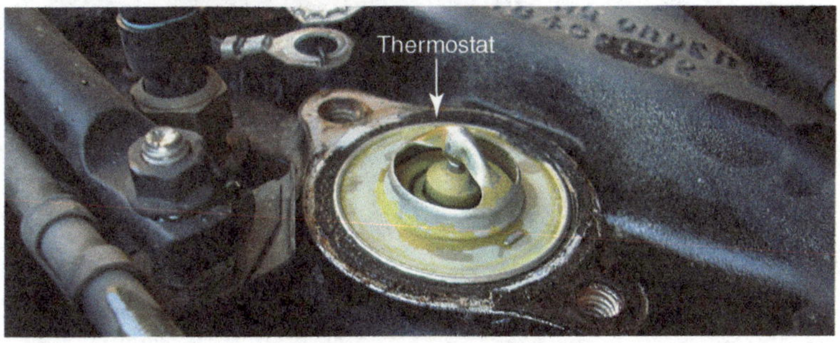

☐ 10. Remove the thermostat from the engine.

☐ 11. Remove any gasket material or seals from sealing areas on the engine and thermostat housing. You may wish to stuff a rag in the thermostat housing to prevent any debris from entering the coolant passages.

Tech Tip

The following step is optional and may be assigned by your instructor.

☐ 12. Test the thermostat by suspending it in a water-filled container over a burner or other source of heat. The thermostat should not touch the sides of the container. Place a thermometer in the water and observe the thermostat as the water is heated. If the thermostat does not begin to open at its rated temperature, or is not fully open before the water begins boiling, it is defective.

☐ 13. If the thermostat is being replaced, compare the old and new thermostats. The new thermostat should be the same size as the original thermostat. The thermostat opening temperature should match the manufacturer's specifications. This temperature is usually stamped on the thermostatic element, as shown in **Figure 37-2**.

Do the sizes match? Yes ___ No ___

Do the opening temperatures match? Yes ___ No ___

Caution

Do *not* install a thermostat with a lower operating temperature than the original thermostat. This will affect emissions control operations and may set a trouble code on OBD II–equipped vehicles.

☐ 14. Place the thermostat in position. The heat-sensing element should face the interior of the engine.

Is the thermostat installed properly? Yes ___ No ___

☐ 15. If specified, coat the thermostat housing and engine sealing surfaces with nonhardening sealer.

☐ 16. Install the thermostat gasket or seals on the engine.

Figure 37-2. The opening temperature is usually stamped on the thermostatic element of the thermostat. Most thermostats have both Fahrenheit and Celsius values.

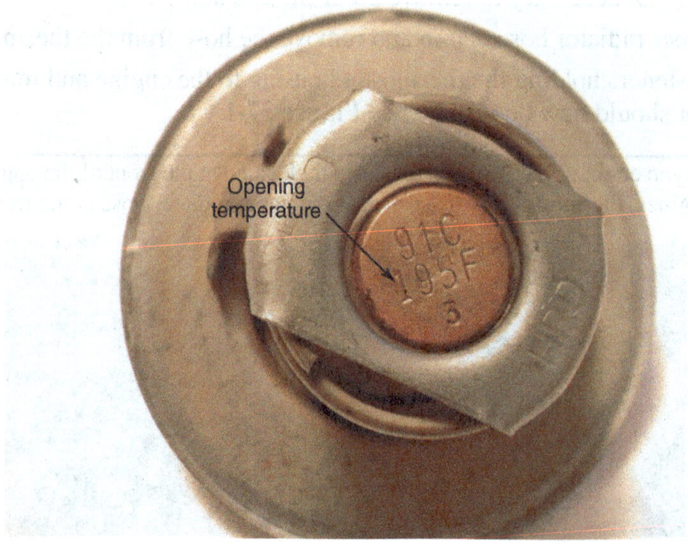

Name ____

Project 7: Job 37 *(continued)*

☐ 17. Place the thermostat housing on the engine and install the housing fasteners. If the fasteners extend into the coolant passage, the threads should be coated with nonhardening sealer.

☐ 18. Tighten the thermostat housing fasteners in an alternating pattern to prevent distortion. Be careful not to overtighten the fasteners. Overtightening the fasteners can cause distortion of the housing, resulting in leaks, and may break the housing.

☐ 19. Refill the system with the proper coolant. Many modern vehicles use special long-life coolant. Do not mix coolant types.

☐ 20. Start the engine and check for leaks and proper thermostat operation.

Job Wrap-Up

☐ 1. Clean the work area, including coolant spills, and return any equipment to storage.

☐ 2. Did you encounter any problems during this procedure? Yes ___ No ___

If Yes, describe the problems: ____

____

What did you do to correct the problems? ____

____

☐ 3. Have your instructor check your work and sign this job sheet.

Performance Evaluation—Instructor Use Only

How would you rate this student's overall performance on this task/job?

4 Competent/Proficient. Able to perform all elements of the task/job successfully and independently.

3 Satisfactory performance of the task/job. Able to perform elements of the task/job with minimal instructor assistance.

2 Completed the task/job with significant instructor assistance.

1 Unsuccessfully attempted the task/job.

0 No exposure. Note reason below (absence, skill not covered, etc.).

Comments:

____

____

____

____

Instructor's Signature: ____

Notes

PROJECT 8

Diagnosing and Servicing Stop-Start Systems and Hybrid Vehicles

Introduction

This project covers diagnosis and service of stop-start systems and hybrids. Review electrical diagnostic methods such as voltage drops, scopes, and amp clamps for this project. Both systems can develop problems due to a low battery. Both systems use a 12-volt battery, and both rely on the 12-volt battery heavily. A low or drained 12-volt battery will disable both, as well. That's why you will see a repeat of the 12-volt battery testing job.

For hybrids, the 12-volt battery is normally an AGM, absorbed glass mat, battery if the battery will be in any space a person can be. That includes the trunk. If the low-voltage battery is mounted under the hood, it will be a lead-acid battery.

Testing and servicing a 12-volt battery is Job 38. Testing the stop-start system is Job 39. Testing and servicing the 12-volt battery, also called the auxiliary battery, is Job 40. Job 41 is testing the motors associated with the high-voltage cooling system for hybrids. Job 42 covers maintenance on a hybrid. Hybrid maintenance is as lengthy as an ICE vehicle but focuses on other components related to the cabin.

Project 8 Jobs

- Job 38—Testing the Starting Battery on a Stop-Start System
- Job 39—Testing a Stop-Start System
- Job 40—Testing the Auxiliary Battery in a Hybrid
- Job 41—Diagnosing the Cooling Motors of a Hybrid Vehicle
- Job 42—Hybrid Vehicle Maintenance

The following list contains the tools and materials that may be needed to complete the jobs in this project. The items used will depend on the make and model of the vehicle being serviced.

- A vehicle requiring service.
- Applicable service information.
- Hand tools.
- Battery tester (capacitance or load tester).
- Scan tool.
- Scope.
- Safety glasses and other protective equipment.

Safety Notice

Before performing these jobs, review all pertinent safety information in the text and review safety information with your instructor.

Name ____________________

Date ____________________ Class ____________________

Project 8: Job 38—Testing the Starting Battery on a Stop-Start System

After completing this job, you will be able to test and diagnose a vehicle battery.

Instructions

As you read the job instructions, answer the questions and perform the tasks. Record your answers using complete sentences. Consult the proper service information and ask your instructor for help as needed.

Warning

Before performing this job, review all pertinent safety information in the text and discuss safety procedures with your instructor.

Procedures

- [ ] 1. Obtain a vehicle to use for this job. Your instructor may provide you with the vehicle.
- [ ] 2. Obtain a capacitance tester and/or load tester for the starting battery.
- [ ] 3. What is the cold cranking amp rating of the battery?
- [ ] 4. What is the age of the battery? ____________________

  If the battery is more than 3 years old, it may be near the end of its service life in a stop-start vehicle, but it may be acceptable for vehicles without stop-start.
- [ ] 5. Perform a capacitance test on the battery.

  What are the cranking amps measured? ____________________

  What is the health % of the battery? ____________________

  What is the measured voltage (state of charge) of the battery?
- [ ] 6. Perform a load test on the battery. For old load testers, this means loading the battery to one half of the cold cranking amps for 10 seconds and reading the voltage it was pulled down to.

  Was the voltage pulled below 10 volts? Yes ___ No ___

  Was the battery discharged before the tests? Yes ___ No ___

  If the battery was not discharged before the test and is not an old battery, replace it—it lacks the capacity of a healthy battery.
- [ ] 7. New batteries are only 75% charged upon purchase. Perform a trickle charge on the battery until the charger indicates a full charge. This may take 24 hours.
- [ ] 8. After installing the battery, use a scan tool to check for resets and relearns, **Figure 38-1**, for this vehicle.

  Many vehicles require battery registration with the ECM so that the new charge rate is not the same as the old charge rate. Failure to complete this step will result in shorter battery life.

  Does this vehicle require battery registration? Yes ___ No ___
- [ ] 9. Back out of the scanner completely before removing the DLC from the vehicle.
- [ ] 10. Reset any lost radio stations. Reinitialize any lost automatic features, such as window auto-down and auto-up and the auto-sunroof. To perform this step on most vehicles, the switch must be held for 10 additional seconds after the operation, such as the window being closed. Consult the appropriate service information for more information.

Figure 38-1. Use the resets and relearns feature to perform a battery registration. If the scan tool does not have this feature, the registration procedure may be located in the engine or electrical system tab.

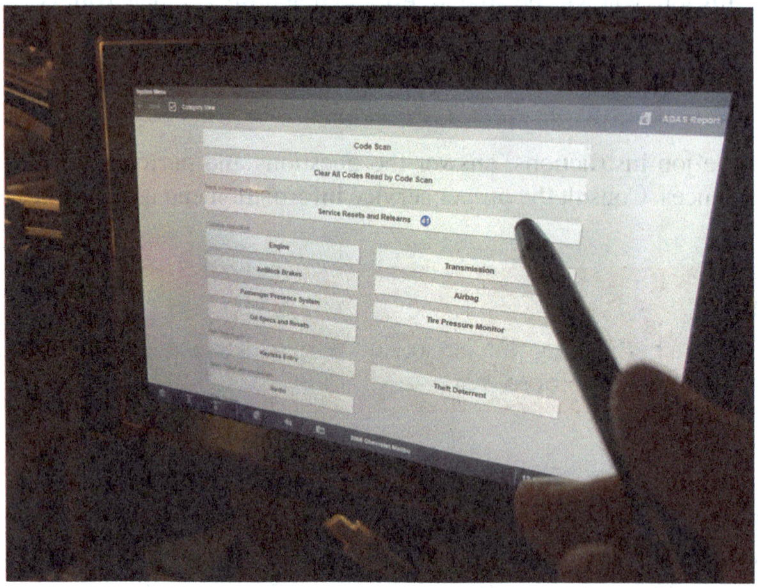

Job Wrap-Up

☐ 1. Clean the work area and return any equipment to storage. Return old battery for the core charge.

☐ 2. Did you encounter any problems during this procedure? Yes ___ No ___

If Yes, what did you do to correct the problem? ______________________________

____

☐ 3. Have your instructor check your work and sign this job sheet.

Performance Evaluation—Instructor Use Only

How would you rate this student's overall performance on this task/job?

4 Competent/Proficient. Able to perform all elements of the task/job successfully and independently.

3 Satisfactory performance of the task/job. Able to perform elements of the task/job with minimal instructor assistance.

2 Completed the task/job with significant instructor assistance.

1 Unsuccessfully attempted the task/job.

0 No exposure. Note reason below (absence, skill not covered, etc.).

Comments:

____

____

____

____

Instructor's Signature: ______________________________

Name ______________________________

Date ____________________ Class ____________________

Project 8: Job 39—Testing a Stop-Start System

After completing this job, you will be able to test and diagnose a vehicle equipped with Stop-Start.

Instructions

As you read the job instructions, answer the questions and perform the tasks. Record your answers using complete sentences. Consult the proper service information and ask your instructor for help as needed.

Warning

Before performing this job, review all pertinent safety information in the text and discuss safety procedures with your instructor.

Procedures

☐ 1. Obtain a vehicle with stop-start or BAS (Belt Alternator Starter) to use for this job. Your instructor may provide you with the vehicle.

Warning

A test drive is necessary to verify stop-start operation. The vehicle must be registered and insured, and it should be driven only by someone with a valid driver's license. When driving while using a scan tool, use the record function of the scan tool when only one person is available. If two people are available, one can drive while the other reads the scan tool.

☐ 2. Obtain a scan tool and/or scope.

☐ 3. Has the customer experienced any stop-start problems, such as slow restarts? Yes ___ No ___

If Yes, list the problems here: ______________________________

____

____

____

____

Tech Tip

Decreased "off-time" during a stop event or less and less time off before restarting are both indications of a declining battery.

☐ 4. Drive the vehicle until it reaches full engine temperature. Make sure the stop-start system is enabled and then verify stop-start system operation. See **Figure 39-1**.

Did the engine stop running when the vehicle was at a stop light or stop sign and motionless for more than 30 seconds? Yes ___ No ___

Did the engine start immediately after releasing the brake pedal? Yes ___ No ___

Figure 39-1. The automatic stop-start is enabled in this vehicle, which is indicated by the white "A" without the "cross out" at the top.

If not, was the problem an extended crank time or a no-start condition?

____Extended crank time

____No-start condition

The remainder of this job will focus on determining the cause of an extended crank or intermittent no-start problem.

Tech Tip

If the vehicle remains off and won't start during a stop-start test drive, put the transmission into PARK and push the START button to shut the vehicle off. Push the START button again to start the engine normally and put the transmission back in DRIVE to begin movement again.

☐ 5. To determine if the health of the battery is sufficient to match the cycling of the alternator during a stop-start event, make sure the engine is off and connect the voltage leads of the scope to the battery.

☐ 6. Set the scope's scale to 20 volts and the sweep to approximately 1 second.

☐ 7. Run the scope leads under the hood to windshield and then into the passenger side of the interior, **Figure 39-2**.

☐ 8. Test drive the vehicle while a helper observes the scope waveform.

Does the alternator cycling occur in intervals of more or less than 1 second? Yes ___ No ___

Does the alternator low cycle ever occur during a stop event? Yes ___ No ___

What is the lowest battery voltage recorded during the stop event? ___ volts

If the stop event occurs during an alternator low cycle, does the start voltage ever go below 10 volts? Yes ___ No ___

If the voltage drops below 10 volts, the battery health may be too low to maintain a reliable stop-start system. This will lead to an intermittent "stall" at some point, as mentioned above. Will the battery be replaced? Yes ___ No ___

Name____

Figure 39-2. To operate the scope and drive the vehicle, the lead wires must be routed from under the hood to the interior.

- [ ] 9. Perform a charging system test to ensure the battery is maintained while the engine is running. Consult the appropriate service information for charging specifications and charging logic. At least one manufacturer will not cycle the alternator until the battery drops to 12.1 volts.

  Does the alternator pass the charging system test? Yes ___ No ___

- [ ] 10. For BAS (Belt Alternator Starter) systems, which can be identified by the lack of a conventional starter on the engine, the alternator will be significantly larger than the traditional alternator, the serpentine belt will be significantly more substantial, and the alternator pully will have heavy-duty pulleys around it to provide more contact area.

  Does this vehicle have a BAS system? Yes ___ No ___

  If Yes, proceed to Step 11. If No, move to Step 12.

- [ ] 11. In addition to the tests outlined earlier in this job, perform a visual inspection of the BAS system.

  Does the serpentine belt glazed or have ribs missing? Yes ___ No ___

  Do any of the alternator tension pulleys have broken springs, worn bearings, or bent/broken pullies? Yes ___ No ___

  Does the belt squeal upon start-up? Yes ____No ____

  If the answer to any of the above questions is yes, explain the problem(s): ____________________

  ____

  ____

- [ ] 12. Using the scan tool in scanner mode (not OBD II since this is not emissions related), note any codes associated with the stop-start system and list them here:

  ____

  ____

- [ ] 13. Consult your instructor and replace any parts or wiring as necessary based on the results found with these diagnostic tests.

Job Wrap-Up

☐ 1. Clean the work area and return any equipment to storage. Return old battery and/or alternator for the core charge if necessary.

☐ 2. Did you encounter any problems during this procedure? Yes ___ No ___
If Yes, what did you do to correct the problem? ______________________________

____

☐ 3. Have your instructor check your work and sign this job sheet.

Performance Evaluation—Instructor Use Only

How would you rate this student's overall performance on this task/job?

4 Competent/Proficient. Able to perform all elements of the task/job successfully and independently.

3 Satisfactory performance of the task/job. Able to perform elements of the task/job with minimal instructor assistance.

2 Completed the task/job with significant instructor assistance.

1 Unsuccessfully attempted the task/job.

0 No exposure. Note reason below (absence, skill not covered, etc.).

Comments:

____

____

____

Instructor's Signature: ______________________________________

Name ______________________________

Date ______________________ Class ______________________

Project 8: Job 40—Testing the Auxiliary Battery in a Hybrid

After completing this job, you will be able to test and diagnose the auxiliary battery in a hybrid vehicle.

Instructions

As you read the job instructions, answer the questions and perform the tasks. Record your answers using complete sentences. Consult the proper service information and ask your instructor for help as needed.

Warning

Before performing this job, review all pertinent safety information in the text and discuss safety procedures with your instructor.

Warning

Hybrid vehicles have high-voltage cables and connections, which can be identified by their orange conduit, plastic, and covers. For this job, do not operate around any high voltage. Consult the appropriate service information and your instructor for more information on high-voltage safety.

Tech Tip

Hybrid vehices are expected to be driven at least once every two weeks. If the vehicle is underused, the 12-volt auxiliary battery will have a decreased life expectancy. If the vehicle is used less than this or is used primarily for short trips, disconnect the battery during the off time or place it on a trickle charger to maintain it.

Procedures

☐ 1. Obtain a hybrid vehicle to use for this job. Your instructor may provide you with the vehicle.

☐ 2. Does the customer use the vehicle at least once every two weeks? Yes ___ No ___

☐ 3. Obtain a capacitance tester and a load tester for the auxiliary battery.

☐ 4. Record the following:

Cold cranking amp rating of the battery: ___

Age of the battery: ___

☐ 5. Perform a capacitance test on the battery and record the following:

Measured cranking amps: ___

Battery health (%): ___

Measured battery voltage (state of charge): ___

☐ 6. Perform a load test on the battery. For old load testers, this means loading the battery to ½ of the cold cranking amps for 10 seconds and reading the voltage it was pulled down to.

Was the voltage pulled below 10 volts? Yes ___ No ___

Was the battery discharged before the tests? Yes ___ No ___

If the battery was not discharged before the test and is not an old battery, replace it. If the battery was discharged before the test, it will require charging and retesting. If the battery is more than three years old, replacement may be recommended by the manufacturer as a precaution. Check the vehicle manufacturer's maintenance schedule for any hybrid or electric vehicle.

☐ 7. If necessary, install a new battery.

Tech Tip

New batteries are only 75% charged upon purchase. Perform a trickle charge on the battery until the charger indicates a full charge. This may take 24 hours.

☐ 8. After installing the new battery, use a scan tool to check for resets and relearns for this vehicle. Many vehicles require battery registration with the ECM so that the new charge rate is not the same as the old charge rate. Failure to complete this step will result in shorter battery life.

Does this vehicle require a battery registration? Yes ___ No ___

☐ 9. Back out of the scanner completely and then unplug it from the DLC.

☐ 10. Reset any lost radio stations. Reinitialize any lost automatic features, such as window auto-down and auto-up and the auto-sunroof. To perform this step on most vehicles, the switch must be held for 10 additional seconds after the operation, such as the window being closed. Consult the appropriate service information for more detailed instructions.

Job Wrap-Up

☐ 1. Clean the work area and return any equipment to storage. Return old battery for the core charge.

☐ 2. Did you encounter any problems during this procedure? Yes ___ No ___

If Yes, what did you do to correct the problem? ______________________________

____

☐ 3. Have your instructor check your work and sign this job sheet.

Performance Evaluation—Instructor Use Only

How would you rate this student's overall performance on this task/job?

4 Competent/Proficient. Able to perform all elements of the task/job successfully and independently.

3 Satisfactory performance of the task/job. Able to perform elements of the task/job with minimal instructor assistance.

2 Completed the task/job with significant instructor assistance.

1 Unsuccessfully attempted the task/job.

0 No exposure. Note reason below (absence, skill not covered, etc.).

Comments:

____

____

____

____

Instructor's Signature: ______________________________

Name ____________________

Date ____________________ Class ____________________

Project 8: Job 41—Diagnosing the Cooling Motors of a Hybrid Vehicle

After completing this job, you will be able to test and diagnose cooling motors on a hybrid vehicle.

Instructions

As you read the job instructions, answer the questions and perform the tasks. Record your answers using complete sentences. Consult the proper service information and ask your instructor for help as needed.

Warning

Before performing this job, review all pertinent safety information in the text and discuss safety procedures with your instructor.

Procedures

☐ 1. Obtain a hybrid vehicle to use for this job. Your instructor may provide you with the vehicle.

☐ 2. Obtain a scan tool and/or scope with a low-amp clamp.

Warning

Hybrid vehicles have high-voltage cables and connections identified with orange conduit, plastic, and covers. For this job, do not operate around any high voltage. Consult the appropriate service information and your instructor for more information on high-voltage safety.

Testing the Inverter/Converter Coolant Pump

There are three options for testing the pump.

Option 1 would be to amp clamp a wire at the pump directly. This may require some disassembly.

Option 2 would be to find the fuse in the fuse panel that supplies the pump with power if the system is set up that way. Use the wiring diagram to determine this.

Option 3 would be to find the ground wire if it is visible and not shared with another device. This is normally the easiest option for not only this motor, but many 12-volt motors in a vehicle.

Which option will be used? ____________________

Why is this option being used? ____________________

Using a wiring diagram, determine the wire color and connection shape for the inverter/converter coolant pump.

☐ 3. Using component locator in your service data or by following the plumbing, find the inverter/converter coolant pump. It is usually located near the inverter/converter and will have coolant hoses the size of heater hose running from the inverter/converter to the pump. These pumps can be hidden by headlights, or they may be underneath the vehicle. These pumps exist on EVs as well. Have your instructor verify this device.

☐ 4. Using the information from Steps 1 and 2 to ensure that the pump being scoped is the correct one.

☐ 5. With the scope lead setting on low-amp clamp, connect the low-amp clamp to the corresponding channels.

- [ ] 6. Surround one of the pump wires with the low-amp clamp and turn the clamp on.
- [ ] 7. Put the vehicle into READY mode. "READY" will be displayed on the instrument panel or a green vehicle shape will appear to verify. Is the vehicle ready? Yes ___ No ___
- [ ] 8. If the vehicle does not go into READY mode, is the red triangle showing? Yes ___ No ___

  If the red triangle is showing, retrieve trouble codes with the scan tool and consult your instructor for further instruction. The hybrid portion of the vehicle will need to be fixed before continuing.
- [ ] 9. Inspect the wiring and the ground connection to the body.

  Are the wires acceptable with no breaks and no insulation damage? Yes ___ No ___

  Is the ground connection clean and uncorroded? Yes ___ No ___

  If yes, did you clean the ground connection? Yes ___ No ___

  Consult your instructor. ___
- [ ] 10. The set-up should look like **Figure 41-1**. The waveform should look like **Figure 41-1**.

  Is your scope set to the correct settings? Yes ___ No ___

  Is the amp clamp surrounding only 1 wire? Yes ___ No ___

  Does your waveform look like the one in Figure 41-1 with a "hill and spike"? Yes ___ No ___

  Are there any flat spots or jagged spots on the waveform? Yes ___ No ___

  The waveform shown in Figure 41-1 was produced by a healthy pump motor with vanes of the pump that are in good shape. The hills are the commutator sections of the pump motor, and the spikes are the increase in amperage as each vane moves coolant.
- [ ] 11. Does the pump require replacement? Yes ___ No ___
- [ ] 12. Consult your instructor and replace any parts or wiring necessary based on the results found with these diagnostic tests.

Figure 41-1. Scope setup for testing the inverter/converter coolant pump.

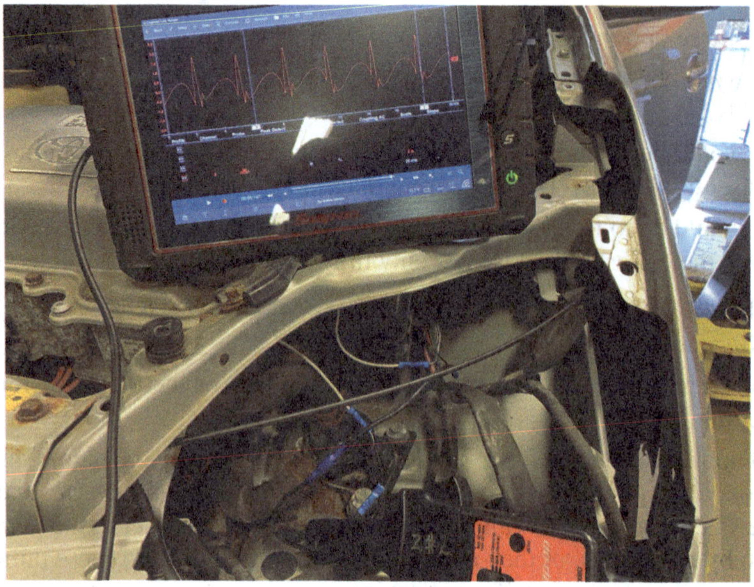

Name ____

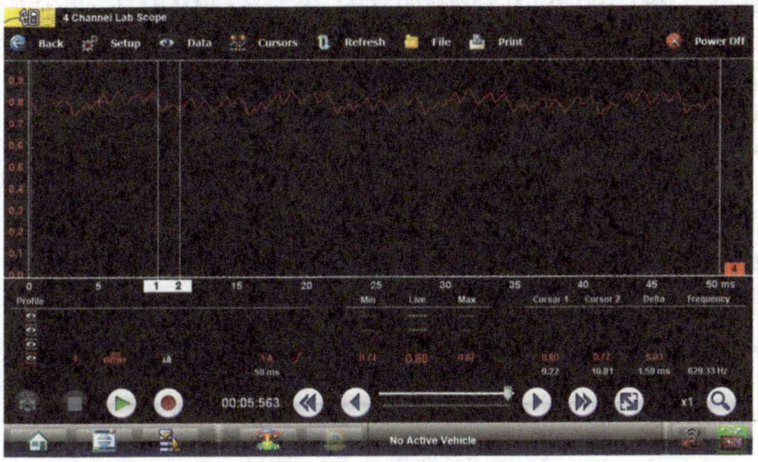

Figure 41-2. Waveform produced by a battery cooling fan motor.

Testing a Battery Cooling Fan Motor

☐ 13. Using a wiring diagram, determine which wire to use on the battery cooling fan motor. If a wiring diagram is not available, put the low-amp clamp around each wire one at a time until a waveform like **Figure 41-2** appears.

The high-voltage battery cooling fan operates on 12 volts like a blower motor, fuel pump, window motor, etc. The waveform will be like those of the other 12-volt brush motors as well. See **Figure 41-2** as an example of an unhealthy motor.

Does your waveform look worse or better than **Figure 41-2**? ____________________

☐ 14. Check the interior blower motor in the same manner as the high-voltage battery cooling fan motor.

What is the health of the interior blower motor? ____________________

☐ 15. Consult your instructor and replace any parts or wiring as necessary based on the results found with these diagnostic tests.

Job Wrap-Up

☐ 1. Clean the work area and return any equipment to storage. Return old battery and/or alternator for the core charge if necessary.

☐ 2. Did you encounter any problems during this procedure? Yes ____No ____

If Yes, what you do to correct the problem? ____________________

____

☐ 3. Have your instructor check your work and sign this job sheet.

Performance Evaluation—Instructor Use Only

How would you rate this student's overall performance on this task/job?

4 Competent/Proficient. Able to perform all elements of the task/job successfully and independently.

3 Satisfactory performance of the task/job. Able to perform elements of the task/job with minimal instructor assistance.

2 Completed the task/job with significant instructor assistance.

1 Unsuccessfully attempted the task/job.

0 No exposure. Note reason below (absence, skill not covered, etc.).

Comments:

____

____

____

____

Instructor's Signature: ____

Name ____________________

Date ____________________ Class ____________________

Project 8: Job 42—Hybrid Vehicle Maintenance

After completing this job, you will be able to maintain a hybrid vehicle.

Instructions

As you read the job instructions, answer the questions and perform the tasks. Record your answers using complete sentences. Consult the proper service information and ask your instructor for help as needed.

Warning

Before performing this job, review all pertinent safety information in the text and discuss safety procedures with your instructor.

Warning

Hybrid vehicles have high-voltage cables and connections, which can be identified by orange conduit, plastic, and covers. For this job, do not operate around any high voltage. Consult the appropriate service information and your instructor for more information on high-voltage safety.

Procedures

☐ 1. Obtain a hybrid vehicle to use for this job. Your instructor may provide you with the vehicle.

☐ 2. Before performing an oil and filter change on a hybrid, take the vehicle out of READY mode. The key must be moved more than 10 feet away from the vehicle so that it cannot go back into READY mode and have the engine start.

☐ 3. Perform the oil and filter change as would be done on any other internal combustion vehicle.

Was the service done? Yes ___ No ___

Was the oil change interval reset? Yes ___ No ___

☐ 4. Inspect the tires.

Are the tires in good condition? Yes ___ No ___

If not, describe the problem(s): ____________________

____

____

Tires are often rotated on the same visit as an oil change.

What is the rotation pattern for this vehicle? ____________________

____

____

Are the tires hybrid- and EV-specific? Look at the sidewall designation. Yes ___ No ___

☐ 5. Check the suspension. Hybrids and EVs are heavier than their equal ICE vehicle. What is the condition of the following?

Ball joints: ____________________

Tie rod ends: ____________________

Struts and springs: ____________________

☐ 6. Check the brakes. Hybrids and EVs do not apply as much pressure to the brakes, but corrosion from under use can shorten brake life.

☐ 7. What is the condition of the brakes? ____________________

☐ 8. Check the cabin filter. Hybrids will often cool the high-voltage battery with cabin air. Therefore, the cabin air filter on a hybrid will require more maintenance than an ICE vehicle. Use your service information to locate the cabin filter.

Where is the cabin filter located? ____________________

____

____

What was removed to access the cabin air filter? ____________________

____

____

Was the cabin air filter replaced? Yes ___ No ___

☐ 9. Check the cabin intake to the battery cooling ducts, **Figure 42-1**. The cooling ducts are normally in the rear of the vehicle around the rear seats.

Tech Tip

This step only applies to air-cooled batteries. Consult the appropriate service information to determine if this vehicle has air or liquid cooling for the high-voltage batteries.

Are the ducts covered or full of debris? Yes ___ No ___

If the ducts are full of debris, the cooling fan will have debris as well. Consult your instructor regarding duct disassembly and cleaning.

Was duct cleaning performed? Yes ___ No ___

Figure 42-1. The battery cooling air ducts must be clean and unobstructed.

Name ____

Project 8: Job 42 *(continued)*

Figure 42-2. Note that this inverter/converter cooling system is separate from the engine cooling system.

☐ 10. Check the age and condition of the coolant. Note that the cooling system for the engine is separate from the cooling system for the inverter/converter that is attached to the engine, **Figure 42-2**.

Is the coolant due for replacement? Yes ___ No ___

The coolant is likely not to be the same as for the engine.

What type of coolant is used in the cooling system for the inverter converter? ________________

____

☐ 11. Some hybrids have water leaks into the interior. Check the battery and spare tire areas for signs of water leaks.

Are there water leaks? Yes ___ No ___

Are all air dams and air ducts properly fastened on the exterior? Yes ___ No ___

☐ 12. Hybrids will run the engine whenever the battery requires charging; therefore, the engine can come on and turn off with no input by the operator. For engine performance diagnosis, the engine may need to run for longer periods of time. Some hybrids have "maintenance mode" where, with a combination of button and throttle applications, the engine will be forced to remain running. Consult the appropriate service information or the scan tool and run the scripted procedure to put the engine into maintenance mode.

Was the vehicle put into maintenance or service mode? Yes ___ No ___

What are codes related to the engine? ________________________________

____

____

____

☐ 13. A hybrid has no starter as the first motor/generator is connected to the engine flywheel, making the motor/generator into the starter. Engine starting rpm is approximately 1000 rpm; therefore, the starting sounds like engine running.

Tech Tip

Being in READY mode does not mean the engine will run when the START button is pushed. READY means ready to move. Application of the throttle pedal does not mean the engine will run to move the vehicle. If the battery is low, the engine will start.

Does the engine crank over when the high voltage battery becomes low, as seen on the display screen in the vehicle? Yes ___ No ___

Does the engine "run" for 30 seconds and stop? Yes ___ No ___

If the answer for the last question is "Yes," consult with your instructor to put the engine into Maintenance Mode and diagnose it as a No-Start as you would with any ICE vehicle.

☐ 14. Consult your instructor and replace any parts as necessary based on the results found with these diagnostic tests.

Job Wrap-Up

☐ 1. Clean the work area and return any equipment to storage.

☐ 2. Did you encounter any problems during this procedure? Yes ___ No ___

If Yes, what did you do to correct the problem? ____

____

☐ 3. Have your instructor check your work and sign this job sheet.

Performance Evaluation—Instructor Use Only

How would you rate this student's overall performance on this task/job?

4 Competent/Proficient. Able to perform all elements of the task/job successfully and independently.

3 Satisfactory performance of the task/job. Able to perform elements of the task/job with minimal instructor assistance.

2 Completed the task/job with significant instructor assistance.

1 Unsuccessfully attempted the task/job.

0 No exposure. Note reason below (absence, skill not covered, etc.).

Comments:

____

____

____

____

Instructor's Signature: ____